Benedictus

Benedictus

"Blessed is he who comes in the name of the Lord."

Day by Day with Pope Benedict XVI

Edited by Rev. Peter John Cameron, O.P.

MAGNIFICAT / ignatius press

Cover: Pope Benedict XVI © Alessia Giuliani/CPP/CIRIC.

Copyright © Ignatius Press / Magnificat SAS 2006.
All rights reserved.
No part of this book may be used or reproduced in any manner whatsoever without written permission except in the case of brief quotations embodied in critical articles or reviews. For information address Magnificat, PO Box 822, Yonkers, NY 10702.

Editor Magnificat, PO Box 822, Yonkers, NY 10702.

The trademark MAGNIFICAT depicted in this publication is used under license from and is the exclusive property of Magnificat Central Service Team, Inc., A Ministry to Catholic Women, and may not be used without its written consent.

Edition number: MGN 12008.

First Edition: October 2006.
Second Edition: December 2006.
Third Edition: September 2007.
Fourth Edition: June 2012.

Printed by Tien Wah Press, Singapour.

ISBN Ignatius Press: 978-0-96761-865-4 – ISBN Magnificat: 978-0-9676186-5-4

Foreword

READERS OF MAGNIFICAT are well-acquainted with the "Meditation of the Day" feature of the magazine which presents a prayerful reflection for each day of the year drawn from the writings of the spiritual masters of the Church. Among the outstanding authors who have appeared in those pages is Cardinal Joseph Ratzinger. When Cardinal Ratzinger was elected to the papacy in 2005, all of us at MAGNIFICAT agreed that an ideal way for the public to meet the new Holy Father, Pope Benedict XVI, would be by publishing his thoughts in the form of an entire volume of yearlong daily meditations.

In 1992, Ignatius Press published a superb book entitled *Co-Workers of the Truth: Meditations for Every Day of the Year*, which excerpts the writings, homilies, and talks of the then Cardinal Ratzinger (the title is his episcopal motto). *Benedictus* carries on this intention. However, in compiling the texts, I began with the most recent works of Pope Benedict XVI (those of May 2006) and then worked back to his earlier ones.

You can find a list of all the sources used in *Benedictus* in the handy *Bibliographical Information* section found on pages 400 to 402. To identify the source of a particular meditation, simply turn to the complete *Index of Meditations*, keyed to each day of the year, that begins on page 403.

There would be no *Benedictus* without the talents and painstaking efforts of Catherine Kolpak and Jeanne Shanahan. Together they tended to the tedium of preparing the final manuscript by typing texts, systematizing them, proofreading, copyediting, and making the bibliography. I cannot thank them enough for all they did to make *Benedictus* a true labor of love.

All of us at MAGNIFICAT hope you enjoy this book of meditations, and that the extraordinary wisdom and grace of Pope Benedict XVI will be a source of profound illumination and countless blessings for you.

Father Peter John Cameron, O.P., Editor
Our Lady of Fatima, 2006

The Theological Heritage of Pope Benedict XVI

Reverend Romanus Cessario, O.P.

The Pope Theologian

*N*o pope in modern times has come to the Chair of Peter with as copious a body of published theological writings as did Joseph Ratzinger. He has written more than eighty-five books as well as over five hundred articles and occasional essays. Although Pope Benedict XVI is knowledgeable in many fields, the majority of his writings exhibit his professional competence as a theologian.

Upon being received into the Pontifical Academy of Sciences, the then Cardinal Ratzinger remarked in 2002: "I did my philosophical and theological studies immediately after the war, from 1946 to 1951. In this period, theological formation in the faculty of Munich was essentially determined by the biblical, liturgical, and ecumenical movement of the time between the two World Wars." Joseph Ratzinger engaged the theological disciplines that prepared him to meet the challenges that the Church would face in the twenty-first century. It is easy to discern in this program of studies the hand of divine providence at work early in the life of a man who would become pope.

Professional theologians will come to recognize what the Pope himself has described recently as the "unfinished character" of his complete works. The unfinishedness that Benedict XVI ascribes to his life-long theological accomplishment does not signal a failure, however. He contemplates what might have been the case if he were not asked to assume responsibilities other than those of a university professor.

Joseph Ratzinger was called to assume pastoral service in the Church: first as cardinal archbishop of Munich and shortly thereafter as prefect of the Congregation for the Doctrine of the Faith. He was not afforded the opportunity to complete the kind of overall systematic account of Catholic theology that finds an original model in the *Summa theologiae* of Saint

Thomas Aquinas. The Pope considers nonetheless that his writings do "amount to something like a single whole."

Pope Benedict XVI makes these remarks on his own writings in his 2005 book, *Values in a Time of Upheaval: How to Survive the Challenge of the Future.*

The Pope's Theology

Pope Benedict XVI has been occupied with theological studies and discussion for more than half a century. No wonder that he has found the occasion to write on nearly every topic that one expects from the pen of an authentic Catholic theologian. This massive accomplishment provides the Pope's blueprint for doing theology.

One way to identify some general themes that emerge in the theological reflections of Joseph Ratzinger is to recall what he reports as the influences that surrounded his own early theological studies: the Holy Bible, the Sacred Liturgy, and Catholic Ecumenism.

The sacred Scriptures introduce Christ. Joseph Ratzinger takes seriously the Church Fathers' insistence on the unity of the Old and New Testament. This unity illuminates the central place that Jesus Christ holds in the salvation of the world. No one is saved without at least implicit faith in the One Mediator between God and men, which in some way associates them with the worldwide communion that we call the Church.

The liturgy of the Church finds its source in the Eucharist. It is said that Pope Benedict had to be persuaded to hold his inaugural Mass as Pope in Saint Peter's Square. He would have preferred to hold the Mass within the Vatican Basilica to make it visually clear that Christ stands at the center of every efficacious liturgical action that the Church celebrates. Each human being is called to participate in the worship that Christ offers to the Father of glory and which is preeminently commemorated in the Catholic Mass.

Ecumenism is ordered to reveal that the one Church of Christ exists in order to communicate the gift of salvation to the whole human race. There is only one saving communion. *People of God and God's House in Augustine's*

Doctrine of the Church is the title of the Pope's doctoral dissertation. From his earliest student days, a principal concern of Pope Benedict XVI has been to point out the legitimate place that the Church holds among the nations; he wants to capture for his contemporaries the important reflections that Saint Augustine first aired in his chapters on the City of God and the City of Man.

The Pope's Mission

In accord with one's personal vocation, each Catholic is obliged to make the mission of the Pope his or her own.

Benedictus offers to those who do not have the time to read everything that Pope Benedict XVI has written a way to benefit from his richly textured insights into divine truth. Father Peter John Cameron, O.P., who is a long-time student of the Pope's writings, has assembled excerpts from them that may serve, among other purposes, as a source for daily meditation. By keeping *Benedictus* close at hand and picking it up frequently, the everyday Catholic will discover the main themes of the Catholic faith that Pope Benedict XVI considers important for Catholics to ponder with love.

Those who make fruitful use of these daily selections from the writings of Pope Benedict XVI will contribute to completing in their own lives and vocations what, for reasons known only to God, Joseph Ratzinger has left "unfinished."

Father Romanus Cessario, O.P., serves as senior editor for MAGNIFICAT, and teaches theology at Saint John's Seminary in Boston, MA.

The Mind of Pope Benedict XVI

Reverend J. Augustine Di Noia, O.P.

*P*erhaps there is no pope in history for whom we have a more complete record of his "mind" upon election than we have for Pope Benedict XVI. A bibliography of his works prepared just before the conclave runs to nearly fifty typewritten pages! And now, in the months since his election, we have been treated to a series of splendid homilies and discourses which provide further insight into the mind of Benedict XVI.

Theologian and Pastor

Pope Benedict was born in Bavaria on Holy Saturday in 1927. Much of his life after his formative years was spent as a priest and a professor of theology, until in 1977 he became the archbishop of Munich, and then in 1981 Pope John Paul II appointed him the prefect of the Congregation for the Doctrine of the Faith. His "mind" was deeply influenced by his wide reading and research in the works of Saint Augustine and Saint Bonaventure. Among the central themes of his work as a theologian and preacher were the mystery of the Church, the centrality of the Eucharist, and the significance of history for the understanding of the Catholic faith. His position as theological advisor to Cardinal Frings at Vatican Council II, his leadership of the Congregation for the Doctrine of the Faith, and his intimate, twenty-year long collaboration with Pope John Paul II — to these areas of new responsibility he brought that unique blend of theological acumen and pastoral sensibility that is a striking characteristic of the mind of Benedict XVI.

The Mind of Christ

If Pope Benedict himself were writing this little introduction to a daybook of meditations drawn from his works, the first thing he would say is that the mind of the pope must be the mind of Christ and the mind of the Church. In the homily of the Mass for the inauguration of his pontificate, he said: "My program of governance is not to do my own will, not to pursue my own ideas, but to listen, together with the whole Church, to the word and will of the Lord, to be guided by him, so that he himself will lead the Church at this hour of our history." The pope is the servant of the saving truth of the Gospel that is Christ's gift to the Church. Indeed, as Pope Benedict has often said in his writings, Christ himself is this gift of truth. The truth of our faith is not solely an intellectual content, expressed in formulas and creeds — important and necessary as these are — but is more fully the living Word of God, given as a transforming personal gift of the Blessed Trinity, to be cherished, pondered, and adored in the community of his holy people that is the Church. Hence, the awesome responsibility of the Pope and the bishops, and of theologians and all teachers of the Catholic faith, to be faithful to the Truth that is in the first place the divine Son himself.

Mirror of the Truth

For Benedict XVI, this truth is a saving truth. In the mirror of the truth of the Gospel which is Christ himself, we see revealed the truth about ourselves, about our relations with others, about the societies and cultures we inhabit — indeed, about every aspect of our existence as human beings called to enjoy the communion of the life of the Blessed Trinity, but still bound by the constraints of our creatureliness and our sinfulness. The authentic proclamation of the truth is not only a matter of doctrinal precision but also and above all of pastoral urgency. The pastors and teachers of the Church must proclaim the full truth about Christ *for the sake of the salvation* of the faithful.

Precisely at this point we can grasp why, for Pope Benedict, one of the great dangers of modern times is the prevailing atmosphere of relativism which recognizes nothing "as definitive and whose ultimate goal consists solely of one's own ego and desires." This atmosphere blocks the communication of the truth that is Christ and with it the possession of "a clear faith based on the Creed of the Church." Relativism is harmful not just as a theoretical philosophical position, but because it prevents people from embracing the truth that would otherwise save and transform them. Friendship with Christ "opens us up to all that is good and gives us a criterion by which to distinguish the true from the false, and deceit from truth."

For in the truth of Christ, we discover "the measure of true humanism." There can be no encounter with this living Truth that does not entail conversion on our part. At the opening Mass of his pontificate, Pope Benedict proclaimed: "If we let Christ into our lives, we lose nothing, nothing, absolutely nothing of what makes life free, beautiful, and great. No! Only in this friendship is the great potential of human existence truly revealed." Everyone who has heard the Pope say these words on that beautiful spring day, and then repeat them again at World Youth Day in Cologne recalls the passion and conviction which rang out in his voice.

As a professor of theology, as a consultant at Vatican Council II, as a diocesan bishop, as prefect of the Congregation for the Doctrine of the Faith — in carrying out these responsibilities, his work was always marked by scrupulous attention to the details of text and language, and to the criteria of doctrinal authenticity for the sake of the truth that contributes to salvation. One finds oneself at the very center of the mind of Benedict XVI in this embrace and proclamation of the Truth that saves and transforms.

Father J. Augustine Di Noia is a Dominican priest and undersecretary of the Congregation for the Doctrine of the Faith.

January

Mother of God

*I*f Mary is really the one giving birth to God, if she bears him who is the death of death and is life in the full sense of the word, this being the Mother of God is really a "new birth" *(nova nativitas)*: a new way of giving birth inserted into the old way, just as Mary is the New Covenant in the midst of the Old Covenant, even as a member of the Old Covenant. This birth is no dying, but only a becoming, a bursting forth of life that casts off dying and leaves it behind once and for all. The title "Mother of God" points, on the one hand, back to the Virgin: this life is not received through the everyday dying and becoming but is pure beginning. On the other hand, the title points to the Assumption: from this birth comes only life, no death. This new "generation" does not demand the surrender of the old self as its *sine qua non*, rather it effects the ultimate validation of the whole.

The Reasonableness of the Universe

The more we know of the universe the more profoundly we are struck by a Reason whose ways we can only contemplate with astonishment. In pursuing them we can see anew that creating Intelligence to whom we owe our own reason. Albert Einstein once said that in the laws of nature "there is revealed such a superior Reason that everything significant which has arisen out of human thought and arrangement is, in comparison with it, the merest empty reflection." In what is most vast, in the world of heavenly bodies, we see revealed a powerful Reason that holds the universe together. And we are penetrating ever deeper into what is smallest, into the cell and into the primordial units of life; here, too, we discover a Reason that astounds us, such that we must say with Saint Bonaventure: "Whoever does not see here is blind. Whoever does not hear here is deaf. And whoever does not begin to adore here and to praise the creating Intelligence is dumb"… God himself shines through the reasonableness of his creation. Physics and biology, and the natural sciences in general, have given us a new and unheard-of creation account with vast new images, which let us recognize the face of the Creator and which make us realize once again that at the very beginning and foundation of all being there is a creating Intelligence. The universe is not the product of darkness and unreason. It comes from intelligence, freedom, and from the beauty that is identical with love. Seeing this gives us the courage to keep on living, and it empowers us, comforted thereby, to take upon ourselves the adventure of life.

Creatures that can be One with Christ

*I*n the New Testament Christ is referred to as the second Adam, as the definitive Adam, and as the image of God (1 Cor 15: 44-48; Col 1: 15). This means that in him alone appears the complete answer to the question about what the human being is. In him alone appears the deepest meaning of what is for the present a rough draft. He is the definitive human being, and creation is, as it were, a preliminary sketch that points to him. Thus we can say that human persons are the beings who can be Jesus Christ's brothers or sisters. Human beings are the creatures that can be one with Christ and thereby be one with God himself. Hence this relationship of creature to Christ, of the first to the second Adam, signifies that human persons are beings en route, beings characterized by transition. They are not yet themselves; they must ultimately become themselves… Human beings must die with Christ like a grain of wheat in order truly to rise, to stand erect, to be themselves (Jn 12: 24). Human persons are not to be understood merely from the perspective of their past histories or from that isolated moment that we refer to as the present. They are oriented toward their future, and only it permits who they really are to appear completely (1 Jn 3: 2). We must always see in other human beings persons with whom we shall one day share God's joy. We must look upon them as persons who are called, together with us, to be members of the Body of Christ, with whom we shall one day sit at table with Abraham, Isaac, and Jacob, and with Christ himself, as their brothers and sisters, as the brothers and sisters of Christ, and as the children of God.

Faith Transforms Time

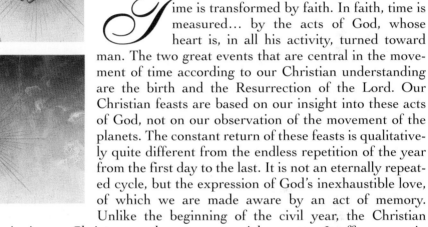

ime is transformed by faith. In faith, time is measured… by the acts of God, whose heart is, in all his activity, turned toward man. The two great events that are central in the movement of time according to our Christian understanding are the birth and the Resurrection of the Lord. Our Christian feasts are based on our insight into these acts of God, not on our observation of the movement of the planets. The constant return of these feasts is qualitatively quite different from the endless repetition of the year from the first day to the last. It is not an eternally repeated cycle, but the expression of God's inexhaustible love, of which we are made aware by an act of memory. Unlike the beginning of the civil year, the Christian beginning — Christmas — has a very special newness. It offers us again and again the opportunity to return in the goodness of the God who became man, in that goodness to become a child again and in it to live a new life… The eighth day in the life of Jesus was the day when he became legally a citizen, a member of his people… When he became a living part of our history, the dark mystery of our own birth was completed; and our beginning, until then situated uneasily between blessing and curse, became a blessing… The eighth day is also the day of his Resurrection and at the same time the day of creation. God's creation does not come to nothing. It is always moving toward the Resurrection… In the midst of passing time there is always a new beginning. This new beginning is eternal love.

The Event of Christianity

*W*e have come to believe in God's love: in these words the Christian can express the fundamental decision of his life. Being Christian is not the result of an ethical choice or a lofty idea, but the encounter with an event, a person, which gives life a new horizon and a decisive direction. Saint John's Gospel describes that event in these words: "God so loved the world that he gave his only Son, that whoever believes in him should… have eternal life" (3: 16). In acknowledging the centrality of love, Christian faith has retained the core of Israel's faith, while at the same time giving it new depth and breadth. The pious Jew prayed daily the words of the Book of Deuteronomy which expressed the heart of his existence: "Hear, O Israel: the Lord our God is one Lord, and you shall love the Lord your God with all your heart, and with all your soul and with all your might" (6: 4-5). Jesus united into a single precept this commandment of love for God and the commandment of love for neighbor found in the Book of Leviticus: "You shall love your neighbor as yourself" (19: 18; cf. Mk 12: 29-31). Since God has first loved us (cf. 1 Jn 4: 10), love is now no longer a mere "command"; it is the response to the gift of love with which God draws near to us.

What the Magi Learned

Going into the house, the Magi saw the child… Outwardly, their journey was now over. But at this point a new journey began for them which changed their whole lives… Deep within themselves they felt prompted to go in search of the true justice that can only come from God, and they wanted to serve this King, to fall prostrate at his feet and so play their part in the renewal of the world. They were among those "who hunger and thirst for justice" (Mt 5: 6). This hunger and thirst had spurred them on in their pilgrimage — they had become pilgrims in search of the justice that they expected from God… The new King, to whom they now paid homage, was quite unlike what they were expecting. In this way they had to learn that God is not as we usually imagine him to be. This was where their inner journey began. It started at the very moment when they knelt down before this child and recognized him as the promised King. But they still had to assimilate these joyful gestures internally. They had to change their ideas about power, about God and about man, and in so doing, they also had to change themselves… They had to learn to give themselves — no lesser gift would be sufficient for this King. They had to learn that their lives must be conformed to this divine way of exercising power, to God's own way of being. They must become men of truth, of justice, of goodness, of forgiveness, of mercy… They will have to ask: How can I serve God's presence in the world? They must learn to lose their life and in this way to find it. Having left Jerusalem behind, they must not deviate from the path marked out by the true King, as they follow Jesus.

The Deep Desire of the Magi

Why did the Magi set off from afar to go to Bethlehem? The answer has to do with the mystery of the "star" which they saw "in the East" and which they recognized as the star of the "King of the Jews," that is to say, the sign of the birth of the Messiah (Mt 2: 2). So their journey was inspired by a powerful hope, strengthened and guided by the star, which led them toward the King of the Jews, toward the kingship of God himself. The Magi set out because of a deep desire which prompted them to leave everything and begin a journey. It was as though they had always been waiting for that star. It was as if the journey had always been a part of their destiny, and was finally about to begin. This is the mystery of God's call, the mystery of vocation. It is part of the life of every Christian… When the Magi came to Bethlehem, "going into the house they saw the child with Mary his Mother, and they fell down and worshiped him" (Mt 2: 11). Here at last was the long-awaited moment — their encounter with Jesus. "Going into the house": this house in some sense represents the Church. In order to find the Savior, one has to enter the house, which is the Church… "They fell down and worshiped him… and offered him gifts: gold, frankincense, and myrrh" (Mt 2: 11-12). Here is the culmination of the whole journey: encounter becomes adoration; it blossoms into an act of faith and love which acknowledges in Jesus, born of Mary, the Son of God made man… The secret of holiness is friendship with Christ and faithful obedience to his will.

The Baptism of the Lord

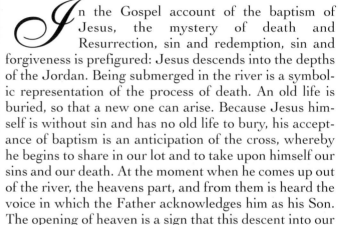

*I*n the Gospel account of the baptism of Jesus, the mystery of death and Resurrection, sin and redemption, sin and forgiveness is prefigured: Jesus descends into the depths of the Jordan. Being submerged in the river is a symbolic representation of the process of death. An old life is buried, so that a new one can arise. Because Jesus himself is without sin and has no old life to bury, his acceptance of baptism is an anticipation of the cross, whereby he begins to share in our lot and to take upon himself our sins and our death. At the moment when he comes up out of the river, the heavens part, and from them is heard the voice in which the Father acknowledges him as his Son. The opening of heaven is a sign that this descent into our night is the dawning of a new day, that the barrier between God and man is being broken down by this identification of the Son with us: God is no longer inaccessible; in the depths of our sins, and even of death, he searches for us and brings us into the light again. To this extent the baptism of Jesus anticipates the entire drama of his life and death and at the same time explains them to us.

Searching for Someone

We are asking: "Where do I find standards to live by, what are the criteria that govern responsible cooperation in building the present and the future of our world? On whom can I rely? To whom shall I entrust myself? Where is the One who can offer me the response capable of satisfying my heart's deepest desires?" The fact that we ask questions like these means that we realize our journey is not over until we meet the One who has the power to establish that universal Kingdom of justice and peace to which all people aspire, but which they are unable to build by themselves. Asking such questions also means searching for Someone who can neither deceive nor be deceived, and who therefore can offer a certainty so solid that we can live for it and, if need be, even die for it. Dear friends, when questions like these appear on the horizon of life, we must be able to make the necessary choices. It is like finding ourselves at a crossroads: which direction do we take? The one prompted by the passions or the one indicated by the star which shines in your conscience? The Magi heard the answer: "In Bethlehem of Judea; for so it is written by the prophet" (Mt 2: 5), and, enlightened by these words, they chose to press forward to the very end. From Jerusalem they went on to Bethlehem. In other words, they went from the word which showed them where to find the King of the Jews whom they were seeking, all the way to the end, to an encounter with the King who was at the same time the Lamb of God who takes away the sins of the world. Those words are also spoken for us.

Faith as an Act of Affirmation

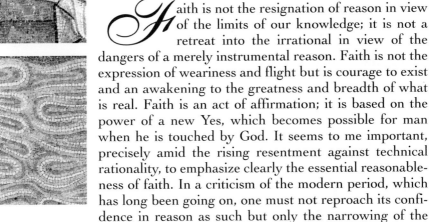

aith is not the resignation of reason in view of the limits of our knowledge; it is not a retreat into the irrational in view of the dangers of a merely instrumental reason. Faith is not the expression of weariness and flight but is courage to exist and an awakening to the greatness and breadth of what is real. Faith is an act of affirmation; it is based on the power of a new Yes, which becomes possible for man when he is touched by God. It seems to me important, precisely amid the rising resentment against technical rationality, to emphasize clearly the essential reasonableness of faith. In a criticism of the modern period, which has long been going on, one must not reproach its confidence in reason as such but only the narrowing of the concept of reason, which has opened the door to irrational ideologies. The *mysterium*, as faith sees it, is not the irrational but rather the uttermost depths of the divine reason, which our weak eyes are no longer able to penetrate. It is the creative reason, the power of the divine knowledge that imparts meaning. It is only from this beginning that one can correctly understand the mystery of Christ, in which reason can then be seen to be the same as love. The first word of faith, therefore, tells us: everything that exists is thought that has poured forth. The Creator Spirit is the origin and the supporting foundation of all things. Everything that is, is reasonable in terms of its origin, for it comes from creative reason… The *mysterium* is not opposed to reason but saves and defends the reasonableness of existence and of man.

Faith as Meeting

*O*ne has never achieved complete faith. Faith has to be lived again and again in life and in suffering, as well as in the great joys that God sends us. It is never something that I can put in my pocket like a coin… The essence of faith is that I do not meet with something that has been thought up, but that here something meets me that is greater than anything we can think of for ourselves… The Christian faith brings us consolation, that God is so great that he can become small. And that is actually for me the unexpected and previously inconceivable greatness of God, that he is able to bow down so low. That he himself really enters into a man, no longer merely disguises himself in him so that he can later put him aside and put on another garment, but that he becomes this man. It is just in this that we actually see the truly infinite nature of God, for this is more powerful, more inconceivable than anything else, and at the same time more saving… This very God, who has the power to realize love in such a way that he himself is present in a man, that he is there and introduces himself to us, that he associates himself with us, is exactly what we need in order to escape from having to live to the end with fragments and half-truths.

Faith is Always a Path

aith in God is not a form of knowledge that can be learned like chemistry or mathematics, but remains a belief… Since faith demands our whole existence, our will, our love, since it requires letting go of ourselves, it necessarily always goes beyond a mere knowledge, beyond what is demonstrable. And because that is so, then I can always turn my life away from faith and find arguments that seem to refute it… We must have the courage not to lose hold of the truth, to stretch toward it and to accept it humbly and thankfully, whenever it is given to us… Belief is never simply there, in a way that would enable me to say at a certain point in time: I have it, and others do not have it. It is something living, which is inclusive of the whole person in all his dimensions — understanding, will, and feelings. It can then fasten its roots ever deeper into my life, so that my life becomes more and more nearly identical with my faith; but for all that it is never just a possession. A man can always still give way to this other tendency within himself and thus fall away. Faith is always a path. As long as we live we are on the way, and on that account faith is always under pressure and under threat. And it is healthy that it can never turn into a convenient ideology. That it does not make me hardened and unable to follow the thoughts of my doubting brother and to sympathize with him. Faith can only mature by suffering anew, at every stage in life, the oppression and the power of unbelief, by admitting its reality and then finally going right through it, so that it again finds the path opening ahead for a while.

Faith as the Seed of Life

The Lord uses the image of the mustard seed, as being the smallest of all grains or seeds, out of which in the end a tree will grow in which all the birds of the air will be able to nest. The mustard seed comprises, on the one hand, smallness — wherein I am wretched — but at the same time the potential for growth. In that way there is in this mustard seed a profound depiction of faith. Faith is seen thereby not as the mere acceptance of certain propositions, but is the seed of life within me. I am only a true believer if faith is present within me as a living seed, from which something is growing and which then truly changes my world and, in doing so, brings something new into the world as a whole... The experiment of life can only become clear for me if I truly give myself up to the will of God, so far as he has made it known to me... Sometimes, precisely by the breadth of our vision, in that we can see so many glimpses of divine reason in reality, this really does add breadth and scope to our image of God, and we stand before him with greater reverence and even with humility and awe.

Celebrating Sunday

*C*hristians are Sunday people. What does that mean? Before we ask ourselves how we "observe Sunday," we have to consider what we Christians actually celebrate on Sunday. The real and first reason for celebrating Sunday lies in the fact that on this day Christ rose from the dead. In doing so, he inaugurated a new age. For the first time someone returns from the dead and will not die again. For the first time someone has broken the bonds of time that hold us all in captivity. But Jesus did not pass quickly into heaven. He did not simply shed time as one might shed a worn-out garment; on the contrary, he remains with us. He has returned and will never leave us again. The feast of Sunday is, therefore, above all a profession of faith in the Resurrection. It is a profession of faith that life is good. Very early in the history of the Church Christians asked themselves: "Why did the Lord choose this day? What meaning did he intend to convey thereby?" According to Jewish reckoning, Sunday was the first day of the week. It was therefore the day on which God created the world. It was the day on which God ended his rest and spoke: "Let there be light" (Gn 1: 3). Sunday is the first day of the week, the day of creation. That means, then, that Sunday is also the day on which we give thanks for creation... Creation has been given us by God as our living space, as the scene of our labor and our leisure, in which we find both the necessities and the superfluities of life, the beauty of images and sounds, which we need precisely as much as we need food and clothing.

Belief in the Personal God

*T*his saying "I believe" is a conscious act of the self. An act in which the will and the understanding, the teaching and the guidance I have been given, are all cooperatively involved. This act comprehends the trusting or, if you like, reaching out, transcending my own limits, turning toward God. And this act is not just a matter of relating to some higher power or other, but to the God who knows me and who speaks to me. Who is truly an "I" — even if in a far higher sense — toward whom I can move and who is moving toward me… God has all the essential characteristics of what we mean by a "person," in particular conscious awareness, the ability to recognize, and the ability to love. In that sense he is someone who can speak and who can listen. That, I think, is what is essential about God. Nature can be marvelous. The starry heaven is stupendous. But my reaction to that remains no more than an impersonal wonder, because that, in the end, means that I am myself no more than a tiny part of an enormous machine. The real God, however, is more than that. He is not just nature, but the One who came before it and who sustains it. And the whole of God, so faith tells us, is the act of relating. That is what we mean when we say that he is a Trinity, that he is threefold. Because he is in himself a complex of relationships, he can also make other beings who are grounded in relationships and who may relate to him, because he has related them to himself.

Faith Resists Brute Force

here's an incident in the storm on the lake, when the disciples are in despair because Jesus does not stir, not even when the boat is filling with water. And after he has stood up and he saves them, he says: "How could you doubt?" Jesus assumes that his disciples really ought to know him. That they ought to know he will not let them drown. He shows them in this way that their faith in what he is, and in what they have actually recognized and accepted, is still so minimal that a puff of wind can, as it were, blow this faith away. The scene described here is concerned with the way Peter no longer looks at Jesus but has earthly elements in view. Naturally, then, by any reckoning of probability, he is bound to sink as soon as he gets out onto the water. But he has left out of this the essential point, that he has been called by Jesus, who is the Lord. Together with him, and by his power, in relation to him, he will so to speak be able to walk right over even what is deadly in this world... If we let our gaze be captivated by the tendency of the moment, by the wind that is blowing around our ears, then really our faith can only sink out of sight... If we do that, then we have already lost our true anchor, which consists in depending on our relationship to the One who can overcome brute force, the brute force of death, the brute force of history and its impossibilities. Faith means resisting the brute force that would otherwise pull us under. Faith means fellowship with him who has the other kind of power, one that draws us up, that holds us fast, that carries us safely over the elements of death.

The Commandments

*T*he whole of man is required for the knowledge of God — understanding, will, and heart. In practice this means that we cannot know God unless we are prepared to accept his will, to take it as the yardstick and the orientation for our lives. In still more practical terms, that means that living in accordance with the commandments is a part of belonging to the pilgrim fellowship of faith, the fellowship of those traveling toward God. That is not a heteronomous rule being imposed upon man. It is in assenting to the will of God that our being made truly similar to God is actually effected, and we become what we are: the image of God. And because God is love, that is why the commandments, in which his will is made known, are the essential variations of the single theme of love. They are the practical rules of love for God, for my neighbor, for creation, for ourselves. And because, again, there exists in Christ the entire assent to God's will, the full stature of being in God's image; that is why living in accordance with love and within the will of God is following Christ, moving toward him and walking together with him.

Authentic Dialogue

What does the word "dialogue" really mean? After all, dialogue does not take place simply because people are talking. Mere talk is the deterioration of dialogue that occurs when there has been a failure to reach it. Dialogue first comes into being where there is not only speech but also listening. Moreover, such listening must be the medium of an encounter; this encounter is the condition of an inner contact which leads to mutual comprehension. Reciprocal understanding, finally, deepens and transforms the being of the interlocutors... To listen means to know and to acknowledge another and to allow him to step into the realm of one's own "I."...

Thus, after the act of listening, I am another man, my own being is enriched and deepened because it is united with the being of the other and, through it, with the being of the world... When we speak of dialogue in the proper sense, what we mean is an utterance wherein something of being itself, indeed, the person himself, becomes speech. This touches the very being of man as such, purifying and intensifying his potency to be who he is... Men are capable of reciprocal comprehension because, far from being wholly separate islands of being, they communicate in the same truth. The greater their inner contact with the one reality which unites them, namely, the truth, the greater their capacity to meet on common ground. Dialogue without this interior obedient listening to the truth would be nothing more than a discussion among the deaf.

Faith is a Meeting with Jesus

aith is not a magic formula. But it does give us the key to learning for ourselves. So that we can get answers and find out for ourselves who we are. It is always the case that a person first recognizes himself in others and through others. No one can arrive at knowledge of himself just by looking within himself and trying to build up his personality from what he finds there. Man as a being is so constructed for relationships that he grows in relation to others. So that his own meaning, his task in life, his advancement in life, and his potential are unlocked in his meetings with others. From the starting point of this basic structure of human existence we can understand faith and our meeting with Jesus. Faith is not just a system of knowledge, things we are told; at the heart of it is a meeting with Jesus. This meeting with Jesus, among all those other meetings we have need of, is the truly decisive one. All our other meetings leave the ultimate goal unclear, where we are coming from, where we are going. At our meeting with him the fundamental light dawns, by which I can understand God, man, the world, mission, and meaning — and by which all the other meetings fall into place.

The Sermon on the Mount and Encounter

People sense very strongly, shall we say, the double implication of the Sermon on the Mount, that this is, on the one hand, the message of a new inwardness, a maturity, and kindness, bringing freedom from superficiality and external things, yet at the same time making a more serious claim on us. And this claim is so great that man, were he left on his own, would be crushed by it. When it is said: I no longer merely say to you, you may not commit adultery, but that you may not look on a woman with lust; when it is said: not only may you not kill, but you may not even be angry at the other person; and when it is said: an eye for an eye, a tooth for a tooth is no longer enough; on the contrary, if anyone strikes you on the cheek, you must offer him the other cheek — then we are confronted by a demand so great that it amazes us but that also seems to ask too much of men. Which would at least be asking too much of them if it were not in the first place lived out in Jesus Christ and if the whole thing were not the result of a personal encounter with God.

The Process of Spiritual Growth

*I*t is important for the process of spiritual growth that you don't just pray and study your faith at times when it happens to cross your mind, when it suits you, but that you observe some discipline... I should say, never begin with thinking alone. For if you try to pull God toward you in the laboratory of rational thought, and to attach him to you in what is to some extent a purely theoretical fashion, you find you can't do it. You always have to combine the questions with action. Pascal once said to an unbelieving friend: Start by doing what believers do, even if it still makes no sense to you... You can never look for faith in isolation; it is only found in an encounter with people who believe, who can understand you, who have perhaps come by way of a similar situation themselves, who can in some way lead you and help you. It is always among us that faith grows. Anyone who wants to go it alone has thus got it wrong from the very start.

The Connection between Faith and Heart

*I*n reality, for the believing Christian the words "I believe" articulate a kind of certainty that is in many respects a higher degree of certainty than that of science yet one that does indeed carry within it the dynamic of the "not yet"… Just as a person becomes certain of another's love without being able to subject it to the methods of scientific experiment, so in the contact between God and man there is a certainty of a quite different kind from the certainty of objectivizing thought. We live faith, not as a hypothesis, but as the certainty on which our life is based… Belief is certainty that God has shown himself and has opened up for us the view of truth itself… In the act of believing the assent comes about in a different way from the way it does in the act of knowing: not through the degree of evidence bringing the process of thought to its conclusion, but by an act of will, in connection with which the thought process remains open and still under way. Here the will commands assent, even though the thought process is still under way… Any perception presupposes a certain sympathy with what is perceived. Without a certain inner closeness, a kind of love, we cannot perceive the other thing or person. In this sense the "will" always somehow precedes the perception and is its precondition; and the more so, the greater and more inclusive is the reality to be perceived. We are able to give the assent of faith because the will — the heart — has been touched by God, "affected" by him. Through being touched in this way, the will knows that even what is still not "clear" to the reason is true.

The Yes of Believing

*A*ssent is produced by the will, not by the understanding's own direct insight: the particular kind of freedom of choice involved in the decision of faith rests upon this... Believing is not an act of the understanding alone, not simply an act of the will, not just an act of feeling, but an act in which all the spiritual powers of man are at work together. Still more: man in his own self, and of himself, cannot bring about this believing at all; it has of its nature the character of a dialogue. It is only because the depth of the soul — the heart — has been touched by God's Word that the whole structure of spiritual powers is set in motion and unites in the Yes of believing. It is through all this that we also begin to see the particular kind of truth with which believing is concerned; theology talks about "saving truth"... Everything a man does or allows to happen to him can, ultimately, be derived from his will to be happy. When the heart comes into contact with God's Logos, with the Word who became man, this inmost point of his existence is being touched. Then, he does not merely feel, he knows from within himself: that is it; that is HE, that is what I was waiting for. It is a kind of recognition. For we have been created in relation to God.

The Commandments As the Form of Our Freedom

*E*very great human utterance reaches beyond what was consciously said into greater, more profound depths; there is always, hidden in what is said, a surplus of what is not said, which lets the words grow with the passing of time... The Ten Commandments can never simply be completely understood... The Ten Commandments appear in ever-new perspectives, and ever-new dimensions of their meaning open up. What is occurring is a process of being guided into the whole of truth, into the truth that absolutely cannot be carried within one historical moment alone (see Jn 16: 12f.). For the Christian, the interpretation that was completed in the words and the life and the death and the Resurrection of Christ represents the ultimate interpretative authority, wherein emerges a depth that could not previously have been foreseen. Because that is so, human listening to the message of faith is no passive reception of hitherto unknown information; rather, it is the awakening of our submerged conscience and the opening up of the powers of understanding that are awaiting the light of truth within us. Thus, such understanding is a highly active process, in which the quite rational search for the standards of our responsibility really gains in strength... If the Ten Commandments, as expounded by rational understanding, are the answer to the inner demands of our nature, then they are not at the opposite pole to our freedom but are rather the concrete form it takes. They are then the foundation for every law of freedom and are the one truly liberating power in human history.

The Conversion of Saint Paul

onversion in the Pauline sense is something much more radical than, say, the revision of a few opinions and attitudes. It is a death-event. In other words, it is an exchange of the old subject for another. The "I" ceases to be an autonomous subject standing in itself. It is snatched away from itself and fitted into a new subject. The "I" is not simply submerged, but it must really release its grip on itself in order then to receive itself anew in and together with a greater "I." In the Letter to the Galatians, the fundamental intuition about the nature of conversion — that it is the surrender of the old isolated subjectivity of the "I" in order to find oneself within the unity of a new subject, which bursts the limits of the "I," thus making possible contact with the ground of all reality — appears again with new emphases in another context… There is only *one* bearer of the promise, outside of which is the chaotic world of self-realization where men compete with one another and desire to compete with God but succeed merely in working right past their true hope… You have become a new, singular subject together with Christ and, in consequence — through the amalgamation of subjects — find yourselves within the purview of the promise.

Conversion and Obedience

*F*aith requires conversion and that conversion is an act of obedience toward a reality which precedes me and which does not originate from me. Moreover, this obedience continues, inasmuch as knowledge never transforms this reality into a constituent element of my own thought, but rather the converse is true: it is I who make myself over to it, while it always remains above me. For Christians, this prior reality is not an "it" but a "he" or, even better, a "you." It is Christ, the Word made flesh. He is the new beginning of our thought. He is the new "I" which bursts open the limits of subjectivity and the boundaries dividing subject from object, thus enabling me to say: "It is no longer I who live." Conversion does not lead into a private relationship with Jesus, which in reality would be another form of mere monologue. It is delivery into the pattern of doctrine, as Paul says, or, as we discovered in John, entrance into the "we" of the Church. This is the sole guarantee that the obedience which we owe to the truth is concrete… Only the concrete God can be something other than a new projection of one's own self. Following in Christ's footsteps is the only way of losing oneself which attains the desired goal… The one who became flesh has remained flesh. He is concrete… Obedience to the Church is the concreteness of our obedience. The Church is that new and greater subject in which past and present, subject and object come into contact. The Church is our contemporaneity with Christ: there is no other.

The Key to Conversion

hristian exodus calls for a conversion which accepts the promise of Christ in its entirety and is prepared to lose its whole life to this promise. Conversion, then, also calls for going beyond self-reliance and for entrusting ourselves to the mystery, the sacrament in the community of the Church, in which God enters my life as agent and frees it from its isolation. Along with faith, conversion entails losing oneself in love, which is a Resurrection since it is a kind of dying. Conversion is a cross held into the Easter mystery, although this does not mean it is less painful. After citing the words of the psalm "pierce my flesh with the nails of thy fear" (Ps 119: 120), Augustine expressed this in his inimitable way: "The nails are the commandments of justice: With these the fear of the Lord nails down the flesh (carnal desire) and crucifies us as a pleasing sacrifice unto himself." In this way eternal life is always present in the midst of this life and exodus shines into a world that is in itself anything but a "promised land." In this manner Christ becomes the way — he himself, not just his words; and also in this way he becomes truly present "today"… Coming from a different angle, we once again encounter the fact that freedom and truth are inseparable. If we can know nothing about God and if God does not want to know anything about us, then we are not free people in a creation that is open to freedom, but elements in a system of necessities in which, inexplicably, the cry for freedom will not die out. The question about God is simultaneously and in one the question about truth and freedom.

JANUARY 28

The Radical Inner Change of Conversion

A mystery can be seen only by one who lives it; the moment of spiritual insight coincides of necessity with the moment of conversion… We have fallen prey to a progressive barbarization of our spiritual vision. Even from a purely human standpoint there is abundant evidence for the thesis that without conversion, without a radical inner change in our thinking and being, we cannot draw closer to one another. For even the simplest intelligence must realize that barbarization cannot be the path to humanization. But where man is barred from every path that leads within, from every means of purification, where, instead, only his envy and his greed are being rekindled, there barbarism becomes method. And we come here upon something unexpected: rightly understood, the path that leads men within and the path that draws them together are not in conflict; on the contrary, they need and support one another. For it is only when men are united inwardly that they can really be united outwardly. But if they are inwardly impenetrable to one another, their outward encounters will serve only to increase their potential for aggressiveness. The Bible portrays this graphically in the story of the tower of Babel: the most advanced union in terms of technical skill turns suddenly into a total incapacity for human communication… That is the logical outcome: where each person wants to be a god, that is, to be so adult and independent that he owes himself to no one but determines his own destiny simply and solely for himself, then every other person becomes for him an antigod, and communication between them becomes a contradiction in itself.

Living Like the Prophets

We can indeed recognize something of God's plan. This knowledge goes beyond that of my personal fate and my individual path. By its light we can look back on history as a whole and see that this is not a random process but a road that leads to a particular goal. We can come to know an inner logic, the logic of God, within apparently chance happenings. Even if this does not enable us to predict what is going to happen at this or that point, nonetheless we may develop a certain sensitivity for the dangers contained in certain things — and for the hopes that are in others. A sense of the future develops, in that I see what destroys the future — because it is contrary to the inner logic of the road — and what, on the other hand, leads onward — because it opens the positive doors and corresponds to the inner design of the whole. To that extent the ability to diagnose the future can develop. It's the same with the prophets. They are not to be understood as seers, but as voices who understand time from God's point of view and can therefore warn us against what is destructive — and, on the other hand, show us the right road forward.

God and Man

I believe that Jesus Christ enables me to divine what God is and what man is. God is not simply the bottomless abyss or infinite height that sustains all things but never itself enters the sphere of the finite. God is not simply infinite distance; he is also infinite nearness. The human person can confide in him and speak to him: He sees and hears and loves... He expresses himself in the man Jesus, although not exhaustively, since Jesus, though one with him, nevertheless addresses him as "Father." God remains the One who is infinitely more than all visible things. Only in the lonely prayer of Jesus, only in Jesus' addressing him as "Father," is he to be known. At the same time, however, he draws very close to us in this utterance of the name "Father." Human beings are such that they cannot stand the person who is wholly good, truly upright, truly loving, the person who does evil to no one. It seems that in this world only momentarily is trust met with trust, justice with justice, love with love. The person who exemplifies all these virtues quickly becomes insupportable to others. People will crucify anyone who is really and fully human. Such is man. And such am I — *that* is the terrifying insight that comes to me from the crucified Christ. Along with this insight, however, goes another: Man is the being who is capable of expressing God himself. Man is so made that God can enter into union with him. The human person, who seems at first sight to be a kind of unfortunate monster produced by evolution, at the same time represents the highest possibility the created order can attain.

Breakthrough to the New Man

The breakthrough to the new man takes place in Jesus Christ. In him the real future of man, what he can be and should be, has in fact begun. The inner self of Jesus, as it is portrayed throughout the whole of his life and finally in his self-sacrifice on the cross, offers a measure and prototype of future humanity. It's not for nothing that we talk of following Christ, of entering upon his way. It is a matter of inner identification with Christ — just as he identified himself with us. That is really what man is moving toward. It is in the great stories of discipleship, which extend across the centuries, that we first see unfolding what is hidden in the figure of Jesus. It is not the case, then, that a schematic pattern is imposed, but that every potential development of true human existence is contained therein. We see how Thérèse of Lisieux or Saint Don Bosco, how Edith Stein, the apostle Paul, or Thomas Aquinas, has learned from Jesus how to go about being human. All these people have become truly like Jesus — and they are nonetheless different and original… The salvation that is offered us is no mechanical process or exterior matter. It has been entrusted to our freedom and has thereby also been rendered vulnerable to the fragility of human freedom and of the human character. Salvation begins anew in every man; it is not simply there. You cannot just cement it on externally or control it by the use of power, but always only enter into the freedom that opens up. But above all and in all is the One who comes to meet us and who gives us a hope that is stronger than all the devastation that men can bring to pass.

February

Beings Moving Toward Another

The essence of an image consists in the fact that it represents something. When I see it I recognize, for example, the person whom it represents, or the landscape, or whatever. It points to something beyond itself. Thus the property of an image is not to be merely what it itself is — for example, oil, canvas, and frame. Its nature as an image has to do with the fact that it goes beyond itself and that it manifests something that it itself is not. Thus the image of God means, first of all, that human beings cannot be closed in on themselves. Human beings who attempt this betray themselves. To be the image of God implies relationality. It is the dynamic that sets the human being in motion toward the totally Other. Hence it means the capacity for relationship; it is the human capacity for God. Human beings are, as a consequence, most profoundly human when they step out of themselves and become capable of addressing God on familiar terms. Indeed, to the question as to what distinguishes the human being from an animal, as to what is specifically different about human beings, the answer has to be that they are the beings that God made capable of thinking and praying. They are most profoundly themselves when they discover their relation to their Creator. Therefore the image of God also means that human persons are beings of word and of love, beings moving toward Another, oriented to giving themselves to the Other and only truly receiving themselves back in real self-giving.

FEBRUARY 2

Jesus the New Temple

*J*esus does not say that he will demolish the temple... But he does prophesy that his accusers will do exactly that. This is a prophecy of the cross: he shows that the destruction of his earthly body will be at the same time the end of the temple. With his Resurrection the new temple will begin: the living body of Jesus Christ, which will now stand in the sight of God and be the place of all worship. Into this body he incorporates men. It is the tabernacle that no human hands have made, the place of true worship of God, which casts out the shadow and replaces it with reality. Interpreted at its deepest level, the prophecy of the Resurrection is also a prophecy of the Eucharist. The body of Christ is sacrificed and precisely as sacrificed is living. This is the mystery made known in the Mass. Christ communicates himself to us and thus brings us into a real bond with the living God... At the moment of Jesus' death, the function of the old temple comes to an end. It is dissolved. It is no longer the place of God's presence, his "footstool," into which he has caused his glory to descend. Theologically, the visible destruction of the temple has already been anticipated. Worship through types and shadows ends at the very moment when the real worship takes place: the self-offering of the Son, who has become man and "Lamb," the "Firstborn," who gathers up and into himself all worship of God, takes it from the types and shadows into the reality of man's union with the living God. The prophetic gesture of cleansing the temple, of renewing divine worship and preparing it for its new form, has reached its goal.

Entrance into Sonship

To share in the Son's relationship: How is this to be done? What did it mean for Jesus himself? It manifests itself in the Gospels primarily in the prayer of Jesus. The fact that he is Son means, above all, that he prays. That, in the ground of his being, whether he works among men or takes his rest, he is always open to the living God, always has his place in him, always regards his existence as an exchange with him and so always lives from this innermost depth... The Son does not simply design his own existence; he receives it in a most profound dialogue with God. It is this dialogue that makes him free to walk among men and makes him free to serve. It is this dialogue that teaches him, without school or teacher, to know Scripture more deeply than anyone else — to know it truly from God himself... Whoever becomes the son of this Father no longer stands alone. Entrance into this sonship is entrance into the great family of those who are sons along with us. It creates a relationship. To draw near to Christ means always to draw near to all those of whom he wants to make a single body.

Returning to the Sabbath Source

*I*n the creation account the Sabbath is depicted as the day when the human being, in the freedom of worship, participates in God's freedom, in God's rest, and thus in God's peace. To celebrate the sabbath means to celebrate the covenant. It means to return to the source and to sweep away all the defilement that our work has brought with it. It also means going forth into a new world in which there will no longer be slaves and masters but only free children of God — into a world in which humans and animals and the earth itself will share together as kin in God's peace and freedom...

People had rejected God's rest, its leisure, its worship, its peace, and its freedom, and so they fell into the slavery of activity. They brought the earth into the slavery of their activity and thereby enslaved themselves. Therefore God had to give them the Sabbath that they denied themselves. In their "no" to the God-given rhythm of freedom and leisure they departed from their likeness to God and so did damage to the earth. Therefore they had to be snatched from their obstinate attachment to their own work. God had to begin afresh to make them his very own, and he had to free them from the domination of activity. *Operi Dei nihil praeponatur*: The worship of God, his freedom, and his rest come first. Thus and only thus can the human being truly live.

The Anointing at Bethany

The story of the anointing at Bethany gives the impression, when one reads it for the first time, of being no more than an anecdote. Yet Jesus himself regarded it as part of the Gospel: "Wherever the Gospel is preached in the whole world what she has done will be told in memory of her" (Mk 14: 9)… Clearly, Jesus was comparing what took place at Bethany with the anointing of kings and rich men at death. This anointing was an attempt to go counter to the event of death in the conviction that death had not completed its work until the corruption of the body. As long as the body continued to exist, man was not completely dead. Jesus therefore regarded Mary's gesture as an attempt to prevent his death. He recognized her helpless, but not insignificant concern — a concern that expresses love — to give life, even immortality, to others. The events that followed show clearly that no human concern, however strong could ever purchase immortality. In the end, any anointing of this kind can only be an attempt to preserve the dead body. It cannot overcome death itself. There is only one anointing that is strong enough to meet death and that is the anointing of the Holy Spirit, the love of God. There is, then, something that is both exemplary and lasting in Mary's anointing of Jesus at Bethany. It was above all a concern to keep Christ alive in this world and to oppose the powers that aimed to silence and kill him. It was an act of faith and love. Every such act can have the same effect.

The Way to Immortality

hat a sensation it would cause if we were to read one day in the newspapers that the remedy for death had been discovered. Ever since man has been on this earth, he has been looking for this remedy. We hope to find it, but at the same time we are afraid of it… Yet the Church proclaims that this remedy has in fact been found. Death has been overcome — Jesus Christ has risen and will die no more. What was possible then is also fundamentally possible and this remedy applies to all of us. With Christ, we can all be Christians and immortal. How can this be?… What was this humanity of Christ that was so closely united with God, the humanity that is the way that we should all follow? It was this: Jesus lived his whole life in contact with God. Jesus lived in close contact with God. He spent his nights in prayer… The crucified Christ died praying. His whole being was driven into God and transmuted into pure human life. Because of this, he breathed God's own atmosphere of love. Because of this too, he was immortal, being raised above death… This is the way to immortality… Victory is with the Son, the living Christ. The more perfectly we follow his way, the more complete will be the victory in this world of his saving power over death.

Human Beings are the Fruit of Love

The great projects of the living creation point to a creating Reason and show us a creating Intelligence, and they do so more luminously and radiantly today than ever before. Thus we can say today with a new certitude and joyousness that the human being is indeed a divine project, which only the creating Intelligence was strong and great and audacious enough to conceive of. Human beings are not a mistake but something willed; they are the fruit of love. They can disclose in themselves, in the bold project that they are, the language of the creating Intelligence that speaks to them and that moves them to say: Yes, Father, you have willed me… Pilate is correct when he says: "Behold the man." In him, in Jesus Christ, we can discern what the human being, God's project, is, and thereby also our own status. In the humiliated Jesus we can see how tragic, how little, how abased the human being can be. In him we can discern the whole history of human hate and sin. But in him and in his suffering love for us we can still more clearly discern God's response: Yes, that is the man who is loved by God to the very dust, who is so loved by God that he pursues him to the uttermost toils of death. And even in our own greatest humiliation we are still called by God to be the brothers and sisters of Jesus Christ and so to share in God's eternal love. The question about what the human being is finds its response in the following of Jesus Christ. Following in his steps from day to day in patient love and suffering we can learn with him what it means to be a human being and to become a human being.

Original Temptation

emptation does not begin with the denial of God and with a fall into outright atheism. The serpent does not deny God; it starts out rather with an apparently completely reasonable request for information, which in reality, however, contains an insinuation that provokes the human being and that lures him or her from trust to mistrust: "Did God say, 'You shall not eat of any tree of the garden'?" (Gn 3: 1). The first thing is not the denial of God but rather doubt about his covenant, about the community of faith, prayer, the commandments — all of which are the context for living God's covenant. There is indeed a great deal of enlightenment when one doubts the covenant, experiences mistrust, demands freedom, and renounces obedience to the covenant as a straitjacket that prevents one from enjoying the real promises of life. It is so easy to convince people that this covenant is not a gift but rather an expression of envy of humankind and that it is robbing human beings of their freedom and of the most precious things of life. With this doubt people are well on their way to building their own worlds. In other words, it is then that they make the decision not to accept the limitations of their existence; it is then that they decide not to be bound by the limitations imposed by good and evil, or by morality in general, but quite simply to free themselves by ignoring them.

The Inner Standard of the Human Person

We should see that human beings can never retreat into the realm of what they are capable of. In everything that they do, they constitute themselves. Therefore they themselves, and creation with its good and evil, are always present as their standard, and when they reject this standard they deceive themselves. They do not free themselves, but place themselves in opposition to the truth. And that means that they are destroying themselves and the world. This, then, is the first and most important thing that appears in the story of Adam, and it has to do with the nature of human guilt and thus with our entire existence. The order of the covenant — the nearness of the God of the covenant, the limitations imposed by good and evil, the inner standard of the human person, creatureliness: all of this is placed in doubt. Here we can at once say that at the very heart of sin lies human beings' denial of their creatureliness, inasmuch as they refuse to accept the standard and the limitations that are implicit in it. They do not want to be creatures, do not want to be subject to a standard, do not want to be dependent. They consider their dependence on God's creative love to be an imposition from without… Human beings who consider dependence on the highest love as slavery and who try to deny the truth about themselves, which is their creatureliness, do not free themselves; they destroy truth and love. They do not make themselves gods, which in fact they cannot do, but rather caricatures, pseudo-gods, slaves of their own abilities, which then drag them down.

Original Sin

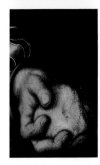

hat does original sin mean when we interpret it correctly? It must once again be stressed that no human being is closed in upon himself or herself and that no one can live of or for himself or herself alone. We receive our life not only at the moment of birth but every day from without — from others who are not ourselves but who nonetheless somehow pertain to us. Human beings have their selves not only in themselves but also outside of themselves: they live in those whom they love and in those who love them and to whom they are "present." Human beings are relational, and they possess their lives — themselves — only by way of relationship. I alone am not myself, but only in and with you am I myself. To be truly a human being means to be related in love, to be *of and for*. But sin means the damaging or the destruction of relationality. Sin is a rejection of relationality because it wants to make the human being a god. Sin is loss of relationship, disturbance of relationship, and therefore it is not restricted to the individual. When I destroy a relationship, then this event — sin — touches the other person involved in the relationship. Consequently sin is always an offense that touches others, that alters the world and damages it… At the very moment that a person begins human existence, which is a good, he or she is confronted by a sin-damaged world. Each of us enters into a situation in which relationality has been hurt. Consequently each person is, from the very start, damaged in relationships and does not engage in them as he or she ought. Sin pursues the human being, and he or she capitulates to it.

The Attempt to Save Ourselves

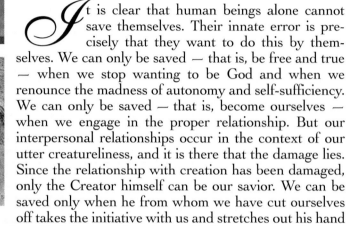

*I*t is clear that human beings alone cannot save themselves. Their innate error is precisely that they want to do this by themselves. We can only be saved — that is, be free and true — when we stop wanting to be God and when we renounce the madness of autonomy and self-sufficiency. We can only be saved — that is, become ourselves — when we engage in the proper relationship. But our interpersonal relationships occur in the context of our utter creatureliness, and it is there that the damage lies. Since the relationship with creation has been damaged, only the Creator himself can be our savior. We can be saved only when he from whom we have cut ourselves off takes the initiative with us and stretches out his hand to us. Only being loved is being saved, and only God's love can purify damaged human love and radically reestablish the network of relationships that have suffered from alienation… The One who is truly like God does not hold graspingly to his autonomy, to the limitlessness of his ability and his willing. He does the contrary: he becomes completely dependent, he becomes a slave. Because he does not go the route of power but that of love, he can descend into the depths of Adam's lie, into the depths of death, and there raise up truth and life. Thus Christ is the new Adam, with whom humankind begins anew. The Son, who is by nature relationship and relatedness, reestablishes relationships. His arms, spread out on the cross, are an open invitation to relationship, which is continually offered to us. The cross, the place of his obedience, is the true tree of life.

Humans are Dependent

*H*umans *are* dependent. They cannot live except from others and by trust. But there is nothing degrading about dependence when it takes the form of love, for then it is no longer dependence, the diminishing of self through competition with others. Dependence in the form of love precisely constitutes the self as self and sets it free, because love essentially takes the form of saying, "I want you to be." It is creativity, the only creative power, which can bring forth the other as other without envy or loss of self. Humans are dependent — that is the primary truth about them. And because it is, only love can redeem them, for only love transforms dependence into freedom. Thus human beings will only succeed in destroying their own redemption, destroying themselves, if they eliminate love "to be on the safe side." For humans, the crucified God is the visible certainty that creation is already an expression of love: we exist on the foundation of love. It is therefore a constitutive part of Christian faith to accept mystery as the center of reality, that is to say, to accept love, creation as love, and to make that love the foundation of one's life.

The Lord is Peace

*I*n giving his peace to his friends, Jesus was simply bidding them farewell before going out into the darkness of the Mount of Olives... But this "peace" was also Jesus' last farewell before he set off on the way of the cross. It was more than a merely conventional word. Jesus, on his way to the cross, could not have been superficially wishing his friends an easy, comfortable existence in his absence. Nor could he, about to bring salvation to the world by experiencing the depths of human suffering, have been wanting his disciples to experience the peace of forgetfulness. Real peace can only be brought by release from the captivity of comfortable lies and the acceptance of suffering. Repression is the most common cause of mental illness, and healing can be found only in a descent into the suffering of truth. Psychotherapists cannot, however, tell us what this truth is or whether it is ultimately good. The two liturgical formulae, "The Lord be with you" and "Peace be with you" are interchangeable and for a very good reason. The Lord himself is peace. He did not simply use words when he took his leave of his friends. He who, on the cross, suffered and overcame the lie and the hatred of mankind was peace itself. He himself came through his cross and in giving his peace he did not simply give something — he gave himself. The Lord gives himself to his own as peace. He places himself in their hands... We must ask him, then, to teach us how to celebrate the Eucharist truly and how to receive the truth that is love and in this way to become, through him, people of peace.

FEBRUARY 14

Forty Days of Preparation

*I*n the forty days of the preparation for Easter, we endeavor to get away from the heathenism that weighs us down, that is always driving us away from God, and we set off toward him once again. So, too, at the beginning of the Eucharist, in the confession of sin, we are always trying to take up this path again, to set out, to go to the mountain of God's word and God's presence… We must learn that it is only in the silent, barely noticeable things that what is great takes place, that man becomes God's image and the world once more becomes the radiance of God's glory. Let us ask the Lord to give us a receptivity to his gentle presence; let us ask him to help us not to be so deafened and desensitized by this world's loud outcry that our receptivity fails to register him. Let us ask him that we may hear his quiet voice, go with him, and be of service together with him and in his way, so that his kingdom may become present in this world… We imitate God, we live by God, like God, by entering into Christ's manner of life. He has climbed down from his divine being and become one of us; he has given himself and does so continually… It is by these little daily virtues, again and again, that we step out of our bitterness, our anger toward others, our refusal to accept the other's otherness; by them, again and again, we open up to each other in forgiveness. This "littleness" is the concrete form of our being like Christ and living like God, imitating God; he has given himself to us so that we can give ourselves to him and to one another.

The Church and the Forty Days

The Church is being urged ever more loudly and insistently to exchange a distant and unreal redemption by the Word for a more robust redemption by bread and the sure path of politicization. Our experience, then, is of a Church in the wilderness, a Church in her forty-day period. It is one of exposure to emptiness, to a world that seems, religiously speaking, to have become wordless, imageless, soundless; exposure to a world in which the heavens over us are dark and distant and impalpable. And yet for us too and for the Church of our day this time in the wilderness can become a time of grace in which a new love can grow out of the suffering induced by God's distance from us. We often have the oppressive feeling that the manna of our faith will be enough only for the present day — but God gives us that manna new each day if we allow him to do so. We must live in a world in which God is seemingly to be found only as One who is dead — but he can strike living water even from dead stones. A Church in her Lent, in her "forty days" in the wilderness. I believe that during this season of fasting we must hearten ourselves anew to accept our situation in patience and faith and to follow fearlessly after our hidden God. If we journey on in patient faith, then for us too a new day can dawn out of the darkness. And God's bright world, the lost world of images and sounds, will be restored to us again; there will be a new morning in God's good creation.

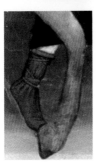

The Purpose of Lent

The purpose of Lent is to keep alive in our consciousness and our life the fact that *being a* Christian can only take the form of *becoming a* Christian ever anew; that it is not an event now over and done with but a process requiring constant practice. Let us ask, then: What does it mean to become a Christian? How does this take place?… If individuals are to become Christians they need the strength to overcome; they need the power to stand fast against the natural tendency to let themselves be carried along. Life in the most inclusive sense has been defined as "resistance to the pull of gravity." Only where such effort is expended is there life; where the effort ceases life too ceases. If this is true in the biological sphere, it is all the more true in the spiritual. The human person is the being which does not become itself automatically. Nor does it do so simply by letting itself be carried along and surrendering to the natural gravitational pull of a kind of vegetative life. It becomes itself always and only by struggling against the tendency simply to vegetate and by dint of a discipline that is able to rise above the pressures of routine and to liberate the self from the compulsions of utilitarian goals and instincts. Our world is so full of what immediately impinges on our senses that we are in danger of seeing only details and losing sight of the whole. It takes effort to see beyond what is right in front of us and to free ourselves from the tyranny of what directly presses upon us.

The Primacy of Peter

*E*very single biblical logion about the primacy remains from generation to generation a signpost and a norm, to which we must ceaselessly resubmit ourselves. When the Church adheres to these words in faith, she is not being triumphalistic but humbly recognizing in wonder and thanksgiving the victory of God over and through human weakness. Whoever deprives these words of their force for fear of triumphalism or of human usurpation of authority does not proclaim that God is greater but diminishes him, since God demonstrates the power of his love, and thus remains faithful to the law of the history of salvation, precisely in the paradox of human impotence. For with the same realism with which we declare today the sins of the popes and their disproportion to the magnitude of their commission, we must also acknowledge that Peter has repeatedly stood as the rock against ideologies, against the dissolution of the word into the plausibilities of a given time, against subjection to the powers of this world. When we see this in the facts of history, we are not celebrating men but praising the Lord, who does not abandon the Church and who desired to manifest that he is the rock through Peter, the little stumbling stone: "flesh and blood" do not save, but the Lord saves through those who are of flesh and blood. To deny this truth is not a plus of faith, not a plus of humility, but is to shrink from the humility that recognizes God as he is.

Authority in the Church

*W*hat makes the Church real is not that there are likable people in her... The reality is her *exousia*: she is given the power, the authority to speak words of salvation and to perform deeds of salvation which humans need and can never achieve on their own. No one can usurp the "I" of Christ or the "I" of God. The priest speaks with this "I" when he says: "This is my body" and when he says "I forgive you your sins." It is not the priest who forgives them but God who forgives them, and this definitely changes everything. But what a shaking event it is that a human being is permitted to utter the "I" of God! The priest can do it only on the basis of that authority which the Lord has given his Church. Without this authority he is nothing but a social worker. That is an honorable profession, but in the Church we are looking for higher hopes, which come from a greater power. If these words of authority are no longer spoken and if they no longer remain transparent so that their foundation is visible, then the human warmth of the small group is of little use. What is essential has been lost, and the group will become aware of this very soon. It must not be spared the pain of conversion, which expects of us what we cannot achieve on our own and leads us precisely in this way into that sphere of God's power which is our true hope. The authority of the Church is transparent to God's power and consequently our hope. For this reason the inner commitment to the authority of the Church in an act of profound obedience is the fundamental decision of priestly existence.

What is Truth

*T*homas Aquinas, as is well known, defined truth as the adequation of the intellect to reality… The perception of the truth is a process which brings man into conformity with being. It is a becoming one of the "I" and the world, it is consonance, it is being gifted and purified. To the extent that men allow themselves to be guided and cleansed by the truth, they find the way not only to their true selves but also to the human "you." Truth, in fact, is the medium in which men make contact, whereas it is the absence of truth which closes them off from one another. Accordingly, movement toward the truth implies temperance. If the truth purifies man from egotism and from the illusion of absolute autonomy, if it makes him obedient and gives him the courage to be humble, it thereby also teaches him to see through producibility as a parody of freedom and to unmask undisciplined chatter as a parody of dialogue. It is victorious over the tendency to mistake the absence of all ties for freedom. Thus, the truth is fruitful precisely by being loved for its own sake.

FEBRUARY 20

The Essence and Dignity of Truth

*H*ow is it that to become true is to become good and that truth is good, indeed the good? How is it that the truth has value of itself, without having to validate itself with reference to exterior aims? These affirmations are correct only if the truth possesses its worth in itself, if it subsists in itself and has more being than everything else; if the truth itself is the ground upon which I stand. To think through the essence of truth is to arrive at the notion of God. In the long run, it is impossible to maintain the unique identity of the truth, in other words, its dignity (which in turn is the basis of the dignity both of man and of the world), without learning to perceive in it the unique identity and dignity of the living God. Ultimately, therefore, reverence for the truth is inseparable from that disposition of veneration which we call adoration. Truth and worship stand in an indissociable relationship to each other; one cannot really flourish without the other, however often they have gone their separate ways in the course of history.

Entering into Lent

*L*ent is a propitious time in which the Church invites Christians to be more intensely aware of Christ's redeeming work and to live our baptism more profoundly... With its duration of forty days, Lent tries to recall some of the events that marked the life and history of ancient Israel, presenting to us again its paradigmatic value... The Lenten season is an invitation to relive with Jesus the forty days he spent in the desert, praying and fasting, before undertaking his public mission... This is the authentic and central program of the Lenten Season: to listen to the Word of truth, to live, speak, and do the truth, to reject lies that poison humanity and are the door to all evils. It is urgent, therefore, during these forty days, to listen again to the Gospel, the Lord's Word, Word of truth, so that in every Christian, in each one of us, the awareness be reinforced of the truth that has been given, that he has given us, to live it and be his witnesses. Lent stimulates us to let the Word of God penetrate our life and in this way to know the fundamental truth: who we are, where we come from, where we must go, what path we must take in life. Thus, the Lenten season offers us an ascetic and liturgical journey that, helping us to open our eyes in face of our weakness, makes us open our hearts to the merciful love of Christ.

The Chair of Saint Peter

Peter expressed in the first place, in the name of the apostles, the profession of faith: "You are the Christ, the Son of the living God" (Mt 16: 16). This is the task of all the successors of Peter: to be the leader in the profession of faith in Christ, the Son of the living God. The chair of Rome is, first of all, the chair of this creed. From the loftiness of this chair, the Bishop of Rome is obliged to repeat constantly: "Dominus Iesus." "Jesus is Lord," as Paul wrote in his Letters to the Romans (10: 9), and to the Corinthians (1 Cor 12: 3). To the Corinthians he said, with particular emphasis: "For although there may be so-called gods in heaven or on earth... yet for us there is one God, the Father... and one Lord, Jesus Christ, through whom are all things and through whom we exist" (1 Cor 8: 5). The chair of Peter obliges its incumbents to say, as Peter did at a moment of crisis of the disciples, when many wished to go away: "Lord, to whom shall we go? You have the words of eternal life; and we have believed, and have come to know, that you are the Holy One of God" (Jn 6: 68 and following). Whoever sits on the chair of Peter must remember the words that the Lord said to Simon Peter at the Last Supper: "And when you have returned again, strengthen your brethren" (Lk 22: 32). The holder of the Petrine ministry must be conscious of being a frail and weak man, as his own strength is frail and weak, constantly needing purification and conversion. But he can also be conscious that from the Lord he receives strength to confirm his brethren in the faith and to keep them united in the confession of Christ, crucified and risen.

The Process of Becoming a Christian

*N*o one becomes a Christian by his own unaided power. No one can make himself a Christian. It is not within the human being's power to shape himself as it were into a great-souled person and finally into a Christian. On the contrary, the process of becoming a Christian begins only when a person sloughs off any illusion of independence and self-sufficiency; when he or she acknowledges that human beings do not create themselves and cannot bring themselves to fulfillment but must open themselves and allow themselves to be led, as it were, to their own true selves. To be a Christian, then, means first and foremost that we acknowledge our own insufficiency and allow him — the Other who is God — to act in us… Adam imagined that he would be like God if he could subsist solely by his own power and could be self-sufficient in giving life to himself as he saw fit. In reality, such a mistaken quest of an imagined divinization leads to self-destruction, for even God himself… does not exist in isolated self-sufficiency but is fully divine only as infinitely needing and receiving in a dialogue of love and as giving himself freely and without limit. Human beings become like God only when they enter into this same movement; when they stop trying to create themselves and, instead, allow God to create them.

The Denial of Sin

*I*t is precisely the existence of sin that modern man is unable to take seriously. Because of this rejection of the concept of sin, no one is directly touched today by the Gospel claim that the evidence of Jesus' divine nature is based on his power to forgive sin. Most people do not explicitly deny the existence of God, but they do not believe that he is of any importance in the realm of human life. Hardly anyone seriously thinks nowadays that men's wrong actions may concern God so much that he regards them as sinful and offensive to himself, with the result that such sin must be forgiven by him alone. Even theologians have discussed the possibility of replacing the practice of confessing sin by conversations with psychologists, sociologists, and lawyers. Sin does not really exist. There are only problems, and these can be settled with the help of experts. Sin has disappeared and with it forgiveness, and behind that disappearance there is also the disappearance of a God who is turned toward man. In this situation, Christians can only turn to the Gospel, which can give us courage to grasp the truth. Only the truth can make us free. But the truth is that there is guilt and that we ourselves are guilty. It is Christ's new truth that there is also forgiveness by the one who has the power to forgive. The Gospel calls on us to accept this truth. There is a God. Sin exists and there is also forgiveness. We need that forgiveness if we are not to seek refuge in the lie of excuses and thus destroy ourselves… Where there is forgiveness, there is also healing.

Reducing Christianity to Moralism

he temptation to turn Christianity into a kind of moralism and to concentrate everything on man's moral action has always been great. God remains invisible, untouchable and, therefore, man takes his support mainly from his own action. But if God is not a true agent in history who also enters into my personal life, then what does redemption mean?… The temptation to reduce Christianity to the level of a type of moralism is very great in our own day. For we are all living in an atmosphere of deism. It seems that there is no room for God himself to act in human history and in my life. And so we have the idea of God who can no longer enter into this cosmos, made and closed against him. What is left? Our action. And we are the ones who must transform the world. We are the ones who must generate redemption. We are the ones who must create the better world, a new world. And if that is how one thinks, then Christianity is dead… We are lacking the force of eternal love to respond to the challenges of our lives and of politics. Love has the capacity to transform the world. It spurs our love and, in this communion of the two wills, one can go on. Christian holiness and rectitude do not consist in any superhuman greatness or in some superior talent. Christian faith is properly the religion of ordinary people… It comes about in a state of obedience that places us at God's disposition wherever he calls. It is the same obedience that does not trust to one's own power or one's own greatness but is founded on the greatness of the God of Jesus Christ.

Happiness and the Passion of Being Human

*I*t is only by enduring himself, by freeing himself through suffering from the tyranny of egoism, that man finds himself, that he finds his truth, his joy, his happiness. He will be all the happier the more ready he is to take upon himself the abysses of existence with all their misery. The measure of one's capacity for happiness depends on the measure of the premiums one has paid, on the measure of one's readiness to accept the full passion of being human. The crisis of our age is made very real by the fact that we would like to flee from it; that people mislead us into thinking that one can be human without overcoming oneself, without the suffering of renunciation and the hardship of self-control; that people mislead us by claiming that there is no need for the difficulty of remaining true to what one has undertaken and the patient endurance of the tension between what one ought to be and what one actually is. An individual who has been freed from all effort and led into the fool's paradise of his dreams loses what is most essential, himself. There is, in fact, no other way in which one can be saved than by the cross. All offers that promise a less costly way will founder, will prove to be false. The hope of Christianity, the outlook of faith, ultimately rest quite simply on the fact that faith tells the truth. The outlook of faith is the outlook of the truth that may be obscured and trampled upon, but can never perish.

Egoism, the I, and the You

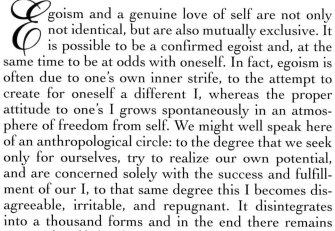

*E*goism and a genuine love of self are not only not identical, but are also mutually exclusive. It is possible to be a confirmed egoist and, at the same time to be at odds with oneself. In fact, egoism is often due to one's own inner strife, to the attempt to create for oneself a different I, whereas the proper attitude to one's I grows spontaneously in an atmosphere of freedom from self. We might well speak here of an anthropological circle: to the degree that we seek only for ourselves, try to realize our own potential, and are concerned solely with the success and fulfillment of our I, to that same degree this I becomes disagreeable, irritable, and repugnant. It disintegrates into a thousand forms and in the end there remains only a dissatisfaction with self that leads to flight from oneself and a turning to drugs or one of the many other forms of a self-destructive egoism. Only the yes that comes to me from a you makes it possible for me to say yes to myself in and through this you. The I realizes itself through a you. It is true, moreover, that only when we have accepted ourselves can we address a genuine yes to anyone else. To accept, to "love," oneself presumes the existence of truth and requires that we never relinquish our quest for that truth.

FEBRUARY 28

Forgiveness as the Restoration of Truth

A Jesus who agrees with everyone and everything, a Jesus without his holy anger, without the hardness of truth and genuine love is not the real Jesus as he is depicted in the Scriptures, but a pitiable caricature. A concept of "Gospel" that fails to convey the reality of God's anger has nothing to do with the Gospel of the Bible. True forgiveness is something quite different from weak indulgence. Forgiveness is demanding and requires both parties, the one who forgives and the one who is forgiven, to do so with all their minds and hearts. A Jesus who sanctions everything is a Jesus without the cross, for such a Jesus would not need the torment of the cross to save mankind. As a matter of fact, the cross is being increasingly banished from theology and reinterpreted as just a vexatious mischance or a purely political event. The cross as reconciliation, as a means of forgiving and saving, is incompatible with a certain modern mode of thought. Only when the relationship between truth and love is rightly comprehended can the cross be comprehensible in its true theological depth. Forgiveness has to do with truth. That is why it requires the Son's cross and our conversion. Forgiveness is, in fact, the restoration of truth, the renewal of being, and the vanquishment of the lies that lurk in every sin; sin is by nature a departure from the truth of one's own nature and, by consequence, from the truth of the Creator God.

Joy, Mercy, Faith, Peace, Presence

*I*f the loved one, love, the greatest gift of my life, is close to me, if I can be convinced that the one who loves me is close to me, even in situations of suffering, the joy that remains in the depth of my heart is ever greater than all sufferings... Fraternal correction is a work of mercy. None of us can see himself well, see his shortcomings well. So it is an act of love, to be a complement to one another, to help each other see one another better, and to correct each other. Of course, this great work of mercy, helping each other so that each one can really find his or her own integrity, and functionality as an instrument of God, demands great humility and love. Only if this comes from a humble heart, from someone who does not place himself above another, who does not consider himself better than the other, but only a humble instrument mutually to help each other. Only if one feels this deep and true humility, if one feels that these words come from common love, from the collegial affection in which we wish to serve God together, can we in this way help each other with a great act of love... We can have the faith of the Church together, because with this faith we enter in the thoughts and feelings of the Lord... We are in inner peace, because being in the thought of Christ unites our real being... However, this is valid to the extent in which we really enter this presence which he gave us, in this gift which is already present in our being.

March

Faith and Our I

*T*he act of faith is a deeply personal act, anchored in the innermost depths of the human I. But precisely because it is so personal, it is also an act of communication. In the depths of its being, the *I* is always related to the *you* and vice versa: that true relationship that becomes "communion" can be born only in the deep places of the human *I*. The act of faith is a participation in the seeing of Jesus, a dependence on Jesus. John, who reclined next to Jesus at the Last Supper, is a symbol of what faith actually means. Faith is communication with Jesus and, consequently, a liberation of my I from its preoccupation with self, a liberation that sets me free to respond to the Father, to speak the Yes of love; that sets me free to say Yes to being, free for that Yes that is our salvation and that overcomes the "world." It follows, then, that faith is, in its innermost essence, a "being with," a breaking out of the isolation that is the malady of my *I*. The act of faith is an opening of oneself to the whole world, a breaking open of the door of my subjectivity… The *I* that has been redeemed finds itself again in a greater new *I*. In this new *I*, for which faith has liberated me, I find myself united not only with Jesus, but with all who travel the same road.

Faith Rooted in Christ's Friendship

Today, having a clear faith based on the Creed of the Church is often labeled as fundamentalism. Whereas relativism, that is, letting oneself be "tossed here and there, carried about by every wind of doctrine," seems the only attitude that can cope with modern times. We are building a dictatorship of relativism that does not recognize anything as definitive and whose ultimate goal consists solely of one's own ego and desires. We, however, have a different goal: the Son of God, the true man. He is the measure of true humanism... A mature adult faith is deeply rooted in friendship with Christ. It is this friendship that opens us up to all that is good and gives us a criterion by which to distinguish the true from the false, and deceit from truth... One element Jesus uses to define friendship is the communion of wills. For the Romans *"Idem velle — idem nolle"* (same desires, same dislikes) was also the definition of friendship... Friendship with Christ coincides with the third request of the *Our Father.* "Thy will be done on earth as it is in heaven." At his hour in the Garden of Gethsemane, Jesus transformed our rebellious human will into a will conformed and united with the divine will. He suffered the whole drama of our autonomy — and precisely by placing our will in God's hands, he gives us true freedom: "Not as I will, but as you will" (Mt 26: 39). Our redemption is brought about in this communion of wills: being friends of Jesus, to become friends of God. The more we love Jesus, the more we know him, the more our true freedom develops and our joy in being redeemed flourishes. Thank you, Jesus, for your friendship!

Faith and Our Goal

The Christian faith is not a pastime, and the Church is not one club among others of a similar or even of a different sort. Rather, faith responds to the primordial question of man regarding his origin and goal. It bears on those basic problems which Kant characterized as the essential core of philosophy: What can I know? What may I hope for? What is man? In other words, faith has to do with truth, and only if man is capable of truth can it also be said that he is called to freedom. The first item in the alphabet of faith is the statement: In the beginning was the Word. Faith reveals to us that eternal reason is the ground of all things or, put in other terms, that things are reasonable from the ground up.

Faith does not aim to offer man some sort of psychotherapy; *its* psychotherapy is the truth. This is what makes it universal and by nature missionary. It is also the reason why faith is intrinsically *"quærens intellectum,"* as the Fathers say, that is, in search of understanding. Understanding, hence, rational engagement with the priorly given Word, is a constitutive principle of the Christian faith, which of necessity spawns theology. This trait, moreover, distinguishes the Christian faith from all other religions, even from a purely historical point of view. Theology is a specifically Christian phenomenon which follows from the structure of this faith.

Lenten Transfiguration

Astonished in the presence of the trans-figured Lord, who was speaking with Moses and Elias, Peter, James, and John were suddenly enveloped in a cloud from which a voice arose that proclaimed: "This is my beloved Son, listen to him" (Mk 9: 7). When one has the grace to sense a strong experience of God, it is as though seeing something similar to what the disciples experienced during the Transfiguration: For a moment they experienced ahead of time something that will constitute the happiness of paradise. In general, it is brief experiences that God grants on occasions, especially in anticipation of harsh trials. However, no one lives "on Tabor" while on earth. Human existence is a journey of faith and, as such, goes forward more in darkness than in full light, with moments of obscurity and even profound darkness. While we are here, our relationship with God develops more with listening than with seeing; and even contemplation takes place, so to speak, with closed eyes, thanks to the interior light lit in us by the word of God… This is the gift and commitment for each one of us in the Lenten season: To listen to Christ, like Mary. To listen to him in the word, preserved in Sacred Scripture. To listen to him in the very events of our lives, trying to read in them the messages of providence. To listen to him, finally, in our brothers, especially in the little ones and the poor, for whom Jesus himself asked our concrete love. To listen to Christ and to obey his voice. This is the only way that leads to joy and love.

The Root of Our Wretchedness

*I*n what does man's wretchedness actually consist? Above all, in his insecurity; in the uncertainties with which he is burdened; in the limitations that oppress him; in the lack of freedom that binds him; in the pain that makes his life hateful to him. Ultimately there is, behind all this, the meaninglessness of his existence that offers satisfaction neither to himself nor to anyone else for whom it might have been necessary, irreplaceable, consequential. We can say, then, that the root of man's wretchedness is loneliness, is the absence of love — is the fact that my existence is not embraced by a love that makes it necessary, that is strong enough to justify it despite all the pain and limitations it imposes... What man needs is a communion that goes beyond that of the collective; a unity that reaches deep into the heart of man and endures even in death. The human unity that man requires by nature must know how to answer the problem of death in which it must find its truest confirmation... Man cannot identify himself with God, but God has identified himself with man — that is the content of the communion that is offered us in the Eucharist. A *communio* that offers less offers too little.

Darkness without Truth

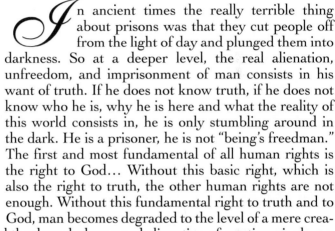

*I*n ancient times the really terrible thing about prisons was that they cut people off from the light of day and plunged them into darkness. So at a deeper level, the real alienation, unfreedom, and imprisonment of man consists in his want of truth. If he does not know truth, if he does not know who he is, why he is here and what the reality of this world consists in, he is only stumbling around in the dark. He is a prisoner, he is not "being's freedman." The first and most fundamental of all human rights is the right to God... Without this basic right, which is also the right to truth, the other human rights are not enough. Without this fundamental right to truth and to God, man becomes degraded to the level of a mere creature of needs. And the deep darkness and alienation of our times is shown in the fact that we have powers and abilities but do not know what they are for; we have so much knowledge that we are no longer able to believe and see truth; we are no longer able to embrace the totality. Our philosophy is that of Pilate: What is truth? This only looks like a question; in fact it is a statement, to the effect that there is no truth, and only idiots and fanatics imagine they have it or argue about it. But if this is how things are, if man has no truth, only abilities, he is fundamentally alienated, and "participation" is only an empty playacting in the dark, deluding man with the notion of freedom and hurting him deeply. There is nothing fortuitous about the strident protests against such empty freedom: man, deprived of truth, has been dishonored.

Moral Obligation is Our Dignity

*M*oral obligation is not man's prison, from which he must liberate himself in order finally to be able to do what he wants. It is moral obligation that constitutes his dignity, and he does not become more free if he discards it: on the contrary, he takes a step backward, to the level of a machine, of a mere thing. If there is no longer any obligation to which he can and must respond in freedom, then there is no longer any realm of freedom at all. The recognition of morality is the real substance of human dignity; but one cannot recognize this without simultaneously experiencing it as an obligation of freedom. Morality is not man's prison but rather the divine element in him… For nature is not — as is asserted by a totalitarian scientism — some assemblage built up by chance and its rules of play but is rather a creation. A creation in which the *Creator Spiritus* expresses himself. This is why there are not only natural laws in the sense of physical functions: the specific natural law itself is a moral law. Creation itself teaches us how we can be human in the right way. The Christian faith, which helps us to recognize creation as creation, does not paralyze reason; it gives practical reason the life-sphere in which it can unfold. The morality that the Church teaches is not some special burden for Christians: it is the defense of man against the attempt to abolish him. If morality — as we have seen — is not the enslavement of man but his liberation, then the Christian faith is the advance post of human freedom.

Liberation and Salvation

The whole argument about Christ revolves around man's "liberation," his "salvation." But what can liberate man? Who liberates him, and to what? Put even more simply: What is "human freedom"? Can man become free without truth, i.e., in falsehood? Liberation without truth would be a lie; it would not be freedom but deception and thus man's enslavement, man's ruin. Freedom without truth cannot be true freedom, so, without truth, freedom is not even freedom. If man is to be free, he must be "like God." Wanting to be like God is the inner motive of all mankind's programs of liberation. Since the yearning for freedom is rooted in man's being, right from the outset he is trying to become "like God." Indeed, anything less is ultimately too little for him... At first sight it may seem to be a rather parochial, merely internal Christian matter, when we speak of the prayer of Jesus as the New Testament's basic affirmation regarding his person. In reality this is precisely the point which concerns us; i.e., it is what is central to humanity. For the New Testament designates it as the place where man may actually become God, where his liberation may take place; it is the place where he touches his own truth and becomes true himself. The question of Jesus' filial relation to the Father gets to the very root of the question of man's freedom and liberation, and unless this is done everything else is futile. Any liberation of man which does not enable him to become divine betrays man, betrays his boundless yearning.

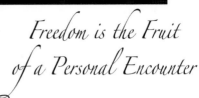

Freedom is the Fruit of a Personal Encounter

God has our freedom very much at heart. He wants us to be free, he loves us inasmuch as we are free... But why does God love our freedom? Because he sees in us the image of his incarnate Son, who has always adhered freely to the Father's plan, who freely accepted a body and freely abased himself to the point of death on the cross, in that sacrificial oblation which the sacrament of the Eucharist actualizes every day on the altar. We can also have the experience of being truly free only when, adhering without reservations to Christ's plan, we also participate in freedom. Genuine freedom is the fruit of a personal encounter with Jesus. In him, God gives us and restores to us that freedom that we had otherwise lost for ever because of the sin of our forbears... The rich youth (see Mt 19: 16-22) did recognize in the Lord the possibility of human fulfillment, but did not have the courage to follow him all the way because, as the Gospel says, he had too many riches. He believed mistakenly that true freedom, which he ardently desired, was [the] absence of links, of ties, and of any obedience. And so, although he remained apparently free to act according to his own autonomous choices, he went away sad. We can undoubtedly try to build our life without Christ, but with the one consequence of remaining always alone and disconsolate. Jesus alone makes us free! One cannot think of freedom without thinking of the term liberation. Jesus is for us liberation! — liberation from sin, from our false desires, and ultimately from ourselves. Liberation is the most beautiful existential reverberation that faith can elicit in our life.

The Glad Tidings of the Cross

*T*he content of the Christian *evangelium* reads: God finds man so important that he himself has suffered for man. The cross is in truth the center of the *evangelium*, the glad tidings: "It is good that you exist" — no, "It is necessary that you exist." The cross is the approbation of our existence, not in words, but in an act so completely radical that it caused God to become flesh and pierced this flesh to the quick; that, to God, it was worth the death of his incarnate Son. One who is so loved that the other identifies his life with this love and no longer desires to live if he is deprived of it; one who is loved even unto death — such a one knows that he is truly loved. But if God so loves us, then we are loved in truth. Then love is truth, and truth is love. Then life is worth living. This is the *evangelium*. This is why, even as the message of the cross, it is glad tidings for one who believes; the only glad tidings that destroy the ambiguity of all other joys and make them worthy to be joy. Christianity is, by its very nature, joy — the ability to be joyful. The "Rejoice!" with which it begins expresses its whole nature. By its very essence, by its very nature, Christian belief is "glad tidings"… deep joy of the heart is also the true prerequisite for a sense of humor, and thus humor is, in a certain sense, the measure of faith.

The Woman at the Well

*T*he account of Jesus' meeting with the Samaritan woman at Jacob's well (Jn 4) opens with the meeting of Jesus and the Samaritan woman in the context of a normal, human, everyday experience — the experience of thirst... The subject shifts to that thirst that is a thirst for life, and the point is made that one must drink again and again, must come again and again to the source. In this way, the woman is made aware of what in actuality she has always known but to which she has not always adverted: that she thirsts for life itself and that all the assuaging that she seeks and finds cannot slake this living, elemental thirst... There comes to light the real dilemma, the deep-seated waywardness, of her existence: she is brought face to face with herself. In general, we can reduce what is happening to the formula: one must know oneself as one really is if one is to know God. The primordial experience of all experiences is that man himself is the place in which and through which he experiences God... The woman stands face to face with herself. It is no longer a question now of *something* but of the depths of the *I* itself and, consequently, of the radical poverty that *is* man's I-myself... The question of all questions arises always and of necessity: the question about oneself becomes a question about God... Only at this point does the offering of Jesus' true gift become possible... Now the woman is aware of the real thirst by which she is driven. Hence she can at last learn what it is for which this thirst thirsts. It is the purpose and meaning of all catechesis to lead to this thirst.

Facing Chaos with Jesus

Passover was celebrated at home. Jesus did this too. But after the meal he got up and went out, and he overstepped the bounds of the law by going beyond the Brook Kidron which marked the boundary of Jerusalem. He went out into the night. He did not fear the chaos, did not hide from it, but plunged into its deepest point, into the jaws of death: as we pray, he "descended into hell"... Faith always means going out together with Jesus, not being afraid of the chaos, because he is the stronger one. He "went out" and we go out with him if we do the same. Faith means emerging from the walls to build places of faith and of love in the midst of the chaotic world by the power of Jesus Christ. The Lord "went out" — it is a sign of his power. He went out into the night of Gethsemane, the night of the cross and the grave. He is the "stronger man" who stands up against the "strong man" — death — (Lk 11: 21-23). The love of God — God's power — is stronger than the powers of destruction. So this very "going out," this setting out on the path of the Passion, when Jesus steps outside the boundary of the protective walls of the city, is a gesture of victory. The mystery of Gethsemane already holds within it the mystery of Easter joy. Jesus is the "stronger man." There is no power that can withstand him now; no place where he is not to be found. He summons us to dare to accompany him on his path; for where faith and love are, he is there, and the power of peace is there which overcomes nothingness and death.

God Loved Us First

"*God loved you first!*"... One should take this sentence as literally as can be, and I try to do that. For it is truly the great power in our lives and the consolation that we need. And it's not seldom that we need it. He loved me first, before I myself could love at all. It was only because he knew me and loved me that I was made. So I was not thrown into the world by some operation of chance, as Heidegger says, and now have to do my best to swim around in this ocean of life, but I am preceded by a perception of me, an idea and a love of me. They are present in the ground of my being. What is important for all people, what makes their life significant, is the knowledge they are loved. The person in a difficult situation will hold on if he knows Someone is waiting for me, Someone wants me, and needs me. God is there first and loves me. And that is the trustworthy ground on which my life is standing and on which I myself can construct it.

MARCH 14

Learning to Love

We are not spared dark nights. They are clearly necessary, so that we can learn through suffering, so that we can acquire freedom and maturity and above all else a capacity for sympathy with others… A part of every human love is that it is only truly great and enriching if I am ready to deny myself for this other person, to come out of myself, to give of myself. And that is certainly true of our relationship with God, out of which, in the end, all our other relationships must grow. I must begin by no longer looking at *myself*, but by asking what *he* wants. I must begin by learning to love. That consists precisely in turning my gaze away from myself and toward him. With this attitude I no longer ask, What can I get for myself, but I simply let myself be guided by him, truly lose myself in Christ; when I abandon myself, let go of myself, then I see, yes, life is right at last, because otherwise I am far too narrow for myself. When, so to speak, I go outside, then it truly begins, then life attains its greatness. Of course it isn't a journey you can make from one day to the next. If you're interested in quick happiness, then faith doesn't work. And perhaps that is one of the reasons for the crisis in faith nowadays, that we want our pleasure and our happiness at once, and not to take the risk of a lifelong venture — a venture made in the trust that this leap will not end in nothingness, but that it is by its nature that act of love for which we were created. And which alone gives me what I want: loving and being loved and thereby finding true happiness.

We are Created to Love

he Christian faith holds that creation has been damaged. Human existence is no longer what was produced at the hands of the Creator. It is burdened with another element that produces, besides the innate tendency *toward God*, the opposite tendency *away from God*. In this way man is torn between the original impulse of creation and his own historical inheritance. The possibility of this is already built into the nature of finite creatures, but has only developed in history. On one hand, man is created to love. He is there in order to lose himself, to give himself. But it is also easy for him to withhold himself, to want to be just himself. This tendency is built up to the point where, on one hand, he can love God and, on the other, can be angry with him and say, I want to be independent, I just want to be myself. If we observe ourselves carefully, we can see this paradox, this inner tension of our existence. On one hand, we recognize that what the Ten Commandments say is right. That's what we want and what we like doing. That is to say, being good to other people, being grateful, respecting other people's property, finding great love in a sexual relationship so that this becomes a lifelong mutual responsibility, telling the truth, not lying. In some sense that is indeed a trend that is not merely *contrary* to our nature and lying on our shoulders like a yoke.

Freedom and Our Essential Being

reedom belongs to the *basic structure* of creation, to the spiritual existence of man. We are not just laid out and determined according to a particular model. Freedom is there so that each one of us can shape his own life and, along with his own inner self, can in the end follow the path that best corresponds to his essential being. Freedom is a *gift* inherent in creation... Freedom means that of my own free will I take upon myself the potential of my being. It is certainly not the case that it is then only a matter of Yes or No. For even beyond the No, there opens up an infinite interplay of creative possibilities for good. Basically, then, our idea that unless I say No to evil, my freedom has already been taken from me is itself a perversion of freedom. Freedom really finds its creative space in the realm of what is good. Love is creative; truth is creative — it is under these conditions that my eyes are truly opened, and I can recognize things for what they are. If we look at the lives of the great men, the saints, we can see how, in the course of history, they bring to light in creative fashion quite new human potentialities, which inwardly blind or stunted people have hitherto been quite unable to perceive. In other words, freedom comes into its own in revealing and developing those things in the realm of good that as yet lie waiting to be discovered and in extending thereby the potentialities of the created order. Freedom is lost whenever it holds that it can only assert its own will in saying No. For in that case I have exercised my freedom but have thereby at the same time distorted it.

Seeing the Father

Whoever sees Christ really sees the Father; in that which is visible one sees that which is invisible, the invisible in person… They who look at the form of Christ are taken up into his exodus, which the Church Fathers explicitly mention in connection with the events on Mount Tabor. They are led on the paschal path of going beyond and learn to see more than just the visible in the visible… In the exodus of Christ's love — that is, in the transition from opposition to community which goes through the cross of obedience — redemption, that is, liberation, truly occurs. This exodus leads from the slavery of *philautia*, the slavery of self-conceit and self-containment, into the love of God… whoever sees Christ, the Crucified One, sees the Father — indeed, the entire Trinitarian mystery… As a consequence, the human person has really become friend, initiated into the innermost mystery of God. This person is no longer a slave in a dark world, but knows the very heart of truth. But this truth is a way; it is the fatal, yet precisely through the losing of oneself life-giving adventure of love which alone is freedom… The truth itself, the real truth, has become bearable for humans — indeed the way for them — by having appeared and appearing in the poverty of the powerless one… In Christ poverty has become the genuine sign, the inner "power" of truth. Only his true existence in poverty, nothing else, has opened the path for him into people's hearts. The humility of God is truth's door into the world; there is no other. Only in this manner can the truth become a way.

When We Say "Father"

The word "Father" makes me sure of one thing: I do not come from myself; I am a child. I am tempted at first to protest against this reminder as the prodigal Son did. I want to be "of age," "emancipated," my own master. But then I ask myself: What is the alternative for me — or for any person — if I no longer have a Father, if I have left my state as child definitively behind me? What have I gained thereby? Am I really free? No, I am free only when there is a principle of freedom, when there is someone who loves and whose love is strong. Ultimately, then, I have no alternative but to turn back again, to say "Father," and in that way to gain access to freedom by acknowledging the truth about myself. Then my glance falls on him who, his whole life long, identified himself as child, as Son, and who, precisely as child and Son, was consubstantial with God himself: Jesus Christ. When I say "Father," the word automatically calls up the word "our." When I speak to God, I cannot address him solely as "Father." When I say "Father," I must include the "we" of all his children. But the opposite is also true: when I say "Father" I know that I have entered the company of all the children of God and that they are at my side. Consequently, talking with God does not distract me from my responsibility for the earth and for all mankind; it gives it to me anew. In the light of prayer, I can venture to accept it.

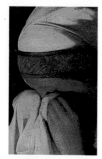

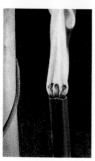

Discovering God in Our Suffering

emarkably enough, the claim that there can no longer be any God, the claim, that is, that God has completely disappeared, is the urgent conclusion drawn by *onlookers* at the terror, the people who view the horrors from the cushioned comfort of their own prosperity and attempt to pay their tribute to it and ward it off from themselves by saying, "If such things can happen, there is no God!" But among those who are themselves immersed in the fearful reality the effect is not infrequently just the opposite: It is precisely then that they discover God. In this world of suffering, adoration has continued to rise up from the fiery furnaces of the crematories and not from the spectators of the horror. It is no accident that the people who in their history have been the most condemned to suffering, who did not have to wait for 1940-1945 to be in "Auschwitz," also became the people of revelation, the people that have known God and made him visible to the world. And it is no accident that the human being who has been the most afflicted and has suffered most — Jesus of Nazareth — was and is revelation itself. It is no accident that faith in God flows from a "head sore-wounded," from a crucified man, and that atheism has Epicurus for father and originates in the world of the satisfied onlooker… We must also learn that in addition to the Real Presence of Jesus in Church and sacrament there is that other, second real presence of Jesus in the least of our brethren, in the downtrodden of this world; he wants us to find him in all of them.

MARCH 20

We are Meant to Rely on Receiving

*M*an is redeemed by the cross; the crucified Christ, as the completely opened being, as the true redemption of man — this is the central principle of Christian faith… in the last analysis of man, it expresses the primacy of acceptance over action, over one's own achievement… Accordingly, from the point of view of the Christian faith, man comes in the profoundest sense to himself not through what he does but through what he accepts. He must wait for the gift of love, and love can only be received as a gift. It cannot be "made" on one's own, without anyone else; one must wait for it, let it be given to one. And one cannot become *wholly* man in any other way than by being loved, by letting oneself be loved. That love represents simultaneously both man's highest possibility and his deepest need, and that this most necessary thing is at the same time the freest and the most unenforceable means precisely that for his "salvation" man is meant to rely on receiving. If he declines to let himself be presented with the gift, then he destroys himself. Activity that makes *itself* into an absolute, that aims at achieving humanity by its own efforts alone, is in contradiction with man's being… The primacy of acceptance is not intended to condemn man to passivity; it does not mean that man can now sit idle. On the contrary, it alone makes it possible to do the things of this world in a spirit of responsibility, yet at the same time in an uncramped, cheerful, free way, and to put them at the service of redemptive love.

Freedom, Responsibility, and the Commandments

*H*uman freedom is a freedom in a coexistence of freedoms; only thus is it true — that is, appropriate to the true reality of man… That means that I have no need at all to seek corrective factors for the freedom of the individual from without; if that were so, then freedom and responsibility, freedom and truth would remain forever opposites, and they are not. Correctly perceived, the reality of the individual carries in it an element of reference to the whole, to others. Accordingly, we shall say that there is such a thing as the common truth of the one human existence within every man, what is referred to in tradition as the "nature" of man. There is one divine idea of man, and our task is to correspond to this… Responsibility would then mean living our existence as a response — as a response to what we are in truth. This one truth of man, in which the good of all and freedom are indissolubly related to each other, is expressed most centrally in the biblical tradition in the Ten Commandments… In the Ten Commandments God presents himself, depicts himself, and at the same time interprets human existence, so that its truth is made manifest, as it becomes visible in the mirror of God's nature, because man can only rightly be understood from the viewpoint of God. Living out the Ten Commandments means living out our own resemblance to God, responding to the truth of our nature, and thus doing good. To say it again, another way: Living out the Ten Commandments means living out the divinity of man, and exactly that is freedom: the fusing of our being with the Divine Being and the resulting harmony of all with all.

The Meaning of Life

*I*f there were not already sense and meaning in the world, then we, too, would be unable to make any. We can indeed carry out actions that have meaning and significance within a particular purposive framework, but these cannot of themselves give meaning to life as a whole. Either it has a sense — or it doesn't. Meaning is not something we can simply manufacture. What we manufacture in that way may be able to grant us a momentary satisfaction, but it will not serve to justify the whole of our existence or to give meaning to it. In all times and all places men have of course asked about meaning and will continue to do so. And in doing so, they will always find fragments of an answer. Of these fragmentary answers, only those elements are valid that men have *discovered*, not those they have *invented*, only what they have found within man as a creature. And what will be of use to them in trying to understand themselves and to live a meaningful life. What the Church says, that meaning is not created by us but is given by God, should be understood in this fashion: Meaning is something that carries us, that goes ahead of us and beyond all our ideas and discoveries — and only in this way has it the strength to sustain our lives.

Love and Eternity

O ur life tends in the end toward a discovery of love, toward receiving love, and giving love. And the crucified Christ, who presents us with love lived out to the end, as he himself says in the Gospel of John, lifts this principle up into the realm of absolute reality. God himself is love. In this sense, love is indeed both the fundamental rule and the ultimate aim of life. Here we come again to the mystery of the grain of wheat, to the mystery of losing oneself and finding oneself. And we must link to this the observation that, as we know, no one can make love. It is given to us. It just happens; it comes to me from someone else; it enters into me. Human love always lays claim to eternity. Love contradicts death, as the French philosopher Gabriel Marcel once said. This human love is turned from a promise into the fulfillment of reality only when it is wrapped in a love that can truly impart eternity. Marcel said that to say to a person "I love you" meant: I refuse to accept your death; I protest against death. Thus we see that human love, in and for itself, represents an unredeemable promise. It strives for eternity, and yet it can offer only mortality. Yet, on the other hand, it knows that this promise is not meaningless and contradictory, and thereby destructive, since ultimately eternity is alive within it nonetheless. Even from a purely human point of view, then, love is what we are looking for and is the goal toward which our lives are directed. But within its own framework and on its own terms it directs our view toward God and brings us to wait upon God.

Jesus' Power as Obedience

The word used in the Bible for Jesus' power already provides a profound interpretation of the essence of this power: it is not just the power of one's own physical or technical strength. It is not the power of an ancient or modern Goliath, but power stemming from obedience, that is, from a relationship that is responsibility for being, the responsibility of truth and the good. As portrayed in the hymn to Christ in Philippians (2: 5-11), it is humble power. Christ does not hold on to equality with God as a thief holds on to his booty, as power captured at last that can be enjoyed to excess... Romano Guardini has very beautifully described the positive content of the fundamental act of Jesus, his crucifixion and attendant exaltation, as it is portrayed in the hymn of Philippians: "Jesus' entire existence is the translation of power into humility... into obedience to the will of the Father. Obedience is not secondary for Jesus, but forms the core of his being..." For his power there is therefore "no limit coming from the outside, but only one from the inside... the will of the Father freely accepted." It is a power that has such complete control over itself "that it is capable of renouncing itself"... Thus, Jesus' power is power based on love, love becoming powerful. It is power that shows us the way from all that is tangible and visible to the invisible and the truly real of God's powerful love. It is power as way that has as its goal setting people on their way: into the transcendence of love.

The Annunciation to a Virgin

*T*hat which is truly great grows unnoticed, and silence at the right moment is more fruitful than the constant activity that only too easily degenerates into spiritual idleness. In the present age, we are all possessed by a strange restlessness that suspects any silence of being a waste of time and any kind of repose as being negligence. We forget the real mystery of time, the real mystery present in growth and activity. That mystery involves silence and stillness. Even in the religious sphere we tend to expect and hope for everything from our own activity. We use all kinds of exercises and involvements to evade the real mystery of interior growth before God. And yet in the religious sphere receptivity is at least as important as activity. The mystery of the Annunciation to Mary is not only a mystery of silence; it is also, and even more, a mystery of grace. We must ask ourselves: What, is the real reason why Christ decided to be born of a Virgin?... Salvation comes not from human beings and their own powers but solely from God and his gracious action. God intervenes where there is a human vacuum; he starts at the point at which, from the human point of view, nothing can be done. He gives life to the bearer of the promise in the dead womb of Sarah, and follows the same pattern through history down to the Lord's birth from the Virgin... The salvation of the world is exclusively God's doing and therefore occurs in the midst of human weakness and powerlessness. From the viewpoint of the Bible the Virgin birth is in the last analysis a sign that what occurs is a pure act of grace on God's part.

MARCH 26

God's Nearness in Us

*T*hat we exist and move within the atmosphere of God the Creator, that is obviously true, first of all, purely from the point of view of our biological existence. And it becomes ever more true, the more we penetrate into the quite specific essence of God. We can put it this way: Wherever one person does something good for another, there God is especially near. Whenever someone opens himself for God in prayer, then he enters into his special closeness... Wherever there is something that best reflects him and makes him present, where there is truth and goodness, in those cases we are in contact with him, the Omnipresent, in a special way... In someone in whom God is present through and through, there is naturally a much stronger presence of God, a greater inner closeness, than in the case of someone who has completely distanced himself from God. Let's consider the Annunciation to Mary. God wishes Mary to become his temple, a living temple, and not merely by physical occupation of her body. But it only becomes possible for God truly to dwell in her because she opens herself to him inwardly; because she develops her inner being to become entirely compatible with him.

Love and Correction

nger is not necessarily always in contradiction with love. A father, for instance, sometimes has to speak crossly to his son so as to prick his conscience, just *because* he loves him. And he would fall short of his loving obligation and his will to love if, in order to make things easier for the other person, and also for himself, he avoided the task of putting him right sometimes by making a critical intervention in his life. We know that spoiled children, to whom everything has been permitted, are often in the end quite unable to come to terms with life, because later on life treats them quite differently, and because they have never learned to discipline themselves, to get themselves on the right track. Or if, for instance, because I want to be nice to him, I give to an addict the drugs he wants instead of weaning him off them (which would seem to him very hard treatment), then in that case you cannot talk of real love. To put it another way: love, in the true sense, is not always a matter of giving way, being soft, and just acting nice. In that sense, a sugar-coated Jesus or a God who agrees to everything and is never anything but nice and friendly is no more than a caricature of real love. Because God loves us, because he wants us to grow into truth, he must necessarily make demands on us and must also correct us. God has to do those things we refer to in the image of "the wrath of God," that is, he has to resist us in our attempts to fall from our own best selves and when we pose a threat to ourselves.

The Richness of Giving

A fantasy of people with property takes no account of the fact that, for the great majority of mankind, life is a struggle. On those grounds I would see this idea of choosing one's own path in life as a selfish attitude and as a waste of one's vocation. Anyone who thinks he already has it all, so that he can take what he wants and center everything on himself, is depriving himself of giving what he otherwise could. Man is not there to make himself, but to respond to demands made upon him. We all stand in a great arena of history and are dependent on each other. A man ought not, therefore, just to figure out what he would like, but to ask what he can do and how he can help. Then he will see that fulfillment does not lie in comfort, ease, and following one's inclinations, but precisely in allowing demands to be made upon you, in taking the harder path. Everything else turns out somehow boring, anyway. Only the man who "risks the fire," who recognizes a calling within himself, a vocation, an ideal he must satisfy, who takes on real responsibility, will find fulfillment. It is not in taking, not on the path of comfort, that we become rich, but only in giving.

Suffering and Love

*P*ain is part of being human. Anyone who really wanted to get rid of suffering would have to get rid of love before anything else, because there can be no love without suffering, because it always demands an element of self-sacrifice, because, given temperamental differences and the drama of situations, it will always bring with it renunciation and pain. When we know that the way of love — this exodus, this going out of oneself — is the true way by which man becomes human, then we also understand that suffering is the process through which we mature. Anyone who has inwardly accepted suffering becomes more mature and more understanding of others, becomes more human. Anyone who has consistently avoided suffering does not understand other people; he becomes hard and selfish... If we say that suffering is the inner side of love, we then also understand why it is so important to *learn how to suffer* — and why, conversely, the avoidance of suffering renders someone unfit to cope with life. He would be left with an existential emptiness, which could then only be combined with bitterness, with rejection, and no longer with any inner acceptance or progress toward maturity.

Christ the Burning Fire

*W*hen Jesus talks about fire, he means in the first place his own Passion, which was a Passion of love and was therefore a fire; the new burning bush, which burns and is not consumed; a fire that is to be handed on. Jesus does not come to make us comfortable; rather he sets fire to the earth; he brings the great living fire of divine love, which is what the Holy Spirit is, a fire that burns. In an apocryphal saying of Jesus that has been transmitted by Origen, he says: "Whoever comes close to me comes close to the fire." Whoever comes close to him, accordingly, must be prepared to be burned… It burns, yet this is not a destructive fire but one that makes things bright and pure and free and grand. Being a Christian, then, is daring to entrust oneself to this burning fire… Christ is the one who brings peace. And I would say that this is the saying that is preeminent and determinative. But we only properly comprehend this peace that Christ brings if we do not understand it in banal fashion as a way of cheating one's way out of pain, or out of the truth and the conflicts that truth brings with it… If the Church simply aims to avoid conflict, merely to ensure that no disturbances arise anywhere, then her real message can no longer make any impact. For this message is in fact there precisely in order to conflict with our behavior, to tear man out of his life of lies and to bring clarity and truth. Truth does not come cheap. It makes demands, and it also burns.

The Personal Dimension of Forgiveness

As sin, despite all our bonds with the human community, is ultimately something totally personal, so also our healing with forgiveness has to be something totally personal. God does not treat us as part of a collectivity. He knows each one by name, and he calls him personally and saves him if he has fallen into sin. Even if in all the sacraments, the Lord addresses the person as an individual, the personalist nature of the Christian life is manifested in a particularly clear way in the sacrament of Penance. That means that the personal confession and the forgiveness directed to this person are constitutive parts of the sacrament... Of course, the confession of one's own sin can seem to be something heavy for the person, because it humbles his pride and confronts him with his poverty. It is this that we need: we suffer exactly for this reason: we shut ourselves up in our delirium of guiltlessness and for this reason we are closed to others and to any comparison with them. In psychotherapeutic treatments a person is made to bear the burden of profound and often dangerous revelations of his inner self. In the sacrament of Penance, the simple confession of one's guilt is presented with confidence in God's merciful goodness. It is important to do this without falling into scruples, with the spirit of trust proper to the children of God. In this way confession can become an experience of deliverance, in which the weight of the past is removed from us and we can feel rejuvenated by the merit of the grace of God who each time gives back the youthfulness of the heart.

April

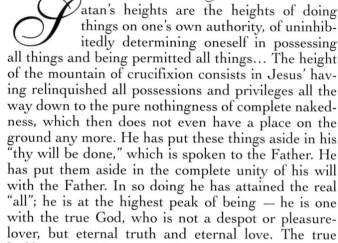

The Highest Peak of Being

atan's heights are the heights of doing things on one's own authority, of uninhibitedly determining oneself in possessing all things and being permitted all things... The height of the mountain of crucifixion consists in Jesus' having relinquished all possessions and privileges all the way down to the pure nothingness of complete nakedness, which then does not even have a place on the ground any more. He has put these things aside in his "thy will be done," which is spoken to the Father. He has put them aside in the complete unity of his will with the Father. In so doing he has attained the real "all"; he is at the highest peak of being — he is one with the true God, who is not a despot or pleasure-lover, but eternal truth and eternal love. The true image of God and of humans is thus restored in contrast to the caricature of God and humans which lay behind the satanic offer of "being like God." In his earthly nothingness but in unity with the will of God, Jesus also stood firm against the power of force and its being able to do all things. He is one with God, and therefore one with the real power that encompasses heaven and earth, time and eternity. He is one with God, so that God's power has become his power. The power he now proclaims from the mountain of exaltation is power coming from the roots of the cross and is thus radically opposed to the unrestrained power of possessing all things, being allowed all things, and being able to do all things.

Imitating Jesus

*T*he call to imitation is concerned not simply with a human agenda or with the human virtues of Jesus, but with his *entire* way, "through the curtain" (Heb 10: 20). What is essential and innovative about the way of Jesus Christ is exactly that he opens *this* way for us, for only in this manner do we come out into the open, into freedom. Imitation has the dimension of moving toward the divine communion, and this is why it is tied to the paschal mystery. For this reason the saying of Jesus about following him that comes after Peter's profession of faith states: "If any want to become my followers, let them deny themselves and take up their cross and follow me" (Mk 8: 34). This is not a narrow moralism that views life principally from the negative side, nor is it a kind of masochism for those who do not like themselves. We also do not track down the real meaning of Jesus' words if we understand them the other way around, as an exalted moralism for heroic souls who are determined to be martyrs. Jesus' call can only be comprehended from the broad paschal context of the entire exodus, which goes "through the curtain." From this goal the age-old wisdom of humans acquires its meaning — that only they who lose themselves find themselves, and only they who give life receive life (Mk 8: 35)... "The plan of God and our Redeemer for human beings consists in calling them back from exile and bringing them back from the alienation which came about because of disobedience"... For the perfection of life it is necessary to imitate Christ, not only in terms of the meekness and patience exhibited in his *life*, but also in terms of his death.

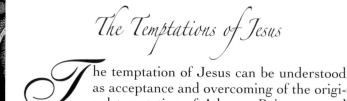

The Temptations of Jesus

The temptation of Jesus can be understood as acceptance and overcoming of the original temptation of Adam… Being tempted is an essential part of his being a man, part of his descent into fellowship with us, into the depths of our need… Temptations depicted in grand images reoccur concretely at particular stages in the life of Jesus. After multiplying the loaves, Jesus sees that the crowds want to make him king, and he flees — to the hills, by himself (Jn 6: 15). In a similar way he resists the temptation to identify himself with his miracles, which would interfere with his preaching — his real mission (cf. Mk 1: 35-39). And when Peter, having declared that Jesus is the Son of God, tries to keep him from the path to suffering, the Lord says to him the same thing that we hear at the climax and conclusion of the temptation story here: "Get behind me, Satan" (Mk 8: 33). Thus the temptation story summarizes the entire struggle of Jesus: it is about the nature of his mission, but at the same time it is also about the right ordering of human life, about the way to be human, about the way of history. Finally, it is about what is really important in the life of man. This ultimate thing, this decisive thing, is the primacy of God. The germ of all temptation is setting God aside, so that he seems to be a secondary concern when compared with all the urgent priorities of our lives. To consider ourselves, the needs and desires of the moment to be more important than he is — that is the temptation that always besets us. For in doing so we deny God his divinity, and we make ourselves, or rather, the powers that threaten us, into our god.

APRIL 4

Judas and Peter

*E*ven where God sets no limits, man can sometimes do so. Two such instances appear here. The first becomes apparent in the figure of Judas: There is the No stemming from greed and lust, from vainglory, which refuses to accept God. This is the No given because we want to make the world for ourselves and are not ready to accept it as a gift from God. "Sooner remain in debt than pay with a coin that does not bear our own portrait — that is what our sovereignty demands," as Nietzsche once said. The camel will not go through the eye of the needle; it sticks its proud hump up, so to speak, and is thus unable to get through the gate of merciful kindness. I think we all ought to ask ourselves, right now, whether we are not just like those people whose pride and vainglory will not let them be cleansed, let them accept the gift of Jesus Christ's healing love. Besides this refusal, which arises from the greed and the pride of man, there is, however, also the danger of piety, represented by Peter: the false humility that does not want anything so great as God bending down to us; the false humility in which pride is concealed, which dislikes forgiveness and would rather achieve its own purity; the false pride and the false modesty that will not accept God's mercy. But God does not wish for false modesty that refuses his kindness; rather, he desires that humility which allows itself to be cleansed and thus becomes pure. This is the manner in which he gives himself to us.

Why Jesus Washes Our Feet

*A*nyone who is not numbered among the powerful will be thankful whenever he sees someone powerful not helping himself at life's table. When the powerful person sees the power or possessions that have been given him as a mandate to be of service to others... As long as power and wealth are seen as ends in themselves, then power is always a power to be used against others and possessions will always exclude others. At that moment when the Lord of the world comes and undertakes the slave's task of foot-washing — which is, in turn, only an illustration of the way he washes our feet all through our lives — we have a totally different picture. God, who is absolute power itself, doesn't want to trample on us, but kneels down before us so as to exalt us. The mystery of the greatness of God is seen precisely in the fact that he can be small. He doesn't always have to take the highest place or the box seats. God is trying in this way to wean us away from our ideas of power and domination. He shows us that it is in fact a trifling matter if I can give orders to a great crowd of people and have everything I could want — and that it is truly great if I undertake the service of others... Only when power is changed from the inside, when our relationship to possessions is changed from within and we accept Jesus and his way of life, whose whole self is there in the action of foot-washing, only then can the world be healed and people be able to live at peace with one another. Jesus shows us what man ought to be, how he ought to live, and what we ought to work toward.

Redemption through Suffering

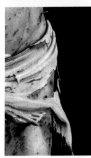

*T*he image of the crucified Christ, which is the focal point of the liturgy of Good Friday, makes us realize the true seriousness of human misery, human aloneness, human sin. Yet, throughout all the centuries of Church history, it has constantly been regarded as an image of consolation and hope. The Isenheim Altar of Matthias Grünewald, which is, perhaps the most moving painting of the crucifixion to be found in all Christendom, was located in a monastery of the Antonian Hospitalers, who cared for victims of the terrible plagues that afflicted the West during the late Middle Ages. The crucified Jesus is depicted as one of these victims; his whole body is disfigured by the boils of bubonic plague, the most terrible of the pestilence of that time... This painting made them realize that precisely by reason of their sickness they were identified with the crucified Christ, who, by his suffering, had become one with all the suffering of history; they felt the presence of the Crucified One in their cross and knew that, in their distress, they were drawn into union with Christ and hence into the abyss of his eternal mercy. They experienced his cross as their redemption... Instead of divine consolation, they want changes that will redeem suffering by removing it: not redemption through suffering, but redemption from suffering is their watchword; not expectation of divine assistance but the humanization of man by man is their goal.

The Easter Flame

*A*s we wait in the night-dark church for the Easter light to be struck, we should experience the consoling realization that God is fully aware of the night by which we are surrounded. In fact, he has already struck his light at the heart of it... The night enables us to appreciate what the light really is. It is brightness or luminousness that enables us to see; that shows the way and gives direction; that helps us to know both others and ourselves. It is warmth that strengthens and brings mobility; that consoles and gladdens. Finally, it is life, and this tiny quivering flame is an image of the wonderful mystery that we call "life" and that is in fact profoundly dependent on light... At this moment we are not only celebrating the Resurrection; we are also being given a distant glimpse of the second coming of the Lord, whom we are advancing to meet with lamps lit... Something of the joy that marks a wedding should be ours on this night so bright with candles. We should also ask ourselves the question: "Will I be one of those who sit at God's table? Will my lamp have enough oil for the everlasting wedding feast?" But perhaps it is even more Christian to ask ourselves the right questions about the present. The world is indeed dark, but even a single candle suffices to bring light into the deepest darkness. Did not God give us a candle at baptism and the means of lighting it? We must be courageous enough to light the candle of our patience, our trust, our love. Instead of bewailing the night, we must dare to light the little lamp that God has loaned us: "The light of Christ! — Thanks be to God!"

Light and Christmas and Easter

uring the two great holy nights of the Church year, Christmas and Easter, the symbolism of light fuses with the symbolism of night. On both occasions the Church uses the interplay of night and light to show in a symbolic manner what the content of the feast in question is: the encounter of God and the world, the victorious entry of God into a world that refuses him room and yet in the end cannot prevent him from taking it. This Christ-centered drama of light and darkness, God and the world, as they encounter each other, begins on Christmas when God knocks on the door of a world that rejects him even though it belongs to him (Jn 1: 5, 11). But the world cannot prevent his coming. He himself becomes "world" in becoming a human being. His coming seems a defeat of the light, which becomes darkness, but at the same time it is the first, hidden victory of the light, since the world has not been able to prevent this coming, however carefully it may have barred the doors of its inns. Now, on Easter, the drama reaches its central act and climax. The darkness has used its ultimate weapon, death... But the Resurrection effects the great reversal. Light has won the victory and now lives on unconquerably... It has made a bit of the world its own and transformed it into itself. Of course, this is not the end of the drama. The end is still awaited; it will arrive with the second coming of the Lord. At present, night continues, but it is a night in which a light has been lit. When the Lord comes again, the day will dawn and last forever.

The Breakthrough of Easter

What would it mean if Easter, the Resurrection of Jesus, had *not* taken place?... Well, if there were no Resurrection, the story of Jesus would have ended with Good Friday. His body would have decayed, and he would have become a has-been. But that would mean that God does not take initiatives in history, that he is either unable or unwilling to touch this world of ours, our human living and dying. And that in turn would mean that love is futile, nugatory, an empty and vain promise. It would mean that there is no judgment and no justice. It would mean that the moment is all that counts and that right belongs to the cunning, the crafty and those without consciences. There would be no judgment. Many people, and by no means only wicked people, would welcome that because they confuse judgment with petty calculation and give more room to fear than to a trusting love... All this makes clear what Easter *does* mean: God has acted. History does not go on aimlessly. Justice, love, truth — these are realities, genuine reality. God loves us; he comes to meet us. The more we go along his path and live in his way, the less we need to fear justice and truth, the more our hearts will be full of Easter joy. Easter is not only a story to be told: it is a signpost on life's way. It is not an account of a miracle that happened a very long time ago: it is the breakthrough which has determined the meaning of all history. If we grasp this, we too, today, can utter the Easter greeting with undiminished joy: Christ is risen; yes, he is risen indeed!

The Completion of the Resurrection

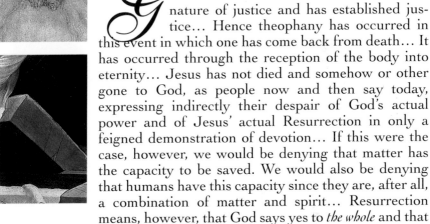

*G*od himself has restored the disturbed nature of justice and has established justice... Hence theophany has occurred in this event in which one has come back from death... It has occurred through the reception of the body into eternity... Jesus has not died and somehow or other gone to God, as people now and then say today, expressing indirectly their despair of God's actual power and of Jesus' actual Resurrection in only a feigned demonstration of devotion... If this were the case, however, we would be denying that matter has the capacity to be saved. We would also be denying that humans have this capacity since they are, after all, a combination of matter and spirit... Resurrection means, however, that God says yes to *the whole* and that he *can* do this... The sin of humans has tried to make God into a liar. It has concluded that his creation is not good at all or that it is really only good for dying. Resurrection means that through the twisted paths of sin and more powerfully than sin God ultimately says: "It *is* good." God speaks his definitive "good" to creation by taking it up into himself and thus changing it into a permanence beyond all transience... Resurrection is the start of a present, a now that will never end. We often live at a great distance from this present. We separate ourselves all the more the more we stick to the merely transient, the more we turn our lives away from that which has proved itself on the cross and in the Resurrection to be the real present in the midst of what passes by: the love that finds itself in losing itself. *It* remains present.

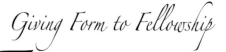

Giving Form to Fellowship

The most beautiful portrayal of the way we are traveling is offered by Luke in the story of the disciples going to Emmaus. This is traveling together with Christ the living Word, who interprets for us the written word, the Bible, and turns that into the path, the path along which our heart starts to burn and thus our eyes are finally opened: Scripture, the true tree of knowledge, opens our eyes for us if at the same time we are eating of Christ, the tree of life. Then we become truly able to see, and then we are truly alive. Three things belong together on this path: the fellowship of the disciples, the Scriptures, and the living presence of Christ. Thus, this journey of the disciples to Emmaus is at the same time a description of the Church — a description of how knowledge that touches on God grows and deepens. This knowledge becomes a fellowship with one another; it ends up with the Breaking of Bread, in which man becomes God's guest and God becomes man's host. Christ is not someone we can have for ourselves alone. He leads us, not just to God, but to each other. That is why Christ and the Church belong together, just as the Church and the Bible belong together. Giving actual form to this great fellowship in the concrete individual fellowships of diocese, of parish, of ecclesial movements, is and remains the central task of the Church, yesterday, today, and tomorrow. It must become possible to experience this fellowship as a pilgrim fellowship with our cares, with the Word of God, and with Christ, and it has to lead us onward to the gift of the Sacrament.

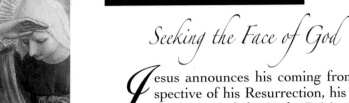

Seeking the Face of God

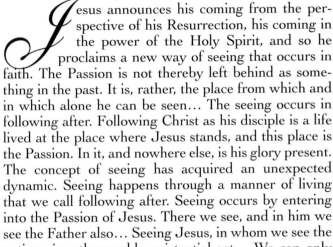

*J*esus announces his coming from the perspective of his Resurrection, his coming in the power of the Holy Spirit, and so he proclaims a new way of seeing that occurs in faith. The Passion is not thereby left behind as something in the past. It is, rather, the place from which and in which alone he can be seen... The seeing occurs in following after. Following Christ as his disciple is a life lived at the place where Jesus stands, and this place is the Passion. In it, and nowhere else, is his glory present. The concept of seeing has acquired an unexpected dynamic. Seeing happens through a manner of living that we call following after. Seeing occurs by entering into the Passion of Jesus. There we see, and in him we see the Father also... Seeing Jesus, in whom we see the Father at the same time, is a thoroughly existential act... We can only encounter God by walking after Jesus; the only way we can see him is by following Jesus, which means walking behind him and thus going along behind God's back. The way that God is seen in this world is by following Christ; seeing is going, is being on the way for our whole life toward the living God, whereby Jesus Christ, by the entire way that he walked, especially by the Paschal Mystery of his suffering, death, Resurrection, and Ascension, presents us with the itinerary... He himself is for us the face of God... What was and is new about biblical religion is the fact that the real "God,"... has a face and a name and is a person... The Christian advances toward this awakening, this satisfaction, by looking upon the Pierced One, by looking upon Jesus Christ.

The Liberation of the Resurrection

O n the night of Passover the angel of death now passes over Egypt and strikes down its firstborn. Liberation is liberation for life. Christ, the firstborn from the dead, takes death upon himself and, by his Resurrection, shatters death's power. Death no longer has the last word. The love of the Son proves to be stronger than death because it unites man with God's love, which is God's very being. Thus, in the Resurrection of Christ, it is not just the destiny of an individual that is called to mind. He is now perpetually present, because he lives, and he gathers us up, so that we may live: "Because I live, you will live also" (Jn 14: 19). In the light of Easter, Christians see themselves as people who truly *live*. They have found their way out of an existence that is more death than life. They have discovered real life: "And this is eternal life, that they know you, the only true God, and Jesus Christ whom you have sent" (Jn 17: 3). Deliverance from death is at the same time deliverance from the captivity of individualism, from the prison of self, from the incapacity to love and make a gift of oneself. Thus Easter becomes the great feast of Baptism, in which man, as it were, enacts the passage through the Red Sea, emerges from his own existence into communion with Christ and so into communion with all who belong to Christ. Resurrection builds communion. It creates the new People of God... The risen Lord does not remain alone. He draws all mankind to himself and so creates a new universal communion of men.

Touching the Risen Jesus

*A*fter the happy reunion on Easter morning Magdalene wants simply to return to the old intimacy and leave the cross behind her like a bad dream… But that is utterly incompatible with what has happened since then. No one can now have Jesus as "his rabbi" without reference to the cross. For Jesus has now become the one who is exalted at the Father's side and accessible to every human being. Consequently, the paradox: Here on earth, in a merely earthly kind of closeness, he is no longer touchable; but he can be touched as the risen Lord! It is possible now to touch Jesus by seeking him at the Father's side and allowing him to draw us after him on his journey. To touch is to worship, and brings with it a mission. That is why Thomas may touch him: the presentation of Jesus' wounds to Thomas is meant not to cause the Passion to be forgotten but, on the contrary, to make it unforgettable. Jesus' action is a call to the mission of witnessing. Consequently, too, Thomas' touching turns into an act of worship: "My Lord and my God!" (Jn 20: 28). The entire Gospel has been leading up to this moment in which the touching of Jesus, the touching of the mortal wounds of him whom the powers of this world had crushed, becomes a recognition of God's glory. Now that he has passed through death, Jesus belongs to all human beings. We can touch him only by entering upon his way, only by ascending with him and, in union with the Father and the Son, belonging to all. The attempt to hold on to him is replaced by a mission: "Go to my brethren" (Jn 20: 17).

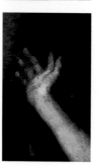

The Resurrection Appearances and Mission

aith in the Risen One is faith in something that has really taken place… Faith stands on the firm basis of reality that has actually taken place; today too, in the words of Scripture, we can as it were touch the Lord's glorified wounds and say, with Thomas, in gratitude and joy: My Lord and my God! (Jn 20: 28). One question, however, continually arises at this point. Not everyone saw the Risen Jesus. Why not? Why did he not go in triumph to the Pharisees and Pilate to show them that he was alive and to let them touch his scars?… The Risen One cannot be seen like a piece of wood or stone. He can only be seen by the person to whom he reveals himself. And he only reveals himself to the one whom he can entrust with a mission. He does not reveal himself to curiosity but to love; love is the indispensable organ if we are to see and apprehend him. This does not mean, however, that the person addressed by the Lord has to be a believer already. Paul was not, nor was Thomas, nor were the Eleven either, for they too were submerged in doubt and sorrow. The only victory they had in mind was the triumph of Jesus in the establishment of the messianic kingdom: the alternative was ruin. Resurrection such as they now encountered was not something they could imagine, nor was it what they were expecting. It was not a prior faith that created a Resurrection vision: rather it is the reality of the Risen One that creates faith where there was only disbelief or a cramped and grudging faith.

Resurrection and the Power for Justice

*C*hrist is risen! There is justice for the world! There is complete justice for all, which is able retroactively to make good all past sufferings, and this is because God exists, and he has the power to do it. As Saint Bernard of Clairvaux once put it, although God cannot suffer, he can be compassionate. And he can be compassionate because he can love. It is this power of compassion, springing from the power of love, which is able to make good the past and create justice. Christ is risen: this means that there is a power that is able to create justice and that is actively creating it. That is why the message of the Resurrection is not only a hymn to God but a hymn to the power of his love and hence a hymn to man, to the earth and to matter. The whole is saved. God does not allow any part of his creation to sink silently into a past that has gone for ever. He has created everything so that it should exist, as the Book of Wisdom says. He has created everything so that all should be one and should belong to him, so that "God shall be all in all."

Faith and the True Self

*F*aith is an orientation of our existence as a whole. It is a fundamental option that affects every domain of our existence. Nor can it be realized unless all the energies of our existence go into maintaining it. Faith is not a merely intellectual, or merely volitional, or merely emotional activity — it is all of these things together. It is an act of the whole self, of the whole person in his concentrated unity. The Bible describes faith in this sense as an act of the "heart" (Rom 10: 9). Faith is a supremely personal act… It transcends the self, the limits of the individual. Augustine remarks that nothing is so little ours as our self. Where man as a whole comes into play, he transcends himself; an act of the whole self is at the same time always an opening to others, hence, an act of being together with others. What is more, we cannot perform this act without touching our deepest ground, the living God who is present in the depths of our existence as its sustaining foundation. Any act that involves the whole man also involves, not just the self, but the we-dimension, indeed, the wholly other "Thou," God, together with the self. But this also means that such an act transcends the reach of what I can do alone. Since man is a created being, the deepest truth about him is never just action but always passion as well; man is not only a giver but also a receiver… Faith is a perishing of the mere self and precisely thus a Resurrection of the true self. To believe is to become oneself through liberation from the mere self, a liberation that brings us into communion with God mediated by communion with Christ.

Christ's Death as Prayer

*J*esus Christ transformed his death into verbal form — into a prayer — and, in so doing, changed the world. As a result, this death is able to be present for us, because it continues to live in the prayer, and the prayer runs right down through the centuries... Because Jesus turned death into a proclamation of thanksgiving and love, he is now able to be present down through all ages as the wellspring of life, and we can enter into him by praying with him. He gathers up, so to speak, the pitiful fragments of our suffering, our loving, our hoping, and our waiting into this prayer, into a great flood in which it shares in his life, so that thereby we truly share in the sacrifice. Christ does not stand facing us alone. It was alone that he died, as the grain of wheat, but he does not arise alone, but as a whole ear of corn, taking with him the communion of the saints. Since the Resurrection, Christ no longer stands alone but is always head and body, open to us all... The magnitude of Christ's achievement consists precisely in his not remaining someone else, over and against us, who might thus relegate us once more to a merely passive role; he does not merely bear with us; rather, he bears us up; he identifies himself with us to such an extent that our sins belong to him and his being to us: *he truly accepts us and takes us up, so that we ourselves become active with his support and alongside him, so that we ourselves cooperate and join in the sacrifice with him, participating in the mystery ourselves.* Thus our own life and suffering, our own hoping and loving, can also become fruitful, in the new heart he has given us.

The Easter Water

*W*ater typifies all that is precious on earth. Anyone who has ever been thirsty knows the truth of this... That is why water awakens in us the memory of Paradise and fruitfulness. Once again, finally, it is the opposite of all this that enables us to grasp fully what a wonderful thing water is. The dirt and burden of the day fall away as we wash ourselves in the bath from which a person emerges as new as a new-born child... The cross of Christ is naught else than his radical gift of himself, the ultimate surrender in which he holds back nothing, not even his very self, but pours himself out totally for others. On the cross, then, the truly marvelous wellspring of pure self-surrender, of self-giving love for God, was unsealed. All the priceless value of water is concentrated in it: the power to cleanse, fruitfulness, all that is refreshing and cheering and invigorating. In baptism this spring flows from Christ's cross through the entire Church like a mighty stream and "gladdens the city of God" (Ps 46: 5). We bathe in this stream and are reborn. It alone constantly transforms the wilderness of the world into fruitful land; for, where hatred and selfishness reign there is a wilderness, and only when the spirit of loving service is effectively at work is anything truly constructive accomplished. We must never forget that the most precious spring in the world pours from the cross and from death, or, rather, from the radical surrender of self.

The Easter Alleluia

*S*inging indicates that the person is passing beyond the boundaries of the merely rational and falling into a kind of ecstasy; the merely rational he can express in ordinary language (that is why overly rational people are seldom tempted to sing). Now singing finds its climactic form in the Alleluia, the song in which the very essence of all song achieves its purest embodiment... In fact we are dealing here with something that cannot be translated. The Alleluia is simply the nonverbal expression in song of a joy that requires no words because it transcends all words. In this it resembles certain kinds of exultation and jubilation that are to be found among all peoples, just as the miracle of joy manifests itself in every nation... What does it mean to sing with "jubilation"? It means: to be unable to express in words, or to verbalize, the song that sings to you in your heart. As the harvesters in field or vineyard experience an increasingly jubilant sense of joy, they become incapable, it seems, of finding words to express this overflowing joy. They abandon syllables and words, and their singing turns into a *jubilus* or cry of exultation. A *jubilus* is a shout that shows the heart is trying to express what it cannot possibly say. And to whom is such a *jubilus* more fittingly directed than to him who is himself ineffable? He is ineffable because your words cannot lay hold of him... The Alleluia is like a first revelation of what can and shall someday take place in us: our entire being shall turn into a single immense joy.

Easter and the Future

A future which we bring about solely by our own power and in which the human person makes himself the sole measure of what is human can only be an inhuman future. In this sense it should be clear to us that only a future which we receive from God can be a "human" future. Consequently, we should regard Easter as being, among other things, a time for reflection on our own history and on the redemption and enslavement that history signifies for us. We may well celebrate Easter as a day of hope in the future. But as soon as we ask what man's hope should rightly be, we cannot look solely to man himself for the answer, since man represents a danger as well as a hope to himself... Faith in the Resurrection of Jesus says that there is a future for every human being; the cry for unending life which is a part of the person is indeed answered. Through Jesus we do know "the room where exiled love lays down its victory." He himself is this place, and he calls us to be with him and in dependence on him. He calls us to keep this place open within the world so that he, the exiled love, may reappear over and over in the world. Admittedly, then, the world is not "intact." "No one can wound the world; only its surface is scratched," says the poet, but over against his words we have the picture of the crucified Christ, and our knowledge that this world is capable of inflicting deadly wounds even on its God. On the other hand, neither is the world the meaningless plaything of voracious death. It provides a place for exiled love, because through the mortal wounds of Jesus Christ God has entered this world.

Resurrection Certainty

The Omega Point represents a real hope for us because we can rightly expect to be integrated into it; because an irrevocability attaches to the human person, who will not be reduced to nothingness but will be delivered from his isolation and taken into the unity of the everlasting Man… The Resurrection of Jesus gives us the certainty that God exists and that, as Father of Jesus Christ, he is a God of human beings. The Resurrection of Jesus is the definitive theophany and the triumphant answer to the question of which really reigns: death or life. God exists: that is the real message of Easter. Anyone who even begins to grasp what this means also knows what it means to be redeemed.

He knows why in her prayers on this day the Church sings endless Alleluias, thus giving expression to the wordless jubilation that is too intense to be articulated in everyday language because its object is our life in its entirety, with all that is effable and ineffable in it. Celebrating Easter means experiencing something of this joy.

APRIL 23

The Priest as Believer

The priest must be a believer, one who converses with God. If this is not the case, then all his activities are futile. The most important thing a priest can do for people is first of all being what he is: a believer. Through faith he lets God, the other, come into the world. And if the other is not at work, our work will never be enough. When people sense that one is there who believes, who lives with God and from God, hope becomes a reality for them as well. Through the faith of the priest, doors open up all around for the people: it is really possible to believe, even today. All human believing is a believing-with, and for this reason the one who believes before us is so important. In many ways this person is more exposed in his faith than the others, since their faith depends on his and since, at any given time, he has to withstand the hardships of faith for them… There is a mutual give-and-take in faith in which priests and lay people become mediators of the nearness of God for one another. The priest must also nurture the humility of such receiving in himself… The first "task" a priest has to do is to be a believer and to become one ever anew and ever more. Faith is never simply there automatically; it must be lived. It leads us into conversation with God which involves speaking and listening to the same degree. Faith and prayer belong together; they cannot be separated. The time spent by a priest in prayer and listening to Scripture is never time lost to pastoral care or time withheld from others. People sense whether the work and words of their pastor spring from prayer or are fabricated at his desk.

Our Capacity for Eucharistic Transformation

here is something new there that was not before. Knowing about a transformation is part of the most basic eucharistic faith… Whenever the Body of Christ, that is, the risen and bodily Christ, comes, he is greater than the bread, other, not of the same order. The transformation happens, which affects the gifts we bring by taking them up into a higher order and changes them, even if we cannot measure what happens. When material things are taken into our body as nourishment, or for that matter whenever any material becomes part of a living organism, it remains the same, and yet as part of a new whole it is itself changed. Something similar happens here. The Lord takes possession of the bread and the wine; he lifts them up, as it were, out of the setting of their normal existence into a new order; even if, from a purely physical point of view, they remain the same, they have become profoundly different… Wherever Christ has been present, afterward it cannot be just as if nothing had happened. There, where he has laid his hand, something new has come to be. This points us back again to the fact that being a Christian as such is to be transformed, that it must involve repentance and not just some embellishment added onto the rest of one's life. It reaches down into our depths and renews us from those very depths. The more we ourselves as Christians are renewed from the root up, the better we can understand the mystery of transformation.

Eucharistic Adoration

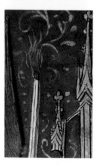

The Eucharist, and its fellowship, will be all the more complete, the more we prepare ourselves for him in silent prayer before the eucharistic presence of the Lord, the more we truly receive Communion. Adoration such as that is always more than just talking with God in a general way… The Eucharist means God has answered: The Eucharist is God as an answer, as an answering presence. Now the initiative no longer lies with us, in the God-man relationship, but with him, and it now becomes really serious. That is why, in the sphere of eucharistic adoration, prayer attains a new level; now it is two-way, and so now it really is a serious business.

Indeed, it is now not just two-way, but all-inclusive: whenever we pray in the eucharistic presence, we are never alone. Then the whole of the Church, which celebrates the Eucharist, is praying with us. Then we are praying within the sphere of God's gracious hearing, because we are praying within the sphere of death and Resurrection, that is, where the real petition in all our petitions has been heard: the petition for the victory over death; the petition for the love that is stronger than death. In this prayer we no longer stand before an imagined God but before the God who has truly given himself to us; before the God who has become for us Communion and who thus frees us and draws us from the margin into communion and leads us on to Resurrection. We have to seek again this kind of prayer.

Resurrection Discipleship

*R*esurrection-faith is a stepping forward along the way. It can be nothing else than a following in the steps of Christ, a discipleship of Christ. In his Easter Gospel, John has expressed very clearly where and how Christ has gone and whither we are to follow him: "I am ascending to my Father and your Father, to my God and your God" (Jn 20: 17). He tells Magdalene that she cannot touch him now but only when he has ascended. We cannot touch him in such a way as to bring him back into this world, but we can touch him by following him, by ascending with him. That is why Christian tradition deliberately speaks not simply of following Jesus but of following Christ. We follow, not a dead man, but the living Christ. We are not trying to imitate a life that is past and gone nor to turn it into a program for action with all kinds of compromises and revaluations. We must not rob discipleship of what is essential to it, namely, cross and Resurrection and Christ's divine Sonship, his being "with the Father." These things are fundamental. Discipleship means that now we can go where (again according to John) Peter and the Jews initially could *not* go. But now that he has gone before us, we can go there too. Discipleship means accepting the entire path, going forward into those things that are above, the hidden things that are the real ones: truth, love, our being children of God... Discipleship is a stepping-forward into what is hidden in order to find, through this genuine loss of self, what it is to be a human being.

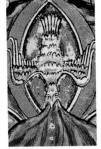

How to Reach the Dignity of Christ

*T*he Church must always become anew what she already is; she must open the borders between peoples and break down the barriers between class and race. In her, there cannot be those who are forgotten or looked down upon. The wind and fire of the Holy Spirit must continually break down those barriers that we men and women continue to build between us; we must continually pass from Babel — being closed in on ourselves — to Pentecost. We continually close our doors; we continually want to feel secure and do not want to be disturbed by others and by God. And so, we can continually implore the Lord just for this, that he come to us, overcoming our closure. It is in lowering ourselves, together with Christ, that we rise up to him and up to God. God is Love, and so the descent, the lowering that love demands of us, is at the same time the true ascent. Exactly in this way, lowering ourselves, coming out of ourselves, we reach the dignity of Jesus Christ, the human being's true dignity. In people, notwithstanding all of their limitations, there is now something absolutely new: the breath of God. The life of God lives in us. The breath of his love, of his truth and of his goodness. To his breath the Lord joins the power of forgiveness. The strength that opens up and overcomes Babel is the strength of forgiveness. Forgiveness comes from the cross; he transforms the world with the love that is offered. His heart opened on the cross is the door through which the grace of forgiveness enters into the world. And this grace alone is able to transform the world and build peace. Evil can be overcome only by forgiveness.

Christ the Good Shepherd

*I*f "sacrifice" in its essence is simply returning to love and therefore divinization, worship now has a new aspect: the healing of wounded freedom, atonement, purification, deliverance from estrangement. The essence of worship, of sacrifice — the process of assimilation, of growth in love, and thus the way into freedom — remains unchanged. But now it assumes the aspect of healing, the loving transformation of broken freedom, of painful expiation. Worship is directed to the Other in himself, to his all-sufficiency, but now it refers itself to the Other who alone can extricate me from the knot that I myself cannot untie. Redemption now needs the Redeemer. The Fathers saw this expressed in the parable of the Lost Sheep. For them, the sheep caught in the thorn bush and unable to find its way home is a metaphor for man in general. He cannot get out of the thicket and find his way back to God. The shepherd who rescues him and takes him home is the Logos himself, the eternal Word, the eternal Meaning of the universe dwelling in the Son. He it is who makes his way to us and takes the sheep onto his shoulders, that is, he assumes human nature, and as the God-Man he carries man the creature home to God. Man is given a homecoming. But now sacrifice takes the form of the cross of Christ, of the love that in dying makes a gift of itself. Such sacrifice has nothing to do with destruction. It is an act of new creation, the restoration of creation to its true identity. All worship is now a participation in this "Pasch" of Christ, in his "passing over" from divine to human, from death to life, to the unity of God and man.

The Good Shepherd

The human race — every one of us — is the sheep lost in the desert which no longer knows the way. The Son of God will not let this happen; he cannot abandon humanity in so wretched a condition. He leaps to his feet and abandons the glory of heaven, in order to go in search of the sheep and pursue it, all the way to the cross. He takes it upon his shoulders and carries our humanity; he carries us all — he is the good shepherd who lays down his life for the sheep… When the shepherd of all humanity, the living God, himself became a lamb, he stood on the side of the lambs, with those who are downtrodden and killed… It is not power, but love that redeems us! This is God's sign: he himself is love… God, who became a lamb, tells us that the world is saved by the Crucified One, not by those who crucified him. The world is redeemed by the patience of God. It is destroyed by the impatience of man. One of the basic characteristics of a shepherd must be to love the people entrusted to him, even as he loves Christ whom he serves. "Feed my sheep," says Christ to Peter. Feeding means loving, and loving also means being ready to suffer. Loving means giving the sheep what is truly good, the nourishment of God's truth, of God's word, the nourishment of his presence, which he gives us in the Blessed Sacrament.

Actualization of the Presence of Jesus

cclesial communion embraces all times and all generations. Thanks to the action of the Holy Spirit, the early apostolic community experienced the Risen Lord. Successive generations do the same, as the faith is transmitted and lived through worship and the communion of the pilgrim People of God. From the beginning, Jesus intended that his saving work would extend to all the world and indeed... the Risen Lord entrusted to the Apostles the task of making disciples of all nations while guaranteeing his own presence with them. This ongoing actualization of the presence of Jesus — through the work of the Spirit and through the Church's apostolic ministry and fraternal communion — is what we mean by the term Tradition; it is not just a transmission of "things" but the efficacious presence of the Lord who accompanies and guides the gathered community. The Holy Spirit nurtures this communion, assuring the connection between the apostolic faith experienced by the first communities of disciples and our experience today of Christ in his Church. Let us rejoice in the presence of the Savior who comes to meet us, to redeem us, and to sanctify us through the ministry of his Church!

May

Mary the Great Believer

M
ary is the great believer who humbly offered herself to God as an empty vessel for him to use in his mysterious plan. She did not try to live according to human calculation but put herself completely at the disposal of God's mysterious, incomprehensible design. All she wanted to be was the instrument and servant of the Word. Therein lies her true fame: that she remained a believer despite all the darkness and all the inexplicable demands God made on her. She believed even in the face of certain incomprehensible facts… Today God is still mysterious; indeed he seems to have a special kind of obscurity in store for each person's life. But could he ever render any life as dark and incomprehensible as he did Mary's? This is the real reason for her greatness and her being called blessed: she is the great believer. Consequently, she is represented to us not as a distant haloed figure but as for ever the young girl who entered Elizabeth's house with the shining light of mystery on her brow and surrounded by the radiance of purity and half hope. But, like Elizabeth, Mary cannot remain silent at this moment. It is said that, even today, under the influence of a great joy simple Arabian women will improvise a song in which they pour forth the hidden poetry a simple heart composes when moved by a powerful joy. "My soul magnifies the Lord, and my spirit rejoices in God my Savior." Mary deflects Elizabeth's praise from herself to God the Lord. It is he who deserves all praise. In so acting, Mary has shown the way for all future praise of herself: it is to be praise of God as he is mirrored in his graciousness to human beings.

The Reversal of the Magnificat

*I*n archaic modes of thought, fertility is a blessing, infertility is a curse. Yet here all is reversed: the infertile one ultimately turns out to be the truly blessed, while the fertile one recedes into the ordinary or even has to struggle against the curse of repudiation, of being unloved. The theological implication of this overthrow of values becomes clear only gradually; from it Paul developed his theology of spiritual birth: the true son of Abraham is not the one who traces his physical origin to him, but the one who, in a new way beyond mere physical birth, has been conceived through the creative power of God's word of promise. Physical life as such is not really wealth; this promise, which endures beyond life, is what first makes life fully itself (cf. Rom 4; Gal 3: 1-14). At an earlier stage of the Old Testament's evolution, a theology of grace was developed from this reversal of values in the song of Hannah, which is echoed in Mary's Magnificat: the Lord raises the humble from the dust, he lifts the poor from the ashes (I Sam 2: 8). God bends down to the humble, the powerless, the rejected, and in this condescension the love of God, which truly saves, shines forth both for Hannah and for Mary, in the remarkable phenomenon of unblessed-blessed women. The mystery of the last place (Lk 14: 10), the exchange between the first and the last place (Mk 10: 31), the reversal of values in the Sermon on the Mount, the reversal of earthly values founded upon *hybris*, all of this is intimated. Here also the theology of virginity finds its first, still hidden formulation: earthly infertility becomes true fertility.

The Role of Woman in Salvation

*I*t is significant that the woman always figures in Israel's thought and belief, not as a priestess, but as prophetess and judge-savior. What is specifically hers, the place assigned to her emerges from this. The essence of what has previously been seen is repeated and strengthened: the infertile one, the powerless one becomes the savior because it is there that the locus for the revelation of God's power is found. After every fall into sin, the woman remains "mother of life"… God's divinity is no longer revealed in his ability to punish but in the indestructibility and constancy of his love… To leave woman out of the whole of theology would be to deny creation and election (salvation history) and thereby to nullify revelation. In the women of Israel, the mothers and the saviors, in their fruitful infertility is expressed most purely and most profoundly what creation is and what election is, what "Israel" is as God's people. And because election and revelation are one, what ultimately becomes apparent in this for the first time is who and what God is.

Mary, the Fruitfulness of Grace

"*S*ophia" signifies the answer which emerges from the divine call of creation and election. It expresses precisely this: that there is a pure answer and that God's love finds its irrevocable dwelling place within it... From the viewpoint of the New Testament, wisdom refers, on one side, to the Son as the Word, in whom God creates, but on the other side to the creature, to the true Israel, who is personified in the humble maid whose whole existence is marked by the attitude of *Fiat mihi secundum verbum tuum*. Sophia refers to the Logos, the Word who establishes wisdom, and also to the womanly answer which receives wisdom and brings it to fruition... The figure of the woman is indispensable for the structure of biblical faith. She expresses the reality of creation as well as the fruitfulness of grace. The abstract outlines for the hope that God will turn toward his people receive, in the New Testament, a concrete, personal name in the figure of Jesus Christ. At that same moment, the figure of the woman... also emerges with a name: Mary... To deny or reject the feminine aspect in belief, or, more concretely, the Marian aspect, leads finally to the negation of creation and the invalidation of grace. It leads to a picture of God's omnipotence that reduces the creature to a mere masquerade and that also completely fails to understand the God of the Bible, who is characterized as being the creator and the God of the covenant — the God for whom the beloved's punishment and rejection themselves become the passion of love, the cross.

The Magnificat

he Magnificat reveals the spirituality of those faithful who not only recognize themselves as "poor" in the detachment from all idolatry of riches and power, but also in the profound humility of a heart emptied of the temptation to pride and open to the bursting in of the divine saving grace. The soul of the prayer is the celebration of the divine grace which has burst into the heart and life of Mary, making her Mother of the Lord. We hear the Virgin's own voice speaking of her Savior who has done great things in her soul and body. The intimate structure of her prayerful canticle, therefore, is praise, thanksgiving, and grateful joy. But this personal witness is neither solitary nor purely individualistic, because the Virgin Mother is aware that she has a mission to fulfill for humanity and her experience fits into the history of salvation. The Lord takes the part of the lowly. His plan is one that is often hidden beneath the opaque context of human events that see "the proud, the mighty and the rich" triumph. Let us accept the invitation of Saint Ambrose: "May Mary's soul be in each one to magnify the Lord, may Mary's spirit be in each one to rejoice in God; if, according to the flesh, the Mother of Christ is one alone, according to the faith all souls bring forth Christ; each welcomes the Word of God within… Mary's soul magnifies the Lord and her spirit rejoices in God because she adores with devout affection one God, from whom come all things… If, according to the flesh, the Mother of Christ is one alone, according to the faith all souls bring forth Christ: each one intimately welcomes the Word of God."

Mary the Holy Soil

The Word of God really penetrated the earth and became bread for us all. He is the seed, the fruitful answer in which God's speech has taken living root in this world. The mystery of Christ is almost nowhere so palpable and intimately connected with the mystery of Mary as in the perspective of this promise. When the text says that the word, or the seed, bears fruit, it means that the seed actually sinks into the earth, assimilates the earth's energies, and changes them into itself. It thus brings about something truly new, for now it carries the earth in itself and turns the earth into fruit. The grain of wheat does not remain alone, for it includes the maternal mystery of the soil — Mary, the holy soil of the Church, is an essential part of Christ. The mystery of Mary means precisely that God's Word did not remain alone; rather, it assimilated the other — the soil — into itself, became man in the "soil" of his Mother, and then, fused with the soil of the whole of humanity, returned to God in a new form... Men can become fruitful soil for God's Word. They can become this soil by providing, as it were, the organic elements in which life can grow and mature; by drawing life themselves from this organic matter; by becoming themselves a word formed by the penetration of the Word; by sinking the roots of their life into prayer and thus into God... To be soil for the Word means that the soil must allow itself to be absorbed by the seed... Mary's maternity means that she willingly places her own substance, body and soul, into the seed so that new life can grow.

Why the Church Needs the Marian Mystery

*W*e must become a longing for God. The Fathers of the Church say that prayer, properly understood, is nothing other than becoming a longing for God. In Mary this petition has been granted: she is, as it were, the open vessel of longing, in which life becomes prayer and prayer becomes life. Saint John wonderfully conveys this process by never mentioning Mary's name in his Gospel. She no longer has any name except "the Mother of Jesus." It is as if she had handed over her personal dimension in order now to be solely at his disposal, and precisely thereby had become a person... It is, I believe, no coincidence, given our Western, masculine mentality, that we have increasingly separated Christ from his Mother, without grasping that Mary's motherhood might have some significance for theology and faith. This attitude characterizes our whole approach to the Church... What we need, then, is to abandon this one-sided, Western activistic outlook, lest we degrade the Church to a product of our creation and design. The Church is not a manufactured item; she is, rather, the living seed of God that must be allowed to grow and ripen. This is why the Church needs the Marian mystery; this is why the Church herself is a Marian mystery. There can be fruitfulness in the Church only when she has this character, when she becomes holy soil for the Word. We must retrieve the symbol of the fruitful soil; we must once more become waiting, inwardly recollected people who in the depth of prayer, longing, and faith give the Word room to grow.

Authentic Mariology

e must avoid relegating Mary's maternity to the sphere of mere biology… If, therefore, Christ and *ecclesia* are the hermeneutical center of the scriptural narration of the history of God's saving dealings with man, then and only then is the place fixed where Mary's motherhood becomes theologically significant as the ultimate personal concretization of Church. At the moment when she pronounces her Yes, Mary is Israel in person; she is the Church in person and as a person. She is the personal concretization of the Church because her *Fiat* makes her the bodily Mother of the Lord. But this biological fact is a theological reality, because it realizes the deepest spiritual content of the covenant that God intended to make with Israel. Luke suggests this beautifully in harmonizing 1: 45 ("blessed is she who believed") and 11: 28 ("blessed… are those who hear the word of God and keep it"). We can therefore say that the affirmation of Mary's motherhood and the affirmation of her representation of the Church are related as *factum* and *mysterium facti*, as the fact and the sense that gives the fact its meaning. The two things are inseparable: the fact without its sense would be blind; the sense without the fact would be empty. Mariology cannot be developed from the naked fact, but only from the fact as it is understood in the hermeneutics of faith. In consequence, Mariology can never be purely mariological. Rather, it stands within the totality of the basic Christ-Church structure and is the most concrete expression of its inner coherence.

Mary the Woman

*M*ary is the believing other whom God calls. As such, she represents the creation, which is called to respond to God, and the freedom of the creature, which does not lose its integrity in love but attains completion therein. Mary thus represents saved and liberated man, but she does so precisely as a woman, that is, in the bodily determinateness that is inseparable from man: "Male and female he created them" (Gen 1: 27). The "biological" and the human are inseparable in the figure of Mary, just as are the human and the "theological."... Mary's virginity, no less than her maternity, confirms that the "biological" is human, that the whole man stands before God, and that the fact of being human only as male and female is included in faith's eschatological demand and its eschatological hope. It is no accident that virginity — although as a form of life it is also possible, and intended for, the man — is first patterned on the woman, the true keeper of the seal of creation, and has its normative, plenary form — which the man can, so to say, only imitate — in her.

Authentic Marian Piety

*I*t is necessary to maintain the distinctiveness of Marian devotion precisely by keeping its practice constantly and strictly bound to Christology. In this way, both will be brought to their proper form. Marian piety must not withdraw into partial aspects of the Christian mystery, let alone reduce that mystery to partial aspects of itself. It must be open to the whole breadth of the mystery and become itself a means to this breadth. Marian piety will always stand within the tension between theological rationality and believing affectivity. This is part of its essence, and its task is not to allow either to atrophy. Affectivity must not lead it to forget the sober measure of ratio, nor must the sobriety of a reasonable faith allow it to suffocate the heart, which often sees more than naked reason. It was not for nothing that the Fathers understood Matthew 5: 8 as the center of their theological epistemology: "Blessed are the pure in heart, for they shall see God." The organ for seeing God is the purified heart. It may just be the task of Marian piety to awaken the heart and purify it in faith. If the misery of contemporary man is his increasing disintegration into mere bios and mere rationality, Marian piety could work against this "decomposition" and help man to rediscover unity in the center, from the heart.

Mary's Faith

*J*ust as Abraham's faith was the beginning of the Old Covenant, Mary's faith, enacted in the scene of the Annunciation, is the inauguration of the New. For Mary, as for Abraham, faith is trust in, and obedience to, God, even when he leads her through darkness. It is a letting go, a releasing, a handing over of oneself to the truth, to God. Faith, in the luminous darkness of God's inscrutable ways, is thus a conformation to him... Mary, saying Yes to the birth of the Son of God from her womb by the power of the Holy Spirit, places her body, her entire self, at God's disposal as a place for his presence. In her Yes, then, Mary's will coincides with her Son's. The unison of these Yesses — "a body you have prepared for me" — makes the Incarnation possible, for, as Augustine says, Mary conceived in Spirit before she conceived in her body. The cruciformity of faith, which Abraham had to experience in such a radical way, becomes evident for Mary, first in her meeting with the aged Simeon, then, in a new way, in her losing, and finding again, the twelve-year-old Jesus in the Temple... Even in the midst of the closest intimacy, the mystery remains a mystery, and even Mary touches it only in faith. But precisely thus she remains truly in contact with this new self-revelation of God, that is, with the Incarnation. Precisely because she belongs to "the little ones" who accept the measure of faith, she is included in the promise: "Father,... you have hidden these things from the wise and understanding and revealed them to infants... No one knows the Son except the Father."

Mary the Ark

*T*he reason for our sadness is the futility of our love, the overwhelming power of finitude, death, suffering, and falsehood. We are sad because we are left alone in a contradictory world where enigmatic signals of divine goodness pierce through the cracks yet are thrown in doubt by a power of darkness that is either God's responsibility or manifests his impotence. "Rejoice" — what reason does Mary have to rejoice in such a world? The answer is: "The Lord is with you."... Jesus, whom Mary is permitted to bear, is identified with Yahweh, the living God. When Jesus comes, it is God himself who comes to dwell in her. He is the Savior — this is the meaning of the name Jesus, which thus becomes clear from the heart of the promise... Mary herself thus becomes the true Ark of the Covenant in Israel, so that the symbol of the Ark gathers an incredibly realistic force: God in the flesh of a human being, which flesh now becomes his dwelling place in the midst of creation... Mary is wholly within the measure of Christ and of God, is through and through his habitation. And what other reason could the *ecclesia* have for existing than to become a dwelling for God in the world? God does not deal with abstractions. He is a person, and the Church is a person. The more that each one of us becomes a person, person in the sense of a fit habitation for God, daughter Zion, the more we become one, the more we are the Church, and the more the Church is herself.

Mary Full of Grace

"**F**ull of grace" could be translated as: "You are full of the Holy Spirit; your life is intimately connected with God." Peter Lombard, the author of what was the universal theological manual for approximately three centuries during the Middle Ages, propounded the thesis that grace and love are identical but that love "is the Holy Spirit." Grace in the proper and deepest sense of the word is not some thing that comes from God; it is God himself. Redemption means that God, acting as God truly does, gives us nothing less than himself. The gift of God is God — he who as the Holy Spirit is in communion with us. "Full of grace" therefore means, once again, that Mary is a wholly open human being, one who has opened herself entirely, one who has placed herself in God's hands boldly, limitlessly, and without fear for her own fate. It means that she lives wholly by and in relation to God. She is a listener and a prayer, whose mind and soul are alive to the manifold ways in which the living God quietly calls to her. She is one: who prays and stretches forth wholly to meet God; she is therefore a lover, who has the breadth and magnanimity of true love, but who has also its unerring powers of discernment and its readiness to suffer.

The Meaning of the Ascension

What is the meaning of Christ's "ascension into heaven"? It expresses our belief that in Christ human nature, the humanity in which we all share, has entered into the inner life of God in a new and hitherto unheard of way. It means that man has found an everlasting place in God. Heaven is not a place beyond the stars, but something much greater, something that requires far more audacity to assert: Heaven means that man now has a place in God. The basis for this assertion is the interpenetration of humanity and divinity in the crucified and exalted man Jesus. Christ, the man who is in God and eternally one with God, is at the same time God's abiding openness to all human beings. Thus Jesus himself is what we call "heaven"; heaven is not a place but a person, the person of him in whom God and man are forever and inseparably one. And we go to heaven and enter into heaven to the extent that we go to Jesus Christ and enter into him. In this sense, "ascension into heaven" can be something that takes place in our everyday lives... For the disciples, the "ascension" was not what we usually misinterpret it as being: the temporary absence of Christ from the world. It meant rather his new, definitive, and irrevocable presence by participation in God's royal power... God has a place for man!... In God there is a place for us!... "Be consoled, flesh and blood, for in Christ you have taken possession of heaven and of God's kingdom!" (Tertullian).

The Transformation of Faith

Whenever we encounter Christ, there takes place what theology would call a "dialogic communication," a mutual inner exchange in the great new I into which I am introduced and assimilated by the transformation of faith. The other, consequently, is no longer a stranger for me; he, too, belongs to this great I. Christ wants to use my capabilities in his behalf... Even when there is no mutual attraction between us, I can now pass on to him as my own yes the yes of Christ that penetrates my whole being yet is still his yes. My own private sympathies and antipathies have been replaced by the sympathy of Christ, by his sharing of our sufferings and love. By virtue of this sharing in the sympathy of Christ that is mine in the life of faith, I can pass on a sympathy, a yes, that is greater than my own yes and allows the other to experience that deepest yes that alone gives meaning and stability to every human yes... It requires practice, patience, and a realization that there will always be setbacks. It presumes that, in the life of faith, I have arrived at the inner exchange of my I with that of Christ so that his yes really penetrates me and becomes my own. It also presumes practice: the risk of accomplishing in a concrete instance that for which Christ needs me — the passing of this yes from him to the other. For it is only in such an initially unaccustomed and even mysterious risk that the strength to do so grows and becomes more and more recognizable in the Easter context: this frustration of self leads to a great inner-joy — to "Resurrection."

The Ascension

The Ascension of Christ means that he no longer belongs to the world of corruption and death, which conditions our life. It means that he belongs completely to God. He, the eternal Son, has taken our human being to the presence of God; he has taken with him flesh and blood in a transfigured form. Man finds a place in God through Christ; the human being has been taken into the very life of God. And, given that God embraces and sustains the whole cosmos, the Lord's Ascension means that Christ has not gone far away from us, but that now, thanks to the fact he is with the Father, he is close to each one of us forever. Each one of us may address him familiarly; each one may turn to him. The Lord always hears our voice. We may distance ourselves inwardly from him. We can live with our backs turned to him, but he always awaits us, and is always close to us... Jesus told his disciples everything, as he is the living word of God, and God can give no more than himself. In Jesus, God gave himself totally to us, that is, he gave us everything. In addition to this, or together with this, there can be no other revelation able to communicate something else, or to complete, in a certain sense, the revelation of Christ. In him, in the Son, we were told everything, we were given everything. But our ability to understand is limited; for this reason the mission of the Spirit consists in introducing the Church in an ever new way, from generation to generation, into the grandeur of the mystery of Christ... Thus, the Holy Spirit is the force through which Christ makes us experience his closeness.

How to Understand the Ascension

The Ascension of the Lord was the last appearance of the Risen One; the disciples knew that they would not see him again in this world. Admittedly, this departure was not like that of Good Friday, for on that occasion Jesus obviously died a failure and all the hopes they had centered on him could be regarded as a great mistake. His departure forty days after the Resurrection, on the contrary, has something triumphal, something reassuring, about it: Jesus departs this time, not to go to an ignominious death, but to enter into life. He is not a failure; rather God has vindicated him. Without doubt, there is cause for joy here. But when understanding and will rejoice, it does not necessarily follow that the feelings will do so as well. Even while they recognize Jesus' victory, they can suffer under the loss of his physical presence. Yet we cannot ignore the statement about the great joy of those returning to Jerusalem, even though we will never be able to explain it totally, any more than we can explain the joy of the martyrs: Maximilian Kolbe's singing as he was being starved to death in a Nazi prison; the joyful praise that Polycarp raised to God from the funeral pyre; and many others. From such experiences we can have some presentiment of how Christ's victory can not only touch the understanding, but can also make itself felt in the heart, and in so doing become truly meaningful. Only when we experience something of it ourselves have we understood the feast of Christ's Ascension. What has happened here is a realization in the human heart of the definitiveness of redemption so that knowledge becomes joy.

Hope for Our Infidelity

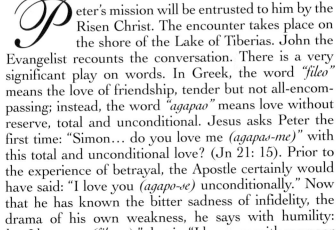

eter's mission will be entrusted to him by the Risen Christ. The encounter takes place on the shore of the Lake of Tiberias. John the Evangelist recounts the conversation. There is a very significant play on words. In Greek, the word *"fileo"* means the love of friendship, tender but not all-encompassing; instead, the word *"agapao"* means love without reserve, total and unconditional. Jesus asks Peter the first time: "Simon… do you love me *(agapas-me)*" with this total and unconditional love? (Jn 21: 15). Prior to the experience of betrayal, the Apostle certainly would have said: "I love you *(agapo-se)* unconditionally." Now that he has known the bitter sadness of infidelity, the drama of his own weakness, he says with humility: "Lord, you know that I love you *(filo-se)*," that is, "I love you with my poor human love." Christ insists: "Simon, do you love me with this total love that I want?" And Peter repeats the response of his humble human love: *"Kyrie, filo-se,"* "Lord, I love you as I am able to love you." The third time, Jesus only says to Simon: *"Fileis-me?,"* "Do you love me?" Simon understands that his poor love is enough for Jesus, it is the only one of which he is capable, nonetheless he is grieved that the Lord spoke to him in this way. He thus replies: "Lord, you know everything; you know that I love you *(filo-se)*." This is to say that Jesus has put himself on the level of Peter, rather than Peter on Jesus' level! It is exactly this divine conformity that gives hope to the Disciple, who experienced the pain of infidelity. From here is born the trust that makes him able to follow Christ to the end.

Priest as Mediator

The primacy of Christ makes the priest humble even while it frees him. It also points us in the right direction. It means that the priest must know in his heart that his place is on the side of the Church, of the people who stand outside before the Holy of Holies and rely on the intercession of him who alone can pass beyond the curtain... The objectivity of salvation must make the priest objective. He preaches, not himself, but the faith of the Church and, in that faith, the Lord Jesus Christ... The holiness of the priest consists in this process of becoming spiritually poor, of decreasing before the other, of losing himself for the other: for Christ — and, in Christ, for others: for those whom the Lord has entrusted to him... When I go to church, it is not to find there my own or anyone else's innovations but what we have all received as the faith of the Church — the faith that spans the centuries and can support us all. Certainly, if it is to remain vital, the objective content of the Church's faith needs the flesh and blood of human beings, the gift of our thinking and willing. But it must be a gift, not just the sacrifice of a moment. The priest always fails in his duty when he wants to stop being a servant: an emissary who knows that it does not depend on him but on what he himself can only receive. Only by letting himself become unimportant can he become truly important, because, in that way, he becomes the gateway of the Lord into this world — of him who is the true Mediator into the immediacy of everlasting Love.

Christ's "I" and the Priesthood

The Eucharistic sacrifice facilitates *communio* with the divinity, and men receive back the divinity's gift in and from the sacrifice… it is God *who gives himself*, taking man up into his action and enabling him to be both gift and recipient… In order that what happened *then* may become present *now*, the words "This is my body — this is my blood" must be said. But the speaker of these words is the "I" of Jesus Christ. Only he can say them; they are his words. No man can dare to take to himself the "I" and "my" of Jesus Christ — and yet the words must be said if the saving mystery is not to remain something in the distant past. So authority to pronounce them is needed, an authority which no one can assume and which no congregation, nor even many congregations together, can confer. Only Jesus Christ himself, in the "sacramental" form he has committed to the whole Church, can give this authority. The word must be located, as it were, in sacrament; it must be part of the "sacrament" of the Church, partaking of an authority which she does not create, but only transmits. This is what is meant by "ordination" and "priesthood." Once this is understood, it becomes clear that, in the Church's Eucharist, something is happening which goes far beyond any human celebration, any human joint activity, and any liturgical efforts on the part of a particular community. What is taking place is the mystery of God, communicated to us by Jesus Christ through his death and Resurrection. This is what makes the Eucharist irreplaceable; this is the guarantee of its identity.

Priest as Servant

*T*here is the term *servus Dei* or *servus Christi*, referring to the priest… What is important for our question is that the concept of servant refers to a relationship. Someone is a servant in relation to someone else. If the priest is defined as being a servant of Jesus Christ, this means that his life is substantially determined in terms of a relationship: being oriented toward his Lord as a servant constitutes the essence of his office, which thus extends to his very being. He is a servant of Christ so as to be, on the basis of Christ, for his sake and along with him, a servant of men. The fact of being oriented toward Christ is not in contradiction to his relation to the congregation (to the Church) but is the basis of that relationship and is what gives it all its depth. Being oriented toward Christ means being received into his own life as a servant and being at the service of the "body," of the Church, with him. Precisely because the priest belongs to Christ, he belongs to men in a quite radical sense. Only in this way is he able to be so profoundly and so unconditionally dedicated to them. That, in turn, means that the ontological conception of the office of priest, as something extending to the very being of the person concerned, does not stand in opposition to the seriousness of the functional concept, the ministry to others, but gives to this service a radical dimension that would be unthinkable in the merely profane sphere.

Priestly Character

We could say that "character" means a belonging that is a part of the person's very existence. To that extent the image of "character" expresses in its turn the same "being related to." And, indeed, this is a kind of belonging we can do nothing about; the initiative for this comes from the proprietor — from Christ. Thereby the nature of the sacrament becomes clear: I cannot simply declare myself as belonging to the Lord in this way. He must first accept me as one of his own, and then I can enter into this acceptance and accept it for my own part, learn to live it. To that extent, then, the term "character" describes the nature of the service of Christ that is contained in the priesthood as having to do with our being; and at the same time it makes clear what is meant by its being sacramental... Belonging to the Lord who became a servant is belonging for the sake of those who are his. This means that the servant can give, in the holy sign, what he is unable to give from his own resources: he is dispensing the Holy Spirit; he is absolving people from sins; he is making present the sacrifice of Christ and Christ himself, in his sacred Body and Blood — all these are privileges reserved by God, which no man can get for himself and no congregation can delegate to him. If "character" is thus the expression of a fellowship of service, then, on the one hand, it shows how ultimately the Lord himself is always acting and how, on the other hand, in the visible Church he nonetheless acts through men.

MAY 23

The Washing of the Feet

*I*n the story of the washing of the disciples' feet the evangelist sums up, as it were, the whole of Jesus' message, his life, and his Passion. As if in a vision, we see what this whole really is. In the washing of the disciples' feet is represented for us what Jesus does and what he is. He, who is Lord, comes down to us; he lays aside the garments of glory and becomes a slave, one who stands at the door and who does for us the slave's service of washing our feet. This is the meaning of his whole life and Passion, that he bends down to our dirty feet, to the dirt of humanity, and that in his greater love he washes us clean. The slave's service of washing the feet was performed in order to prepare a person suitably for sitting at table, to make him ready for company, so that all could sit down together for a meal. Jesus Christ prepares us, as it were, for God's presence and for each other's company, so that we can sit down together at table. We, who repeatedly find we cannot stand one another, who are quite unfit to be with God, are welcomed and accepted by him. He clothes himself, so to speak, in the garment of our poverty, and in being taken up by him, we are able to be with God, we have gained access to God. We are washed through our willingness to yield to his love. The meaning of this love is that God accepts us without preconditions, even if we are unworthy of his love, incapable of relating to him, because he, Jesus Christ, transforms us and becomes a brother to us.

Participation in the Liturgy

he real liturgical action, the true liturgical act, is the *oratio*, the great prayer that forms the core of the Eucharistic celebration, the whole of which was, therefore, called *oratio* by the Fathers... The word *oratio* originally means, not "prayer" (for which the word is *prex*), but solemn public speech. Such speech now attains its supreme dignity through its being addressed to God in full awareness that it comes from him and is made possible by him... This *oratio* — the Eucharistic Prayer, the "Canon" — is really more than speech; it is *actio* in the highest sense of the word. For what happens in it is that the human *actio* (as performed hitherto by the priests in the various religions of the world) steps back and makes way for the *actio divina*, the action of God. In this *oratio* the priest speaks with the I of the Lord — "This is my Body," "This is my Blood." He knows that he is not now speaking from his own resources but in virtue of the Sacrament that he has received, he has become the voice of Someone Else, who is now speaking and acting. This action of God, which takes place through human speech, is the real "action" for which all of creation is in expectation. The elements of the earth are transubstantiated, pulled, so to speak, from their creaturely anchorage, grasped at the deepest ground of their being, and changed into the Body and Blood of the Lord. The New Heaven and the New Earth are anticipated. The real "action" in the liturgy in which we are all supposed to participate is the action of God himself.

Human Thirst and the Holy Spirit

*T*he ultimate thirst of men cries out for the Holy Spirit. He, and he alone, is, at a profound level, the fresh water without which there is no life. In the image of a spring, of the water that irrigates and transforms a desert, that man meets like a secret promise, the mystery of the Spirit becomes visible in an ineffable fashion that no rational meditation can encompass. In man's thirst, and in his being refreshed by water, is portrayed that infinite, far more radical thirst that can be quenched by no other water... The Holy Spirit is eternally, of his very nature, God's gift, God as wholly self-giving, God as sharing himself, as gift. In that sense, the inner reason and basis for creation and salvation history do after all lie in this quality of being of the Holy Spirit, as *donum* and *datum*... He is the content of Christian prayer. He is the only gift worthy of God: as God, God gives nothing other than God; he gives himself and thereby everything. That is why properly Christian prayer, again, does not beg for just anything; rather, it begs for the gift of God that is God himself, begs for him.

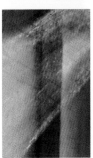

The Holy Spirit is Love

The gift of God is the Holy Spirit. The gift of God is love — God shares himself as love in the Holy Spirit... The presence of the Holy Spirit makes itself known in the manner of love. Love is the criterion of the Holy Spirit as against unholy spirits; indeed, it is the presence of the Holy Spirit himself and, in that sense, the presence of God. The essential and central concept summing up what the Holy Spirit is and what he effects is, in the end, not "knowledge" but love... The basic criterion of love, its "proper work," so to speak — and, thereby, the "proper work" of the Holy Spirit — is this, that it achieves abiding. Love shows itself by being enduring. It can by no means be recognized at a given moment and in the moment alone; but in abiding, it does away with uncertainty and carries eternity within it. And thus in my view the relationship between love and truth is also thereby given: love, in the full sense, can be present only where something is enduring, where something abides. Because it has to do with abiding, it can occur, not just anywhere, but only there where eternity is.

Spirit and Pentecost

Mind, on the one hand, is the sum of the receptive, logical, and pragmatic powers of knowing. Spirit, on the other hand, discovers the values that lie beyond facts, the freedom that lies beyond law, the kind of existence in which justice is given priority over self-interest. Spirit, thus understood, is not the object of calculation and computer storage; it is correlated precisely with what is incalculable. It is a name for an attitude "which brings happiness to the self by bursting through the limitations of self-centeredness"; an attitude, in other words, that requires a decision of the heart, or whole person… What is the real Christian message of Pentecost? What is this "Holy Spirit" of which it speaks?… World history is a struggle between two kinds of love: self-love to the point of hatred for God, and love of God to the point of self-renunciation. This second love brings the redemption of the world and the self. In my opinion it would already be a giant step forward if during the days of Pentecost we were to turn to a reflection on our responsibility; if these days were to become the occasion for moving beyond purely rational thinking, beyond the kind of knowledge that is used in planning and can be stored up, to a discovery of "spirit," of the responsibility truth brings, and of the values of conscience and love… The Holy Spirit is truly "spirit" in the fullest possible sense of the word. In all probability we must make our stumbling way to him anew from the midst of a world profoundly changed.

How the Holy Spirit Operates

How does the Spirit operate? First of all, by bestowing remembrance, a remembrance in which the particular is joined to the whole, which in turn endows the particular, which hitherto had not been understood, with its genuine meaning. A further characteristic of the Spirit is listening: he does not speak in his own name, he listens, and teaches how to listen. In other words, he does not add anything but rather acts as a guide into the heart of the Word, which becomes light in the act of listening. The Spirit does not employ violence; his method is simply to allow what stands before me as an other to express itself and to enter into me. This already entails an additional element: the Spirit effects a space of listening and remembering, a "we," which in the Johannine writings defines the Church as the locus of knowledge. Understanding can take place only within this "we" constituted by participation in the origin. Indeed, all comprehension depends on participation. Bultmann elucidates this point admirably when he says, regarding John's conception of the witness of the Spirit: "It is 'repetition,' a 'calling to mind' in the light of their present relationship with him."

The Grace of Baptism

*B*aptism establishes a communion of name with the Father, Son, and Holy Spirit. It is, in this respect, somewhat analogous to the act of marriage, which establishes between two individuals a communion of name that is, in turn, an expression of the fact that, from now on, they form a new unity by virtue of which they abandon their former mode of existence and are no longer to be met separately but always together. Baptism brings about a communion of name between the human individual and the Father, Son, and Holy Spirit... Being baptized means entering into a communion of name with him who is the Name and thus becoming, more truly than Abraham, Isaac, and Jacob, the attribute of God. From this perspective it is now obvious that baptism is the inception of Resurrection, inclusion in the name of God and, by the same token, in the indestructible aliveness of God. This insight is deepened when we inquire more closely into the "name" of God. God is named here as Father, Son, and Holy Spirit. This means, to begin with, that God himself exists in the relationship of Father and Son as well as in the unity of the Spirit. It means also that we ourselves are destined to be sons, to enter into the Son's relationship with God and so to be transported into the unity of the Spirit with the Father. Being baptized would thus be the call to share in Jesus' relationship with God.

Baptism as Belonging

By his entrance into a communion of name with God, man is drawn into a new existence, that he is, as it were, one who has been born anew, who has already been... The Yes of love for another involves a far-reaching renunciation of self. Only if one risks this giving of oneself to the other, only if existence is, as it were, first given away can a great love ensue. Other examples could be suggested. It will always be hard for man to speak the truth and to abide by the truth. That is why he takes refuge in the lie that will make life easier for him. Truth and witness, witness and martyrdom, are very closely associated in this world. Truth, if it is consistently maintained, is always perilous. But only in the measure in which man risks the passion of truth does he become a man. And in the measure in which he holds fast to himself, in which he withdraws into the safety of a lie, he loses himself... Being baptized means assuming the name of Christ, means becoming a son with and in him. The demand made by the name into which one here enters is more radical than the demand of any earthly name can be. It attacks the roots of our autonomy more deeply than the deepest earthly bond can do. For it demands that our existence become "sonlike," that we belong so totally to God that we become an "attribute" of God. And as sons we are to acknowledge so totally that we belong to Christ that we know ourselves to be one flesh, "one body," with all his brethren. Baptism means, then, that we lose ourselves as a separate, independent "I" and find ourselves again in a new "I."

The Visitation

*S*he who is wholly baptized, as the personal reality of the true Church, is at the same time not merely the Church's *promised* certitude of salvation but its *bodily* certitude also... Luke recounts in the story of Mary's visit to Elizabeth that when Mary's greeting rang out John "leaped for joy in his mother's womb" (1: 44). To express that joy he employs the same word — leap — that he used to express the joy of those to whom the beatitudes are addressed (Lk 6: 23). This word also appears in one of the old Greek translations of the Old Testament to describe David's dance before the Ark of the Covenant after it had returned home (2 Sm 6: 16, Symmachus). Perhaps Laurentin is not entirely off the mark when he finds the whole scene of the visitation constructed as a parallel to the homecoming of the Ark of the Covenant; thus the leaping of the child continues David's ecstatic joy at the guarantee of God's nearness. Be that as it may, something is expressed here that has been almost entirely lost in our century and nonetheless belongs to the heart of faith; essential to it is the joy in the Word become man, the dance before the Ark of the Covenant, in self-forgetful happiness, by one who has recognized God's salvific nearness. Only against this background can Marian devotion be comprehended. Transcending all problems, Marian devotion is the rapture of joy over the true, indestructible Israel; it is a blissful entering into the joy of the Magnificat and thereby it is the praise of him to whom the daughter Zion owes her whole self and whom she bears, the true, incorruptible, indestructible Ark of the Covenant.

June

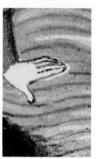

Baptism and the Reality of Easter

*E*aster, the victory in which Jesus Christ breaks down the walls of alienation and leads us out into the open air, is to be heard continually in the sacrament of baptism. In this sacrament he takes us by the hand; in it, Truth speaks to us and shows us the way to freedom. Wherever baptism is celebrated, the reality of Easter takes place here and now. So the annual feast of Easter is an invitation to us to return to our own baptism, to seize the hand of Truth which reaches out to lead us to the light. To renew our baptism, and hence genuinely to celebrate Easter, the feast of liberation, means that we renew our acceptance of the truth of faith; it means entering into the light of this truth and, as believers, overcoming the darkness of truth's absence. In this way we discover the real core of our freedom. "Arise, Christ shall give you light!" The Church's real ministry of liberation is to hold aloft the flame of truth in the world. Liberation is our continual and fresh acceptance of truth as the path of life set before us... The Church's real contribution to liberation, which she can never postpone and which is most urgent today, is to proclaim truth in the world, to affirm that God is, that God knows us, and that God is as Jesus Christ has revealed him, and that, in Jesus Christ, he has given us the path of life. Only then can there be such a thing as conscience, man's receptivity for truth, which gives each person direct access to God and makes him greater than every imaginable world system.

Baptism and Meaning

aptism also serves the purpose of giving a meaning to man's life, above and beyond biological life, so that this life is justified. In an age like today, when the future looks dark, the question can arise of whether it is moral at all to bring someone into the world and thus perhaps to impose upon him a future in which it is no longer possible to be truly human. And indeed, if we no longer know if it makes sense to be human, then this gift of life can only be justified if I can give the new person more than mere biological life. If I can give him, along with it, a meaning that I know to be stronger than all the darkness of history. That is what baptism is, which takes him up into fellowship with Christ. In that sense, infant baptism is clearly justified. It does become a different matter, of course, when in a dechristianized society baptism no longer evolves within the catechumenate. If many still cling to baptism only because it somehow provides the beginning of life with its celebration, with its requisite ritual expression, so to speak, then, at any rate, baptism is called into question from within. Baptism is, in fact, much more than a ritual conferring membership in a community, as many people conceive it nowadays. It is a process of birth, through which a new dimension of life opens out.

The Sustaining Force
of the Blessed Trinity

The Spirit does not speak, as it were, from himself, but is a listening to and a making clear of the Son, who in turn does not speak on his authority, but is, as the one sent by the Father, his distinct presence. The Father also gives himself to the Son so completely that everything that he has belongs to the Son. Each of the three Persons of the Trinity points to the other two. In this circle of love flowing and intermingling, there is the highest degree of unity and constancy and this in turn gives unity and constancy to everything that exists... What sustains us is the movement of the heart and spirit that leaves itself and is on the way to the other... It is only if each Christian makes his whole being available to the Word in the passage of time that time can as a whole be made open to Christ... The Trinity, then, provides us with the means by which both the individual and the community of the Church can disentangle the confusion of time. We shall not solve the problems that trouble us today by theorizing, but by spiritual means, by entering, in other words, into the form of the Trinity... The selflessness of those who bear witness to Christ gives authenticity to the Church, just as Christ's selflessness bore authentic testimony to himself and to the Spirit. It is in this way that a living interrelationship can develop, that growth can come about and that we can be led into the fullness of truth, a truth that is richer and greater than anything that we can invent.

Liturgy as our Bond with Heaven

The beginning of the Gospel stands for the whole; uttering it, one is as it were sending out the breath of the Holy Spirit to engage the four winds, pervading them and turning them to good. The world is thus declared to be the realm of God's creative word; matter is subordinated to the power of his Spirit. For matter too is his creation and hence the sphere of his gracious power. Ultimately we receive the very bread of the earth from his hands. How beautifully the new eucharistic bread is thus related to our daily bread! The eucharistic bread imparts its blessing to the daily bread, and each loaf of the latter silently points to him who wished to be the bread of us all. So the liturgy opens out into everyday life, into our earthly life and cares; it goes beyond the church precincts because it actually embraces heaven and earth, present and future. How we need this sign! Liturgy is not the private hobby of a particular group; it is about the bond which holds heaven and earth together, it is about the human race and the entire created world. In the Corpus Christi procession, faith's link with the earth, with the whole of reality, is represented "in bodily form," by the act of walking, of treading the ground, our ground.

Transcendence vs. Isolation

God brings Abraham out from among his family and sets him on a certain path. When it comes down to it, everyone has to undergo his own exodus. He not only has to leave the place that nurtured him and become independent, but has to come out of his own reserved self. He must leave himself behind, transcend his own limits; only then will he reach the Promised Land, so to speak — the sphere of freedom, in which he plays his part in creation. We have come to recognize this fundamental law of transcendence as being the essence of love. And of course the act of one who loves me is an act of this type. He has to bring me out of the comfortable inclination to stay within myself... Isolation is contrary to man's inmost inclination. If isolation means not being loved, being abandoned, being alone on one's own, this situation is indeed the fear underlying all our fears. Thus we can see again that man is constructed from within, in the image of God, to be loved and to love. At this point I believe we have to refer to man's being in the image of God. God is love. The essence of love portrays its own nature in the Trinity. Man is in God's image, and thereby he is a being whose innermost dynamic is likewise directed toward the receiving and the giving of love.

Eucharist as Blending One's Existence

*T*he most profound content of Christian eucharistic piety is formulated as a standard of conduct… it is based on the *mysterion*, that is, on the descent and self-giving of God, received by us in the Sacrament… According to 1 Corinthians 6: 12-19, receiving the Eucharist means blending one's existence, closely analogical, spiritually, to what happens when man and wife become one on the physical-mental-spiritual plane. The dream of blending divinity with humanity, of breaking out of the limitations of a creature — this dream, which persists through all the history of mankind and in hidden ways, in profane versions, is dreamed anew even within the atheistic ideologies of our time, just as it is in the drunken excesses of a world without God — this dream is here fulfilled. Man's promethean attempts to break out of his limitations himself, to build with his own capacities the tower by which he may mount up to divinity, always necessarily end in collapse and disappointment — indeed, in despair. This blending, this union, has become possible because God came down in Christ, took upon himself the limitations of human existence, suffering them to the end, and in the infinite love of the crucified One opened up the door to infinity. The real end of creation, its underlying purpose — and conversely that of human existence as willed by the Creator — is this very union, "that God may be all in all."

The Multiplication of Loaves

People expected that in the messianic age the miracle of the manna would be repeated. The Messiah, so they believed, would prove his identity in that everyone would have enough to eat and bread would once more come down from heaven. Jesus' intention is to transfer this manna miracle onto a different plane. And to do it with the Eucharist. With the bread in which he gives himself, and in which accordingly the multiplication of loaves takes place henceforth throughout history, down to our own day. He can, in a certain sense, be shared with others to an infinite extent. In this sharing of bread, Jesus is making an advance with this renewed manna miracle, in that he repeats the old manna but also leads to a quite different, shall we say more humble, and at the same time more demanding, form. In its profundity this is a far greater miracle. And also in that bread does not just fall down from heaven; but sharing human togetherness, mutual giving — things that do not just fall down from heaven — are also made part of it.

Corpus Christi and Hope

*I*t is only because God himself is the eternal dialogue of love that he can speak and be spoken to. Only because he himself is relationship can we relate to him; only because he is love can he love and be loved in return. Only because he is threefold can he be the grain of wheat which dies and the bread of eternal life. Ultimately, then, Corpus Christi is an expression of faith in God, in love, in the fact that God is love. All that is said and done on Corpus Christi is in fact a single variation on the theme of love, what it is and what it does. In one of his Corpus Christi hymns Thomas Aquinas puts it beautifully: *nec sumptus consumitur* — love does not consume: it gives and, in giving, receives. And in giving it is not used up but renews itself. Since Corpus Christi is a confession of faith in love, it is totally appropriate that the day should focus on the mystery of transubstantiation. Love is transubstantiation, transformation. Corpus Christi tells us: Yes, there is such a thing as love, and therefore there is transformation, therefore there is hope. And hope gives us the strength to live and face the world. Perhaps it was good to have experienced doubts about the meaning of celebrating Corpus Christi, for it has led us to the rediscovery of a feast which, today, we need more than ever.

The Connection between Joy and Death

*N*othing can make man laugh unless there is an answer to the question of death. And conversely, if there is an answer to death, it will make genuine joy possible — and joy is the basis for every feast. At its very heart the Eucharist is the answer to the question of death, for it is the encounter with that love which is stronger than death. Corpus Christi is the response to this central eucharistic mystery. Once a year it gives demonstrative expression to the triumphal joy in Christ's victory, as we accompany the Victor on his triumphal procession through the streets. So, far from detracting from the primacy of reception which is expressed in the gifts of bread and wine, it actually reveals fully and for the first time what "receiving" really means, namely, giving the Lord the reception due to the Victor. To receive him means to worship him; to receive him means to dare to do as much as you can... The power in virtue of which truth carries the day can be none other than *its own joy*. Unity does not come about by polemics nor by academic argument but by the radiance of Easter joy... This leads, too, to the core of our humanity, which yearns for this joy with its every fiber. So it is this Easter joy which is fundamental to all ecumenical and missionary activity; this is where Christians should vie with each other; this is what they should show forth to the world. This too is the purpose of Corpus Christi... Let beauty shine out in all its radiance when you come to express this joy of all joys. Love is stronger than death; in Jesus Christ God is among us.

JUNE 10

Corpus Christi and Gratitude

The Council of Trent said that the purpose of Corpus Christi was to arouse gratitude in the hearts of men and to remind them of their common Lord. Here, in a nutshell, we have in fact three purposes: Corpus Christi is to counter man's forgetfulness, to elicit his thankfulness, and it has something to do with fellowship, with that unifying power which is at work where people are looking to the one Lord. A great deal could be said about this; for with our computers, meetings, and appointments we have become appallingly thoughtless and forgetful. Psychologists tell us that our rational, everyday consciousness is only the surface of what makes up the totality of our soul. But we are so hounded by this surface awareness that what lies in the depths can no longer find expression. Ultimately man becomes sick for sheer lack of authenticity; he no longer lives as a subject: he exists as the plaything of chance and superficiality. This is connected with our relationship to time. Our relationship to time is marked by forgetting. We live for the moment. We actually *want* to forget, for we do not want to face old age and death. But in reality this desire for oblivion is a lie: suddenly it changes into the aggressive demand for the future, as a way of destroying time. However, this romanticism of the future, this refusal to submit to time, is also a lie, a lie which destroys both man and the world. The only way to master time, in fact, is the way of forgiveness and thankfulness whereby we receive time as a gift and, in a spirit of gratitude, transform it.

Eucharist as the Essential Form of Worship

*I*n the Bible the cross is… the expression of a life that is completely being for others. It is not man who goes to God with a compensatory gift, but God who comes to man, in order to give to him. He restores disturbed right on the initiative of his own power to love, by making unjust man just again, the dead living again, through his own creative mercy. In the New Testament the cross appears primarily as a movement from above to below. It does not stand there as the work of expiation which mankind offers to the wrathful God, but as the expression of that foolish love of God's which gives itself away to the point of humiliation in order thus to save man; it is *his* approach to us, not the other way about… Worship, too, man's whole existence acquires in Christianity a new direction. Worship follows in Christianity *first of all* in thankful acceptance of the divine deed of salvation. The essential form of Christian worship is therefore rightly called *"Eucharistia,"* thanksgiving. In this form of worship human achievements are not placed before God; on the contrary, it consists in man's letting himself be endowed with gifts; we do not glorify God by supposedly giving to him out of our resources… but letting ourselves be endowed with his own gifts and thus recognizing him as the only Lord. We worship him by dropping the fiction of a realm in which we could face him as independent business partners… Christian sacrifice does not consist in a giving of what God would not have without us but in our becoming totally receptive and letting ourselves be completely taken over by him. Letting God act on us — that is Christian sacrifice.

Knowing Christ through Encounter

*W*e need the living Christ, whom we can know only through our encounter with him. But encounter presumes actual presence — the Real Presence, which, in turn, requires the Sacrament and the Church that alone is authorized to give us the Sacrament, the Church that Christ himself willed into existence and continues to support. The Eucharist, at each new celebration, must be recognized anew as the core of our Christian life. But we cannot celebrate the Eucharist adequately if we are content to reduce it to a ritual of — more or less — a half-hour's duration. To receive Christ means to worship him. We welcome him properly and worthily at the solemn moment of receiving him only when we worship him and in worshiping him learn to know him, come to understand his nature, and follow him. We need to learn once more how to rest peacefully in his gentle presence in our churches, where the Eucharist is likewise always present because Christ intercedes for us before the Father, because he always awaits us and speaks to us. We must learn again how to draw inwardly close to him, for it is only thus that we become worthy of the Eucharist. We cannot prepare ourselves to receive the Eucharist simply by thinking about how it should be done. We can prepare for it only when we try to comprehend the depths of its demands on us, of its greatness; when we do not reduce it to our level, but let ourselves be raised to its exalted level; when we become aware of the accumulated sound of the prayers offered during all the centuries in which generations of men have advanced and are still advancing toward Christ.

Orthodoxy and Honoring God

O ften, in the primitive Church, the Eucharist was called simply *"agape,"* that is, "love," or even simply *"pax,"* that is, "peace." The Christians of that time thus expressed in a dramatic way the unbreakable link between the mystery of the hidden presence of God and the praxis of serving the cause of peace, of Christians being peace. For the early Christians, there was no difference between what today is often distinguished as orthodoxy and orthopraxis, as right doctrine and right action. Indeed, when this distinction is made, there generally is a suggestion that the word orthodoxy is to be disdained: those who hold fast to right doctrine are seen as people of narrow sympathy, rigid, potentially intolerant. In the final analysis, for those holding this rather critical view of orthodoxy everything depends on "right action," with doctrine regarded as something always open to further discussion. For those holding this view, the chief thing is the fruit doctrine produces, while the way that leads to our just action is a matter of indifference. Such a comparison would have been incomprehensible and unacceptable for those in the ancient Church, for they rightly understood the word "orthodoxy" not to mean "right doctrine" but to mean the authentic adoration and glorification of God. They were convinced that everything depended on being in the right relationship with God, on knowing what pleases him and what one can do to respond to him in the right way. Israel loved the law: from it they knew God's will... bringing order into the world, opening it to the transcendent.

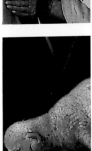

The Sacrificial Aspect of the Eucharist

*I*n the fundamental prayer of the Church, the Eucharist, the heart of our life is not merely expressed but is realized day after day. At the most profound level, the Eucharist has to do with Christ alone. He prays for us; he puts his prayer on our lips, for only he can say: This is my Body — This is my Blood. Thus he draws us into his life, into the act of eternal love by which he gives himself up to the Father, so that we are made over into the Father's possession with him and that through this very act Jesus Christ himself is bestowed upon us. Thus the Eucharist is a *sacrifice*: being given up to God in Jesus Christ and thereby at the same time having the gift of his love bestowed on us, for Christ is both the giver and gift. Through him, and with him, and in him we celebrate the Eucharist. Communion with him is that communion with the whole, without which there is no communion with Christ. A part of Christian prayer and of the Christian act of faith is committing oneself in faith to the whole, overcoming one's own limits. The Liturgy is not the setting up of some club, an association of friends; we receive it from the whole Church, and we have to celebrate it as coming from the whole and directed toward the whole. Only then do we believe and pray aright, when we are living it in the context of this act of self-transcendence, of self-abnegation, directed toward the Church of all times and of all places: this is what Catholicism essentially is. That is what we aim at whenever we step out of the zone of what is ours to unite ourselves with the pope and thus enter into the Church of all nations.

Law is the Inner Direction of Our Lives

At its best periods, Israel saw in the law something that set them free for the truth, free from the burden of uncertainty, the gracious gift of the way. And, indeed, we do know today that man collapses if he has constantly to reinvent himself, if he has to create anew human existence. For man, the will of God is not a foreign force of exterior origin, but the actual orientation of his own being. Thus the revelation of God's will is the revelation of what our own being truly wishes — it is a gift. So we should learn anew to be grateful that in the word of God the will of God and the meaning of our own existence have been communicated to us. God's presence in the word and his presence in the Eucharist belong together, inseparably. The eucharistic Lord is himself the living Word. Only if we are living in the sphere of God's Word can we properly comprehend and properly receive the gift of the Eucharist... The law became a burden the moment it was no longer being lived out from within but was broken down into a series of obligations external in their origin and their nature. Thus the Lord tells us emphatically: The true law of God is not an external matter. It dwells within us. It is the inner direction of our lives, which is brought into being and established by the will of God. It speaks to us in our conscience. The conscience is the inner aspect of the Lord's presence, which alone can render us capable of receiving the eucharistic presence... Faith in Christ simply renders the inmost part of our being, our conscience, once more articulate.

Eucharist and Communion

*I*n Abitene, a small village in present-day Tunisia, forty-nine Christians were taken by surprise one Sunday while they were celebrating the Eucharist, gathered in the house of Octavius Felix, thereby defying the imperial prohibitions. They were arrested and taken to Carthage to be interrogated by the proconsul Anulinus. Significant is the answer a certain Emeritus gave to the proconsul who asked him why on earth they had disobeyed the emperor's severe orders. He replied: We cannot live without joining together on Sunday to celebrate the Eucharist. We would lack the strength to face our daily problems and not to succumb… Christ is truly present among us in the Eucharist… It is a dynamic presence that grasps us, to make us his own, to make us assimilate him. Christ draws us to him, he makes us come out of ourselves to make us all one with him… Communion with the Lord is always also communion with our brothers and sisters… He is the one same Christ who is present in the Eucharistic Bread of every place on earth. This means that we can encounter him only together with all others. We can only receive him in unity… The consequence is clear: we cannot communicate with the Lord if we do not communicate with one another. If we want to present ourselves to him, we must also take a step towards meeting one another. To do this we must learn the great lesson of forgiveness: we must not let the gnawings of resentment work in our soul, but must open our hearts to the magnanimity of listening to others, open our hearts to understanding them, eventually to accepting their apologies, to generously offering our own.

Apostolic Life

*I*f the "apostolic" element is the place of movements in the Church, then the desire for the *vita apostolica* must be fundamental to her in all ages. The renunciation of property, of descendants, of any effort to impose one's own idea of the Church — that is, obedience in following Christ — have in all ages been regarded as the essential elements of the apostolic life, which cannot of course apply in the same way for all those participating in a movement but which are in varying ways points orienting each person's own life that are relevant for everyone. The apostolic life, in turn, is not an end in itself; rather, it creates freedom to serve. An apostolic life calls out for apostolic action: there is in the first place — again, in varying fashion — the proclamation of the Gospel as the missionary element. In following Christ, evangelizing always takes first place: *evangelizare pauperibus* — proclaiming the Gospel to the poor. Yet this never takes place through words alone: love, which constitutes its inner heart, both the center of its truth and the heart of its activity, has to be lived out and has in that sense to be a proclamation. Thus social service is always associated with the Gospel in some form or other. All this presupposes... a personal encounter with Christ at a deep level... Only when a person has been touched by Christ and opened up by him in his deepest heart can the other person also be touched in his heart; only in that case can reconciliation be effected in the Holy Spirit; only then can true community grow.

Corpus Christi Procession

*T*he Holy Thursday procession accompanies Jesus in his loneliness to the *"via crucis."* The Corpus Christi procession, on the contrary, responds symbolically to the mandate of the Risen One... This universal aspect of the eucharistic presence is shown in the procession of our feast. We take Christ, present in the figure of bread, through the streets of our city... With this gesture, we place before his eyes the sufferings of the sick, the loneliness of youth and the elderly, temptations, fears, our whole life. The procession is intended to be a great and public blessing for our city: Christ is, in person, the divine blessing for the world... In the procession of Corpus Christi, we accompany the Risen One on his journey through the whole world, as we have said. And, in this way, we also respond to his mandate: "Take, eat... Drink of it, all of you" (Mt 26: 26 and following). The Risen One, present in the form of bread, cannot be "eaten" as a simple piece of bread. To eat this bread is to enter into communion with the person of the living Lord. This communion, this act of "eating" is really a meeting between two persons; it is to allow oneself to be penetrated by the life of the One who is Lord, who is my Creator and Redeemer. The purpose of this communion is the assimilation of my life with his, my transformation and configuration with the One who is living love. Therefore, this communion implies adoration, the will to follow Christ, to follow the One who goes before us. Adoration and procession form part, therefore, of only one gesture of communion. They respond to his mandate: "Take, eat."

Corpus Christi and God's Tomorrow

he Feast of Corpus Christi is a call of the Lord to us, but also a cry from us to him. The whole Feast is one big prayer: Give us yourself. Give us your true bread. The Feast of Corpus Christi helps us in this way to understand the Lord's Prayer better… The fourth petition, which asks for bread, is the hinge between the three petitions that pertain to the kingdom of God and the three last petitions that have to do with our needs. It joins the two sets together. What do we pray for here? Certainly, for bread for today. It is the petition of the disciples, who live, not on stored-up treasures and investments, but rather on the daily goodness of the Lord and who therefore must live in a constant exchange with him, watching for him and trusting in him. It is the petition, not of people who heap up many possessions and try to gain security for themselves, but rather of the people who are content with the necessities, so as to have time for what is truly important. It is the prayer of the simple… Through this petition, the prayer that God's kingdom will come and earth will become like heaven becomes quite practical: through the Eucharist, heaven comes to earth, God's tomorrow comes today and brings tomorrow's world into today's. But the petitions about deliverance from all evil, from our guilt, from the burden of temptation, too, are practically summed up here: Give us this bread, so that my heart may become watchful, so that it will resist the Evil One, be able to distinguish good and evil, so that it may learn to forgive, so that it will remain strong in temptation.

The Eucharist and the New People

*T*he institution of the most holy Eucharist on the evening before the Passion cannot be regarded as some more or less isolated cultic transaction. It is the making of a covenant and, as such, is the concrete foundation of the new people: the people comes into being through its covenant relation to God. We could also say that by his eucharistic action, Jesus draws the disciples into his relationship with God and, therefore, into his mission, which aims to reach "the many," the humanity of all places and of all times. These disciples become a "people" through communion with the Body and Blood of Jesus which is simultaneously communion with God. The Old Testament theme of covenant, which Jesus incorporates into his preaching, receives a new center: communion with Christ's Body. It could be said that the people of the New Covenant takes its origin as a people from the Body and Blood of Christ; solely in terms of this center does it have the status of a people. We can call it "people of God" only because it is through communion with Christ that man gains access to a relationship with God that he cannot establish by his own power.

Holy Communion and One Body

The body is a man's self, which does not coincide with the corporeal dimension but comprises it as one element among others. Christ gives us himself — Christ, who in his Resurrection has continued to exist in a new kind of bodiliness of that intimate penetration of two subjects. Communion means that the seemingly uncrossable frontier of my "I" is left wide open and can be so because Jesus has first allowed himself to be opened completely, has taken us all into himself and has put himself totally into our hands. Hence, Communion means the fusion of existences; just as in the taking of nourishment the body assimilates foreign matter to itself, and is thereby enabled to live, in the same way my "I" is "assimilated" to that of Jesus, it is made similar to him in an exchange that increasingly breaks through the lines of division. This same event takes place in the case of all who communicate; they are all assimilated to this "bread" and thus are made one among themselves — one body. In this way Communion makes the Church by breaching an opening in the walls of subjectivity and gathering us into a deep communion of existence. It is the event of "gathering," in which the Lord joins us to one another.

Eucharistic Communion

*B*y eating the one bread, Saint Augustine says, we ourselves become what we eat. In the *Confessions* he says that this bread is nourishment for the strong. Normal food is less strong than man, it serves him, is taken into man's body to be assimilated and to build it up. But this special food, the Eucharist, is above man and stronger than man. Consequently the whole process involved is reversed: the man who eats this bread is assimilated *by it*, taken into it; he is fused into this bread and becomes bread, like Christ himself... Eucharist is never merely an event *à deux*, a dialogue between Christ and me. The goal of eucharistic communion is a total recasting of a person's life, breaking up a man's whole "I" and creating a new "We." Communion with Christ is of necessity a communication with all those who are his: it means that I myself become part of this new "bread" which he creates by transubstantiating all earthly reality... The Eucharist is in fact the "healing of our love." Jesus Christ opens the way to the impossible, to communion between God and man, since he, the incarnate Word, is this communion. He performs the "alchemy" which melts down human nature and infuses it into the being of God. To receive the Lord in the Eucharist, therefore, means entering into a community of being with Christ, it means entering through that opening in human nature through which God is accessible — which is the precondition for human beings opening up to one another in a really deep way. Communion with God is the path to interpersonal communion among men.

The Eucharist and Transformation

*I*n the Eucharist, adoration must become union. At the celebration of the Eucharist, we find ourselves in the "hour" of Jesus... Through the Eucharist this "hour" of Jesus becomes our own hour, his presence in our midst... By making the bread into his Body and the wine into his Blood, he anticipates his death, he accepts it in his heart, and he transforms it into an action of love. What on the outside is simply brutal violence — the crucifixion — from within becomes an act of total self-giving love. This is the substantial transformation which was accomplished at the Last Supper and was destined to set in motion a series of transformations leading ultimately to the transformation of the world when God will be all in all (cf. 1 Cor 15: 28). In their hearts, people always and everywhere have somehow expected a change, a transformation of the world. Here now is the central act of transformation that alone can truly renew the world: violence is transformed into love, and death into life. Since this act transmutes death into love, death as such is already conquered from within, the Resurrection is already present in it... Only this intimate explosion of good conquering evil can then trigger off the series of transformations that little by little will change the world. All other changes remain superficial and cannot save. For this reason we speak of redemption: what had to happen at the most intimate level has indeed happened, and we can enter into its dynamic. Jesus can distribute his Body, because he truly gives himself.

What John was Born For

*A*ccording to a splendid saying of Pascal, a single soul is worth more than the entire visible universe. But if we are to grasp this truth in a vivid way, we must be converted; we must as it were do an interior turnabout, overcome the spell visible reality casts over us, and acquire a sensitive touch, ear, and eye for the invisible. We must treat the invisible as more important than all the things that thrust themselves upon us with such force day after day. "Be converted": change your thinking, your outlook, so that you perceive God's presence in the world; change your thinking so that God may become present in you and through you in the world. John himself was not spared the hard task of changing his thinking, of being converted, of undergoing what De Lubac calls "the alchemy of being." His change in thinking began with his having to proclaim, as one crying in the wilderness, a man whom he himself did not know... But John's real suffering, the real recasting as it were of his entire being in relation to God, began in earnest with the activity of Christ during the time when he, John, was in prison. The darkness of the prison cell was not the most fearful darkness John had to endure. The true darkness was what Martin Buber has called "the eclipse of God": the abrupt uncertainty John experienced regarding his own mission and the identity of the one whose way he had sought to prepare.

The Foundation of the Apostles

The Church was built on the foundation of the Apostles as a community of faith, hope, and charity. Through the Apostles, we come to Jesus himself. The Church begins to establish herself when some fishermen of Galilee meet Jesus, allowing themselves to be won over by his gaze, his voice, his warm and strong invitation. After Mary, a pure reflection of the light of Christ, it is from the Apostles, through their word and witness, that we receive the truth of Christ. Their mission is not isolated, however, but is situated within a mystery of communion that involves the entire People of God and is carried out in stages from the Old to the New Covenant. From the first moment of his salvific activity, Jesus of Nazareth strives to gather together the People of God. In reality Jesus continually aims to build the People of God whom he came to bring together, purify, and save. It is clear that the entire mission of the Son-made-flesh has a communitarian finality. He truly came to unite dispersed humanity; he truly came to unite the People of God.

The Call of the Twelve

*I*n our catechesis on Christ and the Church, we have seen how the Church is built "on the foundation of the Apostles." The Gospels show how Jesus, at the beginning of his public ministry, chose the Twelve to become "fishers of men." Saint John in particular presents the calling of the Apostles as the fruit of a life-changing, personal encounter with the Lord. More than just the proclamation of a message, the preaching of the Gospel is seen as a witness to the person of Jesus Christ and an invitation to enter into communion with him. Jesus sent his Apostles first to the "lost sheep of the house of Israel." This prophetic act should be understood in the light of Israel's messianic expectation, according to which God, through his Chosen One, would gather his people like a shepherd his flock. This "gathering" is the sign of the coming of God's Kingdom and the extension of his saving power to every nation and people. After the Resurrection, the universality of the mission entrusted to the Apostles would become explicit. The Risen Lord would send them forth to make disciples of every nation, even "to the ends of the earth!"

JUNE 27

The Destiny of Those Who were Called

he destiny of those who were "called" would henceforth be closely bound to that of Jesus. An apostle is one who is sent, but even before that he is an "expert" on Jesus. This very aspect is highlighted by the Evangelist John from Jesus' very first encounter with the future apostles… The meeting takes place on the banks of the Jordan. The presence of the future disciples, who, like Jesus, also came from Galilee to receive the baptism administered by John, sheds light on their spiritual world. They were men who were waiting for the kingdom of God, anxious to know the Messiah whose coming had been proclaimed as imminent. It was enough for John the Baptist to point out Jesus to them as the Lamb of God, to inspire in them the desire for a personal encounter with the Teacher. The lines of Jesus' conversation with the first two future Apostles are most expressive. To his question "What do you seek?", they replied with another question: "'Rabbi,' where are you staying?" Jesus' answer was an invitation: "Come and see." Come, so that you will be able to see. The Apostles' adventure began as an encounter of people who are open to one another. For the disciples, it was the beginning of a direct acquaintance with the Teacher, seeing where he was staying and starting to get to know him. Indeed, they were not to proclaim an idea, but to witness to a person. Before being sent out to preach, they had to "be" with Jesus, establishing a personal relationship with him. On this basis, evangelization was to be no more than the proclamation of what they felt and an invitation to enter into the mystery of communion with Christ.

The Twelve

e must take note of the fact that the community of Jesus' disciples is not an amorphous mob. At its center are the Twelve, who form a compactly knit core… We should bear in mind that the Twelve receive the title "apostles" only after the Resurrection. Previously they had been called simply "the Twelve." This number, which joins them together into a clearly delineated community, is so important that after Judas' betrayal it is once more completed (Acts 1: 15-26). Mark describes their vocation with the phrase "and Jesus made Twelve" (3: 14). Their primary task is simply to be the community of the Twelve. Two additional functions then come into play: "that they might be with him and that he might send them" (Mk 3: 14). The symbolic value of the Twelve is consequently of decisive significance: twelve is the number of Jacob's sons, the number of the twelve tribes of Israel. In constituting the circle of Twelve, Jesus presents himself as the patriarch of a new Israel and institutes these twelve men as its origin and foundation. There could be no clearer way of expressing the beginning of a new people, which is now no longer formed by physical descent but by "being with Jesus," a reality that the Twelve receive from him and that he sends them to mediate to others. The theme of unity and plurality may already be descried here as well, although the oneness of the new people is the dominant aspect on account of the inseparable communion of the Twelve, who fulfill their symbolism — their mission — only as twelve.

Peter and Paul

he aim of the Church's mission is a humanity that has itself become a living glorification of God, the true worship that God expects: this is the profound meaning of catholicity... Like Paul, Peter also came to Rome, the city that was the place of convergence of all peoples and which precisely because of this could become the first of all expressions of the universality of the Gospel. Undertaking the journey from Jerusalem to Rome, Peter surely felt himself guided by the voices of the prophets, by the faith and by the prayer of Israel... The great psalm of the Passion, Psalm 22, whose first verse "My God, my God, why hast thou forsaken me?" Jesus pronounced on the cross, ended with the vision: "All the ends of the earth shall remember and turn to the Lord; and all the families of the nations shall worship before him" (Ps 22: 28). When Peter and Paul came to Rome the Lord, who invoked that psalm on the cross, was risen; this victory of God would now have to be proclaimed to all peoples, thus fulfilling the promise with which the psalm concluded... The unity of men in their multiplicity became possible because God, this one God of heaven and earth, showed himself to us; because the essential truth of our life, of our "from where?" and "to where?", became visible when he showed himself to us and in Jesus Christ made us see his face, himself. This truth of the essence of our being, of our living and our dying, truth that by God was made visible, unites us and makes us become brothers. Catholicity and unity go together. And unity has a content: the faith that the Apostles transmitted to us on behalf of Christ.

JUNE 30

Peter the Rock

But how are we to understand the new first name Peter? It certainly does not portray the character of this man whom Flavius Josephus' description of the Galilean national temperament so recognizably fits: "brave, kind-hearted, trusting, but also easily influenced and eager for change." The designation "rock" yields no pedagogical or psychological meaning; it can be understood only in terms of mystery, that is to say, christologically and ecclesiologically: Simon Peter will be by Jesus' commission precisely what he is not by "flesh and blood"... A rabbinical text may shed some light on what is meant here: "Yahweh spoke: 'How can I create the world, when these godless men will arise to vex me?' But when God looked upon Abraham, who was also to be born, he spoke: 'Behold, I have found a rock upon which I can build and found the world.' He therefore called Abraham a rock: 'Look upon the rock from which you have been hewn'" (Is 51: 12). Abraham, the father of faith, is by his faith the rock that holds back chaos, the onrushing primordial flood of destruction, and thus sustains creation. Simon, the first to confess Jesus as the Christ and the first witness of the Resurrection, now becomes by virtue of his Abrahamic faith, which is renewed in Christ, the rock that stands against the impure tide of unbelief and its destruction of man.

July

The Heart of God

he Old Testament speaks of God's Heart twenty-six times. It is regarded as the organ of his will, against which man is measured... It is the Logos which is at the center of us all — without our knowing — for the center of man is the heart, and in the heart there is the guiding energy of the whole, which is the Logos. It is the Logos which enables us to be logical, to correspond to the Logos; he is the image of God after which we were created... It is here, in the heart, that the birth of the divine Logos in man takes place, that man is united with the personal, incarnate Word of God... The heart is the locus of the saving encounter with the Logos... The pierced Heart of Jesus... is not concerned with self-preservation but with self-surrender. It saves the world by opening itself... The Heart saves, indeed, but it saves by giving itself away. Thus, in the Heart of Jesus, the center of Christianity is set before us. It expresses everything, all that is genuinely new and revolutionary in the New Covenant. This Heart calls to our heart. It invites us to step forth out of the futile attempt of self-preservation and, by joining in the task of love, by handing ourselves over to him and with him, to discover the fullness of love which alone is eternity and which alone sustains the world.

Sharing God's Wisdom

Wisdom is a sharing in God's ability to see and judge things as they really are. God reveals himself as God by his just judgments; as God, he sees things without disguise, as they really are, and deals with each according to his truth. Wisdom is a sharing in God's way of seeing reality. But there are, obviously, certain preconditions to this knowing from God's perspective. We cannot possess it unless we are united with God. This, in turn, means that this last and deepest mode of knowledge is not just an intellectual experience. In all that is essential, knowledge and life are inseparable. If something of the incorruptibility of God himself belongs to this deepest kind of knowledge, then there belongs to it also that purity of the "I" without which man is not incorruptible. From this, the meaning of the concepts "gifts of God" and "sharing in God's way of thinking" also becomes clear. Only if we let ourselves be cleansed of the corruptibility of the "I" and come thus gradually to live by God, to be united with God, do we come to a true inner freedom of judgment, to a fearless independence of thinking and deciding, that no longer cares about the approval or disapproval of others but clings only to truth. Such a purification is always a process of opening oneself and, at the same time, of receiving oneself. It cannot take place without the suffering of the vine that is pruned. But it makes possible the only form of power that leads, not to slavery, but to freedom.

Christ is the Answer

We ourselves have this very deep certainty that Christ is the answer and that without the concrete God, the God with the Face of Christ, the world destroys itself; and there is growing evidence that a closed rationalism, which thinks that human beings can rebuild the world better on their own, is not true. On the contrary, without the restraint of the true God, human beings destroy themselves. We see this with our own eyes. We ourselves must have a renewed certainty: he is the Truth; only by walking in his footsteps do we go in the right direction, and it is in this direction that we must walk and lead others. In all our suffering, not only should we keep our certainty that Christ really is the Face of God, but we should also deepen this certainty and the joy of knowing it and thus truly be ministers of the future of the world, of the future of every person. We should deepen this certainty in a personal relationship with the Lord because certainty can also grow with rational considerations. A sincere reflection that is also rationally convincing but becomes personal, strong, and demanding by virtue of a friendship lived personally, every day, with Christ, truly seems to me to be very important.

JULY 4

Values Worth Dying For

"Believe that it is the worst crime to prefer your physical life to reverence and to destroy, for the sake of living, the reasons for living" (Juvenal). This means that there are values worth dying for, because a life purchased at the cost of betraying these values is based on the betrayal of the reasons for living and is therefore a life destroyed from within. We could express what is meant here as follows: where there is no longer anything worth dying for, life is no longer worthwhile; it has lost its point. And this is not only true for the individual; a land, too, a common culture, has values that justify the commitment of one's life; if such values no longer exist, we also lose the reasons and the forces that maintain social cohesion and preserve a country as a community of life. Man needs transcendence. Immanence alone is too narrow for him. He is created for more. The denial of an afterlife led initially to a passionate glorification of life, the assertion of life at any price... Man needs morality in order to be himself. But morality requires faith in creation and immortality, that is, it needs the objectivity of obligation and the definitiveness of responsibility and fulfillment.

Moral Force

*I*t is becoming ever clearer that only moral values and strong convictions, and sacrifices, make it possible to live and to build the world. It is impossible to construct it in a mechanical way... If there is no moral force in souls, if there is no readiness to suffer for these values, a better world is not built; indeed, on the contrary, the world deteriorates every day, selfishness dominates and destroys all. On perceiving this the question arises anew: but where does the strength come from that enables us to suffer for good too, to suffer for good that hurts me first, which has no immediate usefulness? Where are the resources, the sources? From where does the strength come to preserve these values? It can be seen that morality as such does not survive and is not effective unless it is deeply rooted in convictions that truly provide certainty and the strength to suffer for — at the same time, they are part of love — a love that grows in suffering and is the substance of life. In the end, in fact, love alone enables us to live, and love is always also suffering: it matures in suffering and provides the strength to suffer for good without taking oneself into account at the actual moment.

JULY 6

Eucharist and Adoration

he process of transformation must now gather momentum. The Body and Blood of Christ are given to us so that we ourselves will be transformed in our turn. We are to become the Body of Christ, his own Flesh and Blood. We all eat the one bread, and this means that we ourselves become one. In this way, adoration becomes union. God no longer simply stands before us as the One who is totally Other. He is within us, and we are in him. His dynamic enters into us and then seeks to spread outwards to others until it fills the world, so that his love can truly become the dominant measure of the world. I like to illustrate this new step urged upon us by the Last Supper by drawing out the different nuances of the word "adoration" in Greek and in Latin. The Greek word is *proskynesis*. It refers to the gesture of submission, the recognition of God as our true measure, supplying the norm that we choose to follow. It means that freedom is not simply about enjoying life in total autonomy, but rather about living by the measure of truth and goodness, so that we ourselves can become true and good. This gesture is necessary even if initially our yearning for freedom makes us inclined to resist it. We can only fully accept it when we take the second step that the Last Supper proposes to us. The Latin word for adoration is *ad-oratio* — mouth to mouth contact, a kiss, an embrace, and hence, ultimately love. Submission becomes union, because he to whom we submit is Love. In this way submission acquires a meaning, because it does not impose anything on us from the outside, but liberates us deep within.

209

The Sacraments

I believe that the seven sacraments truly hold in place the structure and the great events of human life. For these important moments, for birth and death, for growing up and marrying, we need some kind of sign to give to this moment its full stature, its true promise, and thus also the dimension of being shared together… Faith is not something that exists in a vacuum; rather, it enters into the material world. And it is through signs from the material world that we are, in turn, brought into contact with God. These signs are therefore an expression of the corporal nature of our faith. The interpenetration of sensual and spiritual dimensions is the logical extension of the fact that God became flesh and shares himself with us in earthly things. The sacraments are thus a kind of contact with God himself. They show that this faith is not a purely spiritual thing, but one that involves community and creates community and that includes the earth, the creation, which in this way, together with its elements, becomes transparent. The essential point is that the communal aspect, the corporal dimension of faith, expresses itself in the sacraments and that it is made clear, at the same time, that faith is not something produced within us but comes from a higher authority. Certainly, they are entrusted to our freedom, like everything God does.

The Sacrament of Confirmation

he laying on of hands is the sign of being sheltered and protected by God and the sign of the presence of the Spirit. The anointing unites us with the Anointed One himself, who is Christ, and becomes a sign of the Holy Spirit, who inspired and lived in Christ. Confirmation is the completion of Baptism; if Baptism primarily emphasizes our being united with Christ, in Confirmation the emphasis is more on our fellowship with the Holy Spirit. What is also expressed therein is that the confirmed Christian is now a fully active and responsible member of the Church… Undoubtedly one significant aspect of Confirmation is that it means to turn us away from what is merely exterior, from preoccupation with success and achievement, and says to us, you have an inward aspect. And think about it; let the inner man, as Paul puts it, grow strong within you. The stifling of the inner life by practical cares has become one of our greatest problems. In this sense, Confirmation can truly stand as a counterpoise to mere externalizing and thus help to keep the business of being human in a proper balance.

The Power of Confession

*P*eople talk about Christianity having burdened people with guilt and having tried to use this as a lever to oppress them. Well, of course, such a misuse of guilt feelings may occur. But it is worse to extinguish the capacity for recognizing guilt, because man then becomes inwardly hardened and sick. Just think a stage further, to an intensified form of the inability to recognize guilt… The capacity to recognize guilt can be tolerated, and properly developed, whenever there is also healing. And healing, in turn, can only exist when there is absolution. Psychotherapy can indeed do a great deal to help us perceive defective connections in the psychical structure, and to help us put them right, but it cannot overcome guilt. At that point it has passed beyond the limits of its own capabilities, and that is why it so often fails. Only the sacrament, the authority from God, can truly overcome guilt. We must admit, in any case, that in our individualistic age it has become enormously difficult for people to cross the threshold of personal confession. But where the spirit of faith is leading us, then it can be learned anew. Above all because this is not an admission of guilt before men, but before God, and because it ends with the word of forgiveness — and perhaps also with advice that will help us to overcome the after-effects of guilt.

JULY 10

The Sacrament of the Sick

The anointing of the sick is meant to help with a spiritual process that in some circumstances can become a process of healing. This is the Church's sacramental help in the situation of illness. It's less a matter of the moment of death. In that case, the true Viaticum is the Eucharist. And in the prayers for the dying, the benediction of the dying, and the supplementary absolution, the Church has in readiness specific consolations. These strengthen people for their difficult passage over this terrible threshold into a dark that seems to have no light at all. The anointing of the sick is more a help toward the acceptance of suffering. It is meant to help me, by lifting up my pain and suffering into Christ, to enter into sacramental fellowship with him. This is not necessarily a matter of physical healing. For illness can indeed heal me spiritually; I may even have spiritual need of it. Christ, by teaching me how to suffer and by suffering with me, may truly become my doctor, who overcomes the deep spiritual sickness within my soul.

Becoming a Seer and a Pathfinder

*B*y a long and difficult journey, which began in a cave near Subiaco, the man Benedict has climbed up the mountain and finally up the tower. His life has been an inner climb, step by step, up the "vertical ladder." He has reached the tower and, then, the "upper room," which from the time of the Acts of the Apostles has been understood as a symbol of being brought together and drawn up, rising up out of the world of making and doing. He is standing at the window — he has sought and found the place where he can look out, where the wall of the world has been opened up and he can gaze into the open. He is standing. In monastic tradition, someone standing represents a man who has straightened himself up from being crouched and doubled up and is thus, not only able to stare at the earth, but he has achieved upright status and the ability to look up. Thus he becomes a seer. It is not the world that is narrowed down but the soul that is broadened out, being no longer absorbed in the particular, no longer looking at the trees and unable to see the wood, but now able to view the whole. Even better, he can see the whole because he is looking at it from on high, and he is able to gain this vantage point because he has grown inwardly great... He has to stand at the window. He must gaze out. And then the light of God can touch him; he can recognize it and can gain from it the true overview... Those great men who, by patient climbing and by the repeated purification they have received in their lives, have become seers and, therefore, pathfinders for the centuries are also relevant to us today.

Liturgy and Community

*W*e have called to mind once more that Eucharist, in the language of the ancient Church, was called, among other things, *synaxis*, the "meeting together," the assembly. It draws and binds men together, unites them, builds up community. Conversely, the community experiences Eucharist as fulfillment, as the center of its life, something in which it shares as a totality. All this is true, but we must remember that the scope of *synaxis* is much wider than the individual community... The assembly to which Jesus Christ calls us is the assembly of all the children of God. The Lord does not assemble the parish community in order to enclose it but in order to open it up. The man who allows himself to be "assembled" by the Lord has plunged into a river which will always be taking him beyond the limits of his self at any one time. To be with the Lord means to be willing, with him, to seek all the children of God. It is a favorite theme of our time that the Church is "wherever two or three are gathered in my name," but the reverse is also true: the community is only "with the Lord" and "gathered in his name" provided it is entirely at one with the Church, wholly part of the whole... Liturgy is not "made" by the community; the community receives it from the whole, in the same way that it receives its own self, as community, from the whole. And it can only remain an ecclesial community by continually giving itself back in commitment to this whole.

Liturgy and Human Yearning

*I*n the liturgy the absolutely Other takes place, the absolutely Other comes among us. In his commentary on the Song of Songs, that primally and profoundly human poem on the yearning and the tragic quality of love, Gregory of Nyssa describes man as the creature who wants to break out of the prison of finitude, out of the closed confines of his ego and of this entire world. And it is true: this world is too small for man... He yearns for the Other, the totally Other, that which is beyond his own reach. Behind this is the longing to conquer death. In all their celebrations, men have always searched for that life which is greater than death. Man's appetite for joy, the ultimate quest for which he wanders restlessly from place to place, only makes sense if it can face the question of death. Eucharist means that the Lord's Resurrection gives us this joy which no one else can. So it is not enough to describe the Eucharist as the community meal. It cost the Lord his life, and only at this price can we enjoy the gift of the Resurrection... What we need is the presence in our lives of what is real and permanent so that we can approach it. No external participation and creativity is of any use unless it is a participation in this inner reality, in the way of the Lord, in God himself. Its aim is to lead us to this breakthrough to God... Liturgy addresses the human being in all his depth, which goes far beyond our everyday awareness; there are things we only understand with the heart; the mind can gradually grow in understanding the more we allow our heart to illuminate it.

Why Listening is a Part of Life

*M*an ought not to try to be self-sufficient, and he must have the humility to learn, to accept something — "incline thy head." He must find the way to follow the call into listening. And listening means not just giving ear to whatever is going the rounds, but also listening to the depths, or to the heights, since what the Master says is basically the application of Holy Scripture, the application of this fundamental rule of human existence... We can see in the Rule of Saint Benedict how nothing that is truly human ever becomes old-fashioned. Anything that really comes from the depths of our being remains a counsel of life that is always relevant... Perhaps we are beginning to see again that freedom from work, that freedom which is a gift of God's service, stepping outside the mentality of mere achievement, is what we need. That listening — for the service of God is to a great extent a matter of letting God in and of listening — must be a part of life. Just as discipline and right measure and order belong together, just like obedience and freedom, so, equally, tolerating each other in the spirit of faith is not merely a basic rule for any monastic community, but all these things are, when you come down to it, essential elements for building any and every society. This is a rule that springs from what is truly human, and it was able to formulate what was truly human because it looked out and listened beyond what is human and perceived the divine. Man becomes really human when he is touched by God.

Eucharist as Oneness

he Eucharist gathers people together; it creates for human beings a blood relationship, a sharing of blood, with Jesus Christ and, thus, with God, and of people with one another. Yet in order for this, the coming together on the highest level, to come about, there must first be a simpler level of getting together, so to speak, and people have to step outside their own private worlds and meet together. People's coming together in response to the Lord's call is the necessary condition for the Lord's being able to make them into an assembly in a new way... All eucharistic assemblies taken together are still just one assembly, because the body of Christ is just one, and hence the People of God can only be one... If the eucharistic assembly first brings us out of the world and into the "upper room," into the inner chamber of faith, this very upper room is yet the place of meeting, a universal meeting of everyone who believes in Christ, beyond all boundaries and divisions; and it thus becomes the point from which a universal love is bound to shine forth, overcoming all boundaries and divisions: if others are going hungry, we cannot live in opulence. On the one hand, the Eucharist is a turning inward and upward; yet only from the depths within, and from the heights of what is truly above, can come the power that overcomes boundaries and divisions and changes the world.

The Eucharist as Event

he Eucharist unites us with the Lord and does it in fact by limiting us, binding us to him. Only thus are we freed from ourselves… The Incarnation is not a philosophical idea but a historical event, which in its very uniqueness and truth is the point at which God breaks into history and the place at which we come into contact with him. If we deal with it, as is appropriate on the basis of the Bible, not as a principle but as an event, then our conclusion is necessarily the opposite one: God has associated himself with a quite specific point in history, with all its limitations, and wishes us to share in his humility. Allowing oneself to be associated with the Incarnation means accepting this self-limitation of God: these very gifts, which for other spheres of culture are strange and foreign, become for us the sign of his unparalleled and unique action, of his unique historical figure. They are the symbols of God's coming to us, he who is a stranger to us and who makes us his neighbors through his gifts. The response to God's descent can only be one of humble obedience, an obedience that in receiving the tradition and remaining faithful to it is granted as a gift the certainty of his close presence… That is why the "memorial" constituted by the Eucharist is more than a remembrance of something in the past: it is the act of entering into that inner core which can no longer pass away. And that is why the "preaching" of Christ's death is more than mere words: it is a proclamation that bears the truth within it.

Becoming a Eucharist

*I*n the Roman Canon, we ask immediately before the Consecration that our sacrifice may be made *rationabilis*... We are asking that it may become a logos-sacrifice. In this sense we are asking for the gifts to be transformed — and then, again, not just for that... We ask that the Logos, Christ, who is the true sacrifice, may himself draw us into his act of sacrifice, may "logify" us, make us "more consistent with the word," "more truly rational," so that his sacrifice may become ours and may be accepted by God as ours, may be able to be accounted as ours. We pray that his presence might pick us up, so that we become "one body and one spirit" with him... The mysticism of identity, in which the Logos and the inner dimension of man blend together, is transcended by a christological mysticism: the Logos, who is the Son, makes us sons in the sacramental fellowship in which we are living. And if we become sacrifices, if we ourselves become conformed to the Logos, then this is not a process confined to the spirit, which leaves the body behind it as something distanced from God. The Logos himself has become a body and gives himself to us in his Body. That is why we are being urged to present our bodies as a form of worship consistent with the Logos, that is to say, to be drawn into the fellowship of love with God in our entire bodily existence, in bodily fellowship with Christ... The transformation of the gifts which is to be extended to us has to become, for us ourselves, a process of remolding: bringing us out of our restricted self-will, out into union with the will of God.

The Gospel Addresses Culture

The Gospel does not stand "beside" culture. It is addressed, not merely to the individual, but to the culture itself, which leaves its mark on the spiritual growth and development of the individual, his fruitfulness or unfruitfulness with respect to God and to the world. Evangelization is not simply adaptation to the culture, either, nor is it dressing up the Gospel with elements of the culture, along the lines of a superficial notion of inculturation that supposes that, with modified figures of speech and a few new elements in the liturgy, the job is done. No, the Gospel is a slit, a purification that becomes maturation and healing. It is a cut that demands patient involvement and understanding, so that it occurs at the right time, in the right place, and in the right way; a cut, then, that requires sympathy and understanding of the culture from within, an appreciation for its dangers and its hidden or evident potential. Thus it is clear also that this cut "is not a momentary effort that is automatically followed by a ripening process." Rather, an ongoing and patient encounter between the Logos and the culture is necessary, mediated by the service of the faithful... The Christian faith is open to all that is great, true, and pure in world culture... Anyone who evangelizes today will start by looking in our culture for those features in it that are open to the Gospel, the "seeds of the Word," so to speak, and will strive to develop them further.

Saint Benedict's Love for Christ

I would like to emphasize one typical aspect of Saint Benedict's spirituality. Benedict, unlike other great monastic missionaries of his time, did not found a monastic institution whose principal aim was the evangelization of the barbarian peoples; he pointed out to his followers the search for God as the fundamental and, indeed, one and only aim of life: *"Quaerere Deum"* ("to seek God"). He knew, however, that when the believer enters into a profound relationship with God, he cannot be content with a mediocre life under the banner of a minimalistic ethic and a superficial religiosity. In this light one can understand better the expression that Benedict borrowed from Saint Cyprian and summed up in his Rule (IV, 21), the monks' program of life: *"Nihil amori Christi praeponere,"* "Prefer nothing to the love of Christ." Holiness consists of this, a sound proposal for every Christian that has become a real and urgent pastoral need in our time, when we feel the need to anchor life and history to sound spiritual references. Mary Most Holy is a sublime and perfect model of holiness who lived in constant and profound communion with Christ. Let us invoke her intercession, together with Saint Benedict's, so that in our time too the Lord will multiply men and women who, through witnessing to an enlightened faith in their lives, may be the salt of the earth and the light of the world in this new millennium.

The Meaning of a Christian Feast

*I*n a world in which, despite all its progress, injustice and affliction are perhaps more than ever before exercising their fearful reign in many forms: In such a world it must seem like a gesture of contempt when those who are able to do so escape into the happy forgetfulness or expensive pomp of a festive celebration. Well, if celebration means simply a self-satisfied enjoyment of one's own affluence and security, then there is really no place for that kind of celebration today. But is this really the meaning of celebration? It is certainly not the original meaning of a Christian feast. A Christian feast — the birth of the Lord, for example — means something entirely different. It means that the human person leaves the world of calculation and determinisms in which everyday life snares him, and that he focuses his being on the primal source of his existence. It means that for the moment he is freed from the stern logic of the struggle for existence and looks beyond his own narrow world to the totality of things. It means that he allows himself to be comforted, allows his conscience to be moved by the love he finds in the God who has become a child, and that in doing so he becomes freer, richer, purer. If we were to try celebrating in this fashion, would not a sigh of relief pass across the world? Would such a feast not bring hope to the oppressed and be a clarion call to the forgetful folk who are aware only of themselves?

Jesus' Eucharistic Words and His Death

*I*n Jesus' preaching all paths lead into the mystery of him who proves the truth of his love and his message in suffering. The words he spoke at the Last Supper then represent the final shaping of this. They offer nothing entirely unexpected, but rather what has already been shaped and adumbrated in all these paths, and yet they reveal anew what was signified throughout: the institution of the eucharist is an anticipation of his death; it is the undergoing of a spiritual death. For Jesus shares himself out, he shares himself as the one who has been split up and torn apart into body and blood. In the eucharistic words of Jesus he undergoes a spiritual death, or, to put it more accurately, *in these words Jesus transforms death into the spiritual act of affirmation, into the act of self-sharing love*; into the act of adoration, which is offered to God, then from God is made available to men. Both are essentially interdependent: the words at the Last Supper without the death would be, so to speak, an issue of unsecured currency; and again, the death without these words would be a mere execution without any discernible point to it. Yet the two together constitute this new event, in which the senselessness of death is given meaning; in which what is irrational is transformed and made rational and articulate; in which the destruction of love, which is what death means in itself, becomes in fact the means of verifying and establishing it, of its enduring constancy.

Understanding Culture

*W*e can try to give something like a definition of culture. We could say: Culture is the social form of expression, as it has grown up in history, of those experiences and evaluations that have left their mark on a community and have shaped it... Culture has to do with perceptions and values. It is an attempt to understand the world and the existence of man within it; an attempt, however, not of a purely theoretical nature, but rather guided by the fundamental interest of our existence. This understanding is meant to show us how to go about being human, how a man takes his proper place in this world and responds to it, so as to improve himself, to live his life successfully and happily. This question, in turn, does not in the great cultures refer to the individual alone, as if each person could work out for himself a pattern of coping with the world and with living. Each can do this only with the help of others; the question of correct perception is thus also a question concerning the proper shaping of the community. This in turn is the prerequisite for each individual's life being successful. Culture is concerned with understanding, which is a perception that opens the way for practical action, that is, a perception of which the dimension of values, of morality, is an indispensable part... No one can understand the world at all, no one can live his life rightly, so long as the question about the Divinity remains unanswered. Indeed, the very heart of the great cultures is that they interpret the world by setting in order their relationship to the Divinity.

Culture and Divinity

*C*ulture in the classical sense includes going beyond what is visible and apparent to the real basis of things and, at its heart, opens the door to the Divinity. Bound up with that is the other feature, of the individual transcending his own self and finding mutual support for himself in a greater social agency, whose perceptions he can, as it were, borrow and then, of course, also carry farther and develop for himself. Culture is always associated with a social agent, which accepts into itself the experiences of the individuals and, on the other hand, also molds them. This social agent preserves and develops perceptions that go beyond what any individual is capable of — insights we may describe as prerational and suprarational. In doing this, cultures refer to the wisdom of the "elders," who were closer to the gods; to traditions from the beginnings, which have the character of revelation, that is, they are the result, not simply of human questioning and reflection, but of aboriginal contact with the ground of all things; to communications from the Divinity.

Faith and Culture

*F*aith itself is cultural. It does not exist in a naked state, as sheer religion. Simply by telling man who he is and how he should go about being human, faith is creating culture and is culture. This message of faith is not an abstract message; it is one that has matured through a long history and through manifold intercultural fusions, in the course of which it has shaped an entire way of life, a way of man's dealing with himself, with his neighbor, with the world, and with God. Faith itself exists as culture... The cross is, first, a break, the being cast forth, the being lifted up from the earth, but in that very way it becomes a new center of gravity, a point of gravitation drawing things up from the history of the world, for the bringing together of what is divided. Anyone entering the Church has to be aware that he is entering a separate, active cultural entity with her own many-layered intercultural character that has grown up in the course of history. Without a certain exodus, a breaking off with one's life in all its aspects, one cannot become a Christian. Faith is no private path to God; it leads into the people of God and into its history. God has linked himself to a history, which is now also his history and which we cannot simply erase... Because the people of God is not just a single cultural entity but is gathered together from all peoples, therefore the first cultural identity, rising again from the break that was made, has its place therein; and not only that, but it is needed in order to allow the Incarnation of Christ, of the Word, to attain its whole fullness.

The Breakthrough of Christianity

*C*hristianity first brought about a breakthrough, having "broken down the dividing wall" (Eph 2: 14), and it did so in a threefold sense: the blood relationship with the patriarch is no longer necessary, because being united with Jesus brings about full membership, the true relationship. Everyone can now belong to this God; all men are to be permitted and to be able to become his people. The particularist legal and moral structures are no longer binding; they have become a historical prologue, because everything has been brought together in the person of Jesus Christ, and anyone who follows him is carrying within himself, and fulfilling, the whole essence of the law. The old cult has become invalid and has been abolished in Jesus' self-offering to God and to mankind, which now appears as the true sacrifice, as the spiritual worship in which God and man embrace one another and are reconciled — something for which the Lord's Supper, the Eucharist, stands there as a concrete and evermore present assurance. Perhaps the finest and most succinct expression of this new Christian synthesis is to be found in a confession in the First Letter of Saint John: "we know and believe the love" (1 Jn 4: 16). Christ had become for these people the discovery of creative love; the rational principle of the universe had revealed itself as love — as that greater reason which accepts into itself even darkness and irrationality and heals them.

The Humility to Seek the Truth

*S*cience becomes pathological and a threat to life when it takes leave of the moral order of human life, becomes autonomous, and no longer recognizes any standard but its own capabilities. That means that the scope of reason must be enlarged once more. We have to come out of the prison we have built for ourselves and recognize other forms of ascertaining things, forms in which the whole of man comes into play… We need a new readiness to seek the truth and also the humility to let ourselves be found. The strict application of methodical discipline should not mean just the pursuit of success; it should mean the pursuit of truth and the readiness to find it. That methodological strictness, which again and again lays upon us the obligation to subject ourselves to what we have found, and not just to follow our own wishes, can amount to a great school in being human and can make man capable of recognizing and appreciating truth. The humility that gives way to what has been found and does not try to manipulate it should not, however, become a false modesty that takes away our courage to recognize the truth. All the more must it oppose the pursuit of power, which is only interested in dominating the world and is no longer willing to perceive its inner logic, which sets limits to our desire to dominate.

Seeking the Truth and Culture's Role

When man is shut out from the truth, he can only be dominated by what is accidental and arbitrary. That is why it is not "fundamentalism" but a duty of humanity to protect man from the dictatorship of what is accidental and to restore to him his dignity, which consists precisely in the fact that no human institution can ultimately dominate him, because he is open to the truth… The confidence to seek for the truth and to find it is never anachronistic: it is precisely this that maintains the dignity of man, that breaks down particularism, and that leads men toward one another beyond the bounds of their cultural settings on the basis of their common dignity… Cultures are not therefore fixed once and for all in one single form… They are concerned with encounter and with mutual fertilization. Because the inner openness of man to God is more influential in them, the greater and more pure they are, the inward readiness for the revelation of God is written into them. Revelation is not something alien to them; rather, it corresponds to an inner expectation in the cultures themselves… All peoples are now invited to participate in this process of transcending their own heritage that first began in Israel; they are invited to turn to the God who, for his part, transcended his own limits in Jesus Christ, who has broken down "the dividing wall of hostility" between us and in the self-deprivation of the cross has led us toward one another. Faith in Jesus Christ is, therefore, of its nature, a continual opening of oneself, God's action of breaking into the human world and, in response to, this man's breaking out toward God.

Agape Love

irst there is the word *dodim*, a plural form suggesting a love that is still insecure, indeterminate, and searching. This comes to be replaced by the word *ahabà*, which the Greek version of the Old Testament translates with the similar-sounding *agape*, which becomes the typical expression for the biblical notion of love. By contrast with an indeterminate, "searching" love, this word expresses the experience of a love which involves a real discovery of the other, moving beyond the selfish character that prevailed earlier. Love now becomes concern and care for the other. No longer is it self-seeking, a sinking in the intoxication of happiness; instead it seeks the good of the beloved: it becomes renunciation and it is ready, and even willing, for sacrifice. It is part of love's growth towards higher levels and inward purification that it now seeks to become definitive, and it does so in a twofold sense: both in the sense of exclusivity (this particular person alone) and in the sense of being "for ever." Love embraces the whole of existence in each of its dimensions, including the dimension of time. It could hardly be otherwise, since its promise looks towards its definitive goal: love looks to the eternal. Love is indeed "ecstasy," not in the sense of a moment of intoxication, but rather as a journey, an ongoing exodus out of the closed inward-looking self towards its liberation through self-giving, and thus towards authentic self-discovery and indeed the discovery of God.

Eros and Agape

Yet *eros* and *agape* — ascending love and descending love — can never be completely separated. The more the two, in their different aspects, find a proper unity in the one reality of love, the more the true nature of love in general is realized. Even if *eros* is at first mainly covetous and ascending, a fascination for the great promise of happiness, in drawing near to the other, it is less and less concerned with itself, increasingly seeks the happiness of the other, is concerned more and more with the beloved, bestows itself and wants to "be there for" the other. The element of *agape* thus enters into this love, for otherwise *eros* is impoverished and even loses its own nature. On the other hand, man cannot live by oblative, descending love alone. He cannot always give, he must also receive. Anyone who wishes to give love must also receive love as a gift. Certainly, as the Lord tells us, one can become a source from which rivers of living water flow (cf. Jn 7: 37-38). Yet to become such a source, one must constantly drink anew from the original source, which is Jesus Christ, from whose pierced heart flows the love of God (cf. Jn 19: 34).

From the Son's Death Springs Life

The tolerance that admits God as it were as a private opinion but refuses him the public domain, the reality of the world and of our lives, is not tolerance but hypocrisy. But nowhere that the human being makes himself the one lord of the world and owner of himself can justice exist. There, it is only the desire for power and private interests that can prevail. Of course, one can chase the Son out of the vineyard and kill him, in order selfishly to taste the fruits of the earth alone. From the Son's death springs life, a new building is raised, a new vineyard. He, who at Cana changed water into wine, has transformed his Blood into the wine of true love and thus transforms the wine into his Blood. In the Upper Room he anticipated his death and transformed it into the gift of himself in an act of radical love. His Blood is a gift, it is love, and consequently it is the true wine that the Creator was expecting. In this way, Christ himself became the vine, and this vine always bears good fruit: the presence of his love for us which is indestructible. From this death springs life, because Jesus transformed it into a sacrificial gesture, an act of love, thereby profoundly changing it: love has overcome death. In the Holy Eucharist, from the cross, he draws us all to himself (cf. Jn 12: 32) and makes us branches of the Vine that is Christ himself. If we abide in him, we will also bear fruit, and then from us will no longer come the vinegar of self-sufficiency, of dissatisfaction with God and his creation, but the good wine of joy in God and of love for our neighbor.

The Twelve and the People of God

An evident sign of the intention of the Nazarene to gather together the community of the Covenant, to demonstrate in it the fulfillment of the promises made to the Fathers who always speak of convocation, unification, unity, is *the institution of the Twelve*. On the site of the revelation, "the mount," taking initiative that demonstrates absolute awareness and determination, Jesus establishes the Twelve so that, together with him, they are witnesses and heralds of the coming of the Kingdom of God. In choosing the Twelve, introducing them into a communion of life with himself and involving them in his mission of proclaiming the Kingdom in words and works, Jesus wants to say that the definitive time has arrived in which to constitute the new People of God, the people of the twelve tribes, which now becomes a universal people, his Church. We cannot have Jesus without the reality he created and in which he communicates himself. Between the Son of God-made-flesh and his Church there is a profound, unbreakable, and mysterious continuity by which Christ is present today in his people. He is always contemporary with us, he is always contemporary with the Church, built on the foundation of the Apostles and alive in the succession of the Apostles. And his very presence in the community, in which he himself is always with us, is the reason for our joy. Yes, Christ is with us, the Kingdom of God is coming.

August

What it Means to Follow

hat does "the following of Christ" really mean? Is this following a real possibility for modern men and women? Does it perhaps even point out the only way of becoming and being a human person? If so, then a Christian may assert that the following of Christ embodies *the* decisive possibility for the human race and that only this following brings to light the real nature of the enigma that is man… What does "the following of Christ" mean?… "Following" is something quite external but at the same time something very interior as well. Something external: an actual walking behind Jesus on his journey around Palestine. Something interior: a new direction for one's life, which no longer has business, the earning of a livelihood, and one's own wishes and ideas as its central points of reference but is surrendered to the will of another, so that being with this other and being at his disposal are now the really important content of a human existence… To follow really means to go behind, to move in the direction prescribed, even if this direction is completely contrary to one's own wishes. Precisely because the word "follow" is meant so literally, it affects the innermost depths of the human person. The words "Follow me!" contain, first of all, a summons to give up a previous calling. At a deeper level, however, they are a summons to give up one's very self in order to live entirely for him who, for his part, willed to live entirely for the Word of God: so much so that later reflection could recognize in him the incarnate Word of God himself.

AUGUST 2

Following, Believing, Loving

"To follow" means to entrust oneself to the Word of God, to rate it higher than the laws of money and bread and to live by it. In short, to follow means to believe, but to "believe" in the sense of making a radical decision between the two and, in the last analysis, the only two possibilities for human life: bread and the word. The human person does not live on bread alone but also and primarily on the word, the spirit, meaning. It is always this same radical decision that confronts disciples when they hear the call "Follow me!"; the radical decision to stake one's life either on profit and gain or on truth and love; the radical decision to live for oneself or to surrender one's self... Only in losing themselves can human beings find themselves. The real and radical martyrdom of genuine self-renunciation is and remains the basic condition for following Christ... To follow Christ means to accept the *inner* essence of the cross, namely the radical love expressed therein, and thus to imitate God himself. For on the cross God revealed himself as the One who pours himself out in prodigal fashion; who surrenders his glory in order to be present for us; who desires to rule the world not by power but by love, and in the weakness of the cross reveals *his* power which operates so differently from the power of this world's mighty rulers. To follow Christ, then, means to enter into the self-surrender that is the real heart of love. To follow Christ means to become one who loves as God has loved... In the last analysis, to follow Christ is simply for man to become human by integration into the humanity of God.

Breaking of Bread

*U*ltimately, the Church draws her life from the Eucharist, from this real, self-giving presence of the Lord. Without this ever-new encounter with him, she would necessarily wither… Anyone who repeatedly exposes himself to it and confides in it will be changed. You cannot walk constantly with the Lord, cannot ever anew pronounce these tremendous words, *This is my Body and my Blood*, you cannot touch the Body of the Lord again and again, without being affected by him and challenged by him, being changed and led by him. We may of course lag behind him, and will again and again lag immeasurably far behind, but in the long run there are really only two possibilities: either to shake off the Eucharist, with the enormous demands and power it sets up in life, or to surrender to it, to hold fast to it. Anyone who holds fast to the Lord will not be abandoned by him. Anyone who grapples with him calmly and patiently, humbly and sincerely, will be led by him; he will never be denied his light… Christ genuinely shared himself out, gave himself with the torn-up bread, so that his life might be ours: that is the incredible event that occurs ever anew. Herein lies the great significance of the Eucharist, and that is why it is no game, but quite real. When death comes onstage the game is at an end. Man is set before the truth. But only when this encounter reaches right down unto death can true hope arise for man.

The Meaning of Christ's Resurrection

*J*esus is not a character from the past. He lives, and he walks before us as one who is alive, he calls us to follow him, the living one, and in this way to discover for ourselves too the path of life. Christ did not remain in the tomb, his body did not see corruption; he belongs to the world of the living, not to the world of the dead. But somehow the Resurrection is situated so far beyond our horizon, so far outside all our experience that, returning to ourselves, we find ourselves continuing the argument of the disciples: Of what exactly does this "rising" consist? What does it mean for us and the whole of history? The point is that Christ's Resurrection is something more, something different. If we may borrow the language of the theory of evolution, it is the greatest "mutation," absolutely the most crucial leap into a totally new dimension that there has ever been in the long history of life and its development: a leap into a completely new order which does concern us, and concerns the whole of history. The crucial point is that this man Jesus was not alone, he was not an "I" closed in upon itself. He was one single reality with the living God, so closely united with him as to form one person with him. He found himself, so to speak, in an embrace with him who is life itself, an embrace not just on the emotional level, but one which included and permeated his being. His life was a "being taken up" into God. He broke the definitiveness of death, because in him the definitiveness of life was present. He was one single reality with indestructible life, in such a way that it burst forth anew through death.

The Power of Beauty

he beautiful is knowledge certainly, but, in a superior form, since it arouses man to the real greatness of the truth... True knowledge is being struck by the arrow of beauty that wounds man, moved by reality... Being struck and overcome by the beauty of Christ is a more real, more profound knowledge than mere rational deduction... The encounter with the beautiful can become the wound of the arrow that strikes the heart and in this way opens our eyes, so that later, from this experience, we take the criteria for judgment and can correctly evaluate the arguments... The experience of the beautiful has received new depth and new realism. The One who is the beauty itself let himself be slapped in the face, spat upon, crowned with thorns... Whoever has perceived this beauty knows that truth, and not falsehood, is the real aspiration of the world. It is not the false that is "true," but indeed, the truth... Is there anyone who does not know Dostoyevsky's often-quoted sentence: "The beautiful will save us"? However, people usually forget that Dostoyevsky is referring here to the redeeming beauty of Christ. We must learn to see him. If we know him, not only in words, but if we are struck by the arrow of his paradoxical beauty, then we will truly know him, and know him not only because we have heard others speak about him. Then we will have found the beauty of truth, of the truth that redeems. Nothing can bring us into close contact with the beauty of Christ himself other than the world of beauty created by faith and light that shines out from the faces of the saints, through whom his own light becomes visible.

The Transfiguration

T he essential events of Jesus' activity proceeded from the core of his personality and this core was his dialogue with the Father. The very basis and the abiding precondition of the Christian confession of faith: only by entering into Jesus' solitude, only by participating in what is most personal to him, his communication with the Father, can one see what this most personal reality is; only thus can one penetrate to his identity. This is the only way to understand him and to grasp what "following Jesus" means. The Christian confession is not a neutral proposition; it is prayer, only yielding its meaning within prayer. The person who has beheld Jesus' intimacy with his Father and has come to understand him from within is called to be a "rock" of the Church. The Church arises out of participation in the prayer of Jesus (cf. Lk 9: 18-20; Mt 16: 13-20)… "The mountain" is always the realm of prayer, of being with the Father… The Transfiguration only renders visible what is actually taking place in Jesus' prayer: he is sharing in God's radiance and hence in the manner in which the true meaning of the Old Testament — and of all history — is being made visible, i.e., revelation. Jesus' proclamation proceeds from this participation in God's radiance, God's glory, which also involves a seeing with the eyes of God — and therefore the unfolding of what was hidden… The entire person of Jesus is contained in his prayer.

AUGUST 7

The Gift that Overturns Human Ideas

he weight of two millennia of history makes it difficult to grasp the novelty of the captivating mystery of divine adoption. The Father "has made known to us the mystery of his will… as a plan to unite all things in him" (Eph 1: 9-10). And Saint Paul adds, with enthusiasm: "In everything God works for good with those who love him, who are called according to his purpose. For those whom he foreknew he also predestined to be conformed to the image of his Son, in order that he might be the first-born among many brethren" (Rom 8: 28-29). The vision is indeed fascinating: we are called to live as brothers and sisters of Jesus, to feel that we are sons and daughters of the same Father. This is a gift that overturns every purely human idea and plan. The confession of the true faith opens wide our minds and hearts to the inexhaustible mystery of God which permeates human existence. What should be said therefore of the temptation, which is very strong nowadays, to feel that we are self-sufficient to the point that we become closed to God's mysterious plan for each of us? The love of the Father, which is revealed in the person of Christ puts this question to us. In order to respond to the call of God and start on our journey, it is not necessary to be already perfect. We know that the prodigal son's awareness of his own sin allowed him to set out on his return journey and thus feel the joy of reconciliation with the Father Weaknesses and human limitations do not present an obstacle, as long as they help make us more aware of the fact that we are in need of the redeeming grace of Christ.

The Brave Hound

A particular sculptural relief shows three beasts whose reciprocal relationship was evidently intended by the artist to portray the situation of the Church of his day. At the very bottom, one sees a lamb upon which a huge lion has greedily pounced. The lion is holding it fast in its powerful claws and its teeth. The lamb's body is already torn open. Its bones are visible and it is obvious that bits of flesh have already been gobbled away... What the sculpture conveys, then, is a sort of "report on the state of the faith" which seems to be extraordinarily pessimistic. It is the Church in her essence, the Church of faith, which appears already half-devoured by the lion, the symbol of power, in whose clutches it is held prisoner. All it can do now is endure its fate in defenseless misery. But the sculpture, which depicts with due realism the hopelessness of the Church's situation from a human point of view, is also an expression of the hope which knows that faith is invincible. This hope is represented in a remarkable way: a third animal, a small white dog, is falling upon the lion. Though it seems no equal match for the strength of the lion, the dog throws itself with tooth and claw upon the monster... The white hound symbolizes fidelity. It is the sheep dog, which stands for the shepherd himself... The brave hound stands for a theology which understands itself to be the servant of the faith and for that reason agrees to make itself a laughingstock by putting the intemperance and tyranny of naked reason in their place.

The Authority of Preaching

*P*roclamation in the form of preaching does teach bindingly; such is its essence. For it does not suggest some sort of pastime or a kind of religious entertainment. Its aim is to tell man who he is and what he must do to be himself. Its intention is to disclose to him the truth about himself, that is, what he can base his life on and what he can die for. No one dies for interchangeable myths; if one myth leads to difficulties, there is always another to select in its place. Nor is it possible to live on hypotheses: after all, life itself is no hypothesis but rather unrepeatable reality upon which rides an eternal destiny... Proclamation is the measure of theology, and not vice versa. This primacy of simple faith, moreover, is also in perfect accord with a fundamental anthropological law: the great truths about human nature are grasped in a simple apprehension which is in principle available to everyone and which is never wholly retrieved in reflection... Though not all men can be professional theologians, access to the great fundamental cognitions is open to everyone... The very office of preaching the Gospel is the teaching office even for theology.

The Prayer of Jesus

*S*ince the center of the person of Jesus is prayer, it is essential to participate in his prayer if we are to know and understand him... Prayer is the act of self-surrender by which we enter the Body of Christ. Thus it is an act of love. As love, in and with the Body of Christ, it is always both love of God and love of neighbor, knowing and fulfilling itself as love for the members of this Body... The person of Jesus is constituted by the act of prayer, of unbroken communication with the one he calls "Father." If this is the case, it is only possible really to understand this person by entering into this act of prayer, by participating in it. This is suggested by Jesus' saying that no one can come to him unless the Father draws him (Jn 6: 44). Where there is no Father, there is no Son. Where there is no relationship with God, there can be no understanding of him who, in his innermost self, is nothing but relationship with God, the Father... Therefore a participation in the mind of Jesus, i.e., in his prayer,... is the basic precondition if real understanding, in the sense of modern hermeneutics — i.e., the entering-in to the same time and the same meaning — is to take place.

Our Father

*I*n teaching his disciples to pray, Jesus told them to say *"Our* Father" (Mt 6: 9). No one but he can say "my Father." Everyone else is only entitled, as a member of the community, to use that "we" which Jesus made possible for them; i.e., they have the right to address God as Father because they are all created by God and for one another. To recognize and accept God's Fatherhood always means accepting that we are set in relation to one another: man is entitled to call God "Father" to the extent that he participates in that "we" — which is the form under which God's love seeks for him… No one can build a bridge to the Infinite by his own strength. No one's voice is loud enough to summon the Infinite. No intelligence can adequately and securely conceive who God is, whether he hears us and how we should act toward him… Even the awareness that religion must rest on a higher authority than that of one's own reason, and that it needs a community as a "carrier," is part of mankind's basic knowledge, though found in manifold forms and even distortions… Jesus' task was to renew the People of God by deepening its relationship to God and by opening it up for all mankind… He achieved this by transforming his death into an act of prayer, an act of love, and thus by making himself communicable. Jesus has made it possible for people to participate in his most intimate and personal act of being, i.e., his dialogue with the Father. That is the deepest layer of meaning of that process in which he taught his disciples to say "Our Father."

Why We can Speak with God

he basic reason why man can speak with God arises from the fact that God himself is speech, Word. His nature is to speak, to hear, to reply... Only because there is already speech, "Logos," in God can there be speech, "Logos," to God. Philosophically we could put it like this: the Logos in God is the ontological foundation for prayer... In God there is speech and the intercourse of partners in dialogue. Man could speak with God if he himself were drawn to share in this internal speech. And this is what the Incarnation of the Logos means: he who is speech, Word, Logos, in God and to God, participates in human speech. Man is able to participate in the dialogue within God himself because God has first shared in human speech and has thus brought the two into communication with one another. The Incarnation of the Logos brings eternity into time and time into eternity. As a result of the Incarnation, human speech has become a component in divine speech; it has been taken up, unconfusedly and inseparably, into that speech which is God's inner nature. Through the Spirit of Christ, who is the Spirit of God, we can share in the human nature of Jesus Christ; and in sharing in his dialogue with God, we can share in the dialogue which God *is*. This is prayer, which becomes a real exchange between God and man... We could define "Church" as the realm of man's discovery of his identity through the identification with Christ which is its source.

The Prayer "Abba"

A fundamental word in the mouth of "the Son" is "Abba"... It expresses his whole being, and all that he says to God in prayer is ultimately only an explication of his being... First we can say that it is an act of consent. Its basic tenor is affirmatory. Essentially it means this: I can affirm the world, being, myself, because I can affirm the ground of my being, for this ground is good. It is good to *be*... Whenever I am able to say Yes, I can celebrate a feast; whenever I am able to say Yes, I am (to that extent) free, liberated. Christian prayer holds the key to making the whole world a celebration, a feast, namely, affirmation... Prayer is an act of being; it is affirmation, albeit not affirmation of myself as I am and of the world as it is, but affirmation of the ground of being and hence a purifying of myself and of the world from this ground upward... In the purification which issues from this fundamental Yes we discover the active power of prayer, which (a) yields a deep security in the affirmation of being, as a foil to the hectic world of self-made man, yet which (b) is by no means a flight from the world but rather entrusts people with the task of purifying the world and empowers them to carry it out... It is the Son who guides us along the path of purification which leads to the door of the Yes... We encounter him as a living Person only in the foretaste of his presence which is called "Church."

Liturgy and the Search for Joy

*L*iturgy is festal, and the feast is about free-dom, the *freedom of being* which is there beneath the role-playing. But where we speak of being, we also raise the question of death. Therefore the festal celebration, above all else, must address itself to the question of death. Conversely, the feast presupposes joy, but this is only possible if it is able to face up to death. That is why, in the history of religions, the feast has always displayed a cosmic and universal character. It attempts to answer the question of death by establishing a connection with the univer-sal vital power of the cosmos... Christ's Resurrection enables man genuinely to rejoice. All history until Christ has been a fruitless search for this joy. That is why the Christian liturgy — Eucharist — is, of its essence, the Feast of the Resurrection, *Mysterium Paschae*. As such it bears within it the mys-tery of the cross, which is the inner presupposition of the Resurrection... This is why the Church holds fast to the sacrificial char-acter of the Mass; she does so lest we fail to realize the magnitude of what is involved and thus miss both the real depth of what it means to be human and the real depth of God's liberating power. The freedom with which we are concerned in the Christian feast — the feast of the Eucharist — is the liberation of the world and ourselves from death. Only this can make us free, enabling us to accept truth and to love one another in truth.

The Assumption

*W*here the totality of grace is, there is the totality of salvation. Where grace no longer exists in the fractured state of *simul justus et peccator*, but in pure "Yes," death, sin's jailer, has no place. Naturally this involves the question: What does the assumption of body and soul into heavenly glory mean? What, after all, does "immortality" mean? And what does "death" mean? Man is not immortal by his own power, but only in and through another, preliminarily, tentatively, fragmentarily, in children, in fame, but finally and truly only in and from the Entirely-Other, God. We are mortal due to the usurped autarchy of a determination to remain within ourselves, which proves to be a deception...

Nevertheless, where the innate propensity to autarchy is totally lacking, where there is the pure self-dispossession of the one who does not rely upon himself (= grace), death is absent, even if the somatic end is present. Instead, the whole human being enters salvation, because as a whole, undiminished, he stands eternally in God's life-giving memory that preserves him as himself in his *own* life.

Liturgy, Worship, and Freedom

hrist died praying... On the cross, therefore, he held aloft his Yes to the Father, glorifying the Father in the cross, and it was this manner of his dying which led, by an inner logic, to the Resurrection. This means that worship is the context in which we can discover joy, the liberating, victorious Yes to life. The cross is worship, "exaltation;" Resurrection is made present in it. To celebrate the feast of the Resurrection is to enter into worship. If we can describe the central meaning of Christian liturgy as the "feast of the Resurrection," its formative core is "worship." In worship, death is overcome and love is made possible. Worship is truth... Liturgy is a guarantee, testifying to the fact that something greater is taking place here than can be brought about by any individual community or group of people. It expresses the gift of joy, the gift of participation in the cosmic drama of Christ's Resurrection, by which liturgy stands or falls... In the liturgy, we are all given the freedom to appropriate, in our own personal way, the mystery which addresses us.

The Triumph of the Assumption

The feast of the Assumption is a day of joy. God has won. Love has won. It has won life. Love has shown that it is stronger than death, that God possesses the true strength and that his strength is goodness and love. Mary was taken up body and soul into heaven: There is even room in God for the body. Heaven is no longer a very remote sphere unknown to us. We have a Mother in heaven. Heaven is open, heaven has a heart… Only if God is great is humankind also great. With Mary, we must begin to understand that this is so. We must not drift away from God but make God present; we must ensure that he is great in our lives. Thus, we too will become divine; all the splendor of the divine dignity will then be ours. Let us apply this to our own lives… Precisely because Mary is with God and in God, she is very close to each one of us. While she lived on this earth she could only be close to a few people. Being in God, who is close to us, actually, "within" all of us, Mary shares in this closeness of God. Being in God and with God, she is close to each one of us, knows our hearts, can hear our prayers, can help us with her motherly kindness and has been given to us, as the Lord said, precisely as a "mother" to whom we can turn at every moment. She always listens to us, she is always close to us, and being Mother of the Son, participates in the power of the Son and in his goodness. We can always entrust the whole of our lives to this Mother, who is not far from any one of us.

How God Answers Prayer

hy is God silent? Why does he withdraw? Why is it that just the opposite of what I wanted is happening? This distance between what Jesus promised and what we experience in our own lives makes you think, every time — it has that effect in each generation, for each single person, and even for me. Each one of us has to struggle to work out an answer for himself, so that in the end he comes to understand why God has spoken to him precisely like that. Augustine and other great Christians say that God gives us what is best for us — even when we do not recognize this at first. Often, we think that exactly the opposite of what he does would really be best for us. We have to learn to accept this path, which, on the basis of our experience and our suffering, is difficult for us, and to see it as the way in which God is guiding us. God's way is often a path that enormously reshapes and remolds our life, a path in which we are truly changed and straightened out. To that extent, we have to say that this "Ask, and you will receive" certainly cannot mean that I can call God in as a handyman who will make my life easy every time I want something. Or who will take away suffering and questioning. On the contrary, it means that God definitely hears me and what he grants me is, in the way known only to him, what is right for me.

Worship and Our True Self

Withdrawal from God leads inevitably to hiding from God. The confidence of love turns suddenly into fear of the dangerous and frighteningly powerful God... Worship understood in the correct sense, means that I am truly myself only when I form relationships, that only then am I true to the *inner ideal* of my being. And my life is then tending toward the will of God, that is to say, toward a life more closely in agreement with truth and with love. It's not a matter of doing something to please God. Worship means accepting that our life is like an arrow in flight. Accepting that nothing finite can be my goal or determine the direction of my life, but that I myself must pass beyond all possible goals... God always takes up exactly what seems unimportant and shows himself to man in what seems like a speck of dust, or, as in Nazareth, in a little place that is next to nowhere. Thus God always corrects our standards of judgment... Man, in assigning to himself an inflated importance, damages his true self.

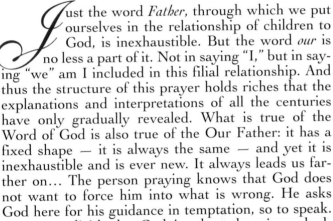

Lead Us Not into Temptation

ust the word *Father*, through which we put ourselves in the relationship of children to God, is inexhaustible. But the word *our* is no less a part of it. Not in saying "I," but in saying "we" am I included in this filial relationship. And thus the structure of this prayer holds riches that the explanations and interpretations of all the centuries have only gradually revealed. What is true of the Word of God is also true of the Our Father: it has a fixed shape — it is always the same — and yet it is inexhaustible and is ever new. It always leads us farther on... The person praying knows that God does not want to force him into what is wrong. He asks God here for his guidance in temptation, so to speak. The Letter of James says explicitly that God, in whom there is no shadow of darkness, does not tempt anyone. But God can put us to the test — think of Abraham — in order to make us more mature, in order to bring us face-to-face with our own depths so as then to be able to bring us back to himself more completely. In that sense, the word "temptation" has various shades of meaning. God never wants to lead us onward to what is evil; that's quite clear. But it could well be that he does not simply keep temptation away from us, that, as we said, he helps us in temptation and leads us through it. We ask him not to allow us to get into temptations that might make us slide into evil ways; that he not subject us to tests that strain us beyond our powers; that he not set aside his power and leave us on our own, that he knows our weakness and therefore will protect us so that we are not lost.

The Father-Son Relationship

*I*t seems important to me to highlight the unique nature of the quite special Father-Son relationship. There is first of all a quite universal rule of knowledge expressed in this sentence about "no one knows the Father except the Son; no one knows the Son but the Father." It signifies that like can only be recognized by like. Where there is no inner correspondence to God, there is no possibility of knowing God. God can be known, in a strict sense, only by himself. Consequently, knowledge of God is bestowed on man, then that assumes that God draws man into a relationship of kinship and that there is then so much alive in man that resembles God that cognition and knowledge become possible. And then Jesus continues: "No one can know this; except those to whom you choose to reveal it." In other words: Recognition and knowledge can only dawn within a community of will... The pattern of relationships between father and son could not serve as an analogy, to pass on to us even a distant glimpse of the inner mystery of God, were there not a trace of God himself to be found in it. This specific relationship of father to son — which is a relationship of giving, of receiving, and of giving in return — is basic to human life. If one continues to philosophize on this basis, then one must of course pose the whole question of the human family, and then one also inevitably runs into limitations. It is in any case right that this particular type of relationship is of such great extent that it can reach right up above, like an outstretched index finger.

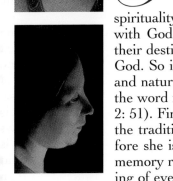

The Quality of Mary's Faithfulness

*I*n Mary the earth has acquired a human face, and more: a Christian face, the face of the Mother of Jesus. By turning to her, nature-spirituality is transformed into faith, into an encounter with God's dealings with men in history, which bear their destined fruit in Mary's life, in the Incarnation of God. So it is quite in order to say that, in Mary, faith and nature-religion have been reconciled... Mary kept the word in her heart and pondered it (Lk 1: 29; 2: 19; 2: 51). First of all, then, she is portrayed as a source of the tradition. The word is kept in her memory; therefore she is a reliable witness for what took place. But memory requires more than a merely external register-ing of events. We can only receive and hold fast to the uttered word if we are involved inwardly. If something does not touch me, it will not penetrate; it will dissolve in the flux of memories and lose its particular face. Above all it is a fact that understanding and preserving what is understood go together. If I have not really understood a thing, I will not be able to communicate it properly. Only by understanding do I receive reality at all; and understanding, in turn, depends on a certain measure of inner identification with what is to be understood. It depends on love. I cannot really understand something for which I have no love whatsoever. So the transmission of the message needs more than the kind of memory that stores telephone numbers: what is required is a memory of the heart, in which I invest something of myself. Involvement and faith-fulness are not opposites: they are interdependent.

The Fatherhood of God

*I*f we look for a moment at pagan mythologies, then the father-god Zeus, for instance is portrayed as moody, unpredictable, and willful: the father does incorporate power and authority, but without the corresponding degree of responsibility, the limitation of power through justice and kindness. The Father as he appears in the Old Testament is quite different, and still more in what Jesus says about the Father: here, power corresponds to responsibility; here we meet a picture of power that is properly directed, that is at one with love, that does not dominate through fear but creates trust. The Fatherhood of God means a devotion toward us, an acceptance of us by God at the deepest level, so that we can belong to him and turn to him in childlike love. Certainly, his Fatherhood does mean that he sets the standards and corrects us with a strictness that manifests his love and that is always ready to forgive. The story of the Prodigal Son is probably the most impressive presentation of the portrait of God the Father that we have from the mouth of Jesus in the entire New Testament. In that sense our human experiences of fathers and fatherhood are corrected; a standard is set up by which they may be measured. The picture of God the Father that we find in the Bible is not a projection upward of our own experiences; rather, the contrary: we are told from on high, in quite a new way, what a father really is and what he could be and should be among us human beings.

AUGUST 24

Salvation, Covenant, and Worship

The Sabbath is the sign of the covenant between God and man; it sums up the inward essence of the covenant. If this is so, then we can define the intention of the account of creation as follows: creation exists to be a place for the covenant that God wants to make with man. The goal of creation is the covenant, the love story of God and man. The freedom and equality of men, which the Sabbath is meant to bring about, is not a merely anthropological or sociological vision; it can only be understood *theo*-logically. Only when man is in covenant with God does he become free. Only then are the equality and dignity of all men made manifest. If, then, everything is directed to the covenant, it is important to see that the covenant is a relationship: God's gift of himself to man, but also man's response to God. Man's response to the God who is good to him is love, and loving God means worshiping him. If creation is meant to be a space for the covenant, the place where God and man meet one another, then it must be thought of as a space for worship... What is worship? What happens when we worship?... It means emerging from the state of separation, of apparent autonomy, of existing only for oneself and in oneself. It means losing oneself as the only possible way of finding oneself (Mk 8: 35; Mt 10: 39). That is why Saint Augustine could say that the true "sacrifice" is the *civitas Dei*, that is, love-transformed mankind, the divinization of creation and the surrender of all things to God: God all in all (1 Cor 15: 28). That is the purpose of the world. That is the essence of sacrifice and worship.

Cooperating with God in the Liturgy

This is what is new and distinctive about the Christian liturgy: God himself acts and does what is essential. He inaugurates the new creation, makes himself accessible to us, so that, through the things of the earth, through our gifts, we can communicate with him in a personal way... Can man, the finite and sinful one, cooperate with God, the Infinite and Holy One? Yes, he can, precisely because God himself has become man, become body, and here, again and again, he comes through his body to us who live in the body. The whole event of the Incarnation, cross, Resurrection, and Second Coming is present as the way by which God draws man into cooperation with himself... True, the sacrifice of the Logos is accepted already and for ever. But we must still pray for it to become *our* sacrifice, that we ourselves, as we said, may be transformed into the Logos, conformed to the Logos, and so be made the true Body of Christ. This petition itself is a way into the Incarnation and the Resurrection, the path that we take in the wayfaring state of our existence... In the words of Saint Paul, it is a question of being "united to the Lord" and thus becoming "one spirit with him" (1 Cor 6: 17). The point is that, ultimately, the difference between the *actio Christi* and our own action is done away with. There is only *one* action, which is at the same time his and ours — ours because we have become "one body and one spirit" with him. The uniqueness of the eucharistic liturgy lies precisely in the fact that God himself is acting and that we are drawn into that action of God.

Priestly Ordination and the Eucharist

The fact that the celebration of the Eucharist is tied to ordination as a priest is not something that the Church has invented... It follows that these words can be pronounced only in the sacrament of the Church as a whole, with the authority that she alone, in her unity and her fullness, possesses. Being entrusted with the mission that the whole Church in her unity has herself received is what we call ordination to the priesthood... Something is happening there that is greater than anything we can do. The magnitude of what is happening is not dependent on the way we perform it, but all our efforts to perform it aright can always be only at the service of the great act that precedes our own and that we cannot achieve for ourselves. We should learn anew that the Eucharist is never merely what a congregation does, but that we receive from the Lord what he has granted to the entirety of the Church. I am always moved by those stories of what happened in concentration camps or Russian prison camps, where people had to do without the Eucharist for a period of weeks or months and yet did not turn to the arbitrary action of celebrating it themselves; rather, they made a eucharistic celebration of their longing, waiting with yearning upon the Lord, who alone can give of himself. In such a Eucharist of longing and yearning they were made ready for his gift in a new way, and they received it as something new, when somewhere or other a priest found a bit of bread and some wine.

The Way of Knowledge that Leads to God

Thinking and living are no longer separable when man confronts the ultimate questions. The decision for God is simultaneously an intellectual and an existential decision — each determines the other reciprocally. Augustine portrayed this connection dramatically in the story of his conversion. He speaks of the misguided patterns of a life that is completely oriented to material things... He speaks about his attempts to break loose and to clear a path to God, to the God who acts, and he compares this with the situation of someone who is dreaming, who is trapped in his dream, who tries to wake up and break loose and yet sinks back again and again into the world of dreams. He describes how he hid himself behind his own back, so to speak, and how God brought him out of his hiding place through the word of a friend, so that he had to look himself in the face. New knowledge should be accompanied by a renewed life, which reopens our closed horizons. Therefore the ancient Church regarded conversion to the faith as... a new life companionship, in which new experiences and interior progress become possible for him... The way of knowledge that leads to God and to Christ is a way of living. In biblical language: in order to know Christ, it is necessary to follow him. Only then do we learn where he lives. To the question, "Where are you staying?" (Who are you?), he always gives the same answer: "Come and see" (Jn 1: 38-39). The disciples were able to give a different answer to the question about Jesus than "men" [in general] did, because they lived in fellowship with him.

Conversion as New Beginning

heology is based upon a new beginning in thought which is not the product of our own reflection but has its origin in the encounter with a Word which always precedes us. We call the act of accepting this new beginning "conversion." Because there is no theology without faith, there can be no theology without conversion. Conversion can take many forms. It need not always be an instantaneous event, as it was in the case of Augustine… In one form or another, however, the convert must consciously pronounce in his own name a Yes to this new beginning and really turn from the "I" to the "no-longer-I"… This is why in every age the path to faith can take its bearings by converts; it explains why they in particular can help us to recognize the reason for the hope that is in us (1 Pt 3: 15) and to bear witness to it. The connection between faith and theology is not, therefore, some sort of sentimental or pietistic twaddle but is a direct consequence of the logic of the thing and is corroborated by the whole of history… Augustine is unthinkable without his passionate journey to a radical Christian life. Moreover, Bonaventure and the Franciscan theology of the thirteenth century would have been impossible without the imposing new representation of Christ in the figure of Saint Francis of Assisi, nor could Thomas Aquinas have existed without Dominic's breakthrough to the Gospel and to evangelization.

John the Baptist's Darkness

his was the task set before the Baptist as he lay in prison: to become blessed by this unquestioning acceptance of God's obscure will; to reach the point of asking no further for external, visible, unequivocal clarity, but, instead, of discovering God precisely in the darkness of this world and of his own life, and thus becoming profoundly blessed. In point of fact, we cannot see God as we see an apple tree or a neon sign, that is, in a purely external way that requires no interior commitment. We can see him only by becoming like him, by reaching the level of reality on which God exists; in other words, by being liberated from what is anti-divine...

John, then, even in his prison cell had to respond once again and anew to his own call for *metanoia* or a change of mentality, in order that he might recognize his God in the night in which all things earthly exist. The Christian of our day, too, can be shown no other way to friendship with God than the way of ceasing to look for external clarity and beginning to turn from the visible to the invisible and thus truly finding the Lord who is the real foundation and support of our existence. Only when we act in this manner does another and doubtless the greatest saying of the Baptist reveal its full significance: "He must increase, but I must decrease" (Jn 3: 30). We will know God to the extent that we are set free from ourselves.

AUGUST 30

How the Liturgy Assimilates Us unto God

"Today" embraces the whole time of the Church. And so in the Christian liturgy we not only receive something from the past but become contemporaries with what lies at the foundation of that liturgy. Here is the real heart and true grandeur of the celebration of the Eucharist, which is more, much more than a meal. In the Eucharist we are caught up and made contemporary with the Paschal Mystery of Christ, in his passing from the tabernacle of the transitory to the presence and sight of God… Now if past and present penetrate one another in this way, if the essence of the past is not simply a thing of the past but the far-reaching power of what follows in the present, then the future, too, is present in what happens in the liturgy: it ought to be called, in its essence, an anticipation of what is to come… This liturgy is founded on the Passion endured by a man who with his "I" reaches into the mystery of the living God himself, by the man who is the Son. Its origin also bears within it its future in the sense that representation, vicarious sacrifice, takes up into itself those whom it represents; it is not external to them, but a shaping influence on them. Becoming contemporary with the Pasch of Christ in the liturgy of the Church is also, in fact, an anthropological reality. The celebration is not just a rite, not just a liturgical "game." It is meant to be indeed the "logicizing" of my existence, my interior contemporaneity with the self-giving of Christ. His self-giving is meant to become mine, so that I become contemporary with the Pasch of Christ and assimilated unto God.

Liturgy as Entering into Reality

*I*t is tempting to say that this dimension of liturgy, its suspension between the cross of Christ and our living entry into him who suffered vicariously for us and wants to become "one" with us (Gal 3: 13, 28), expresses its moral demands. And without doubt Christian worship does contain a moral demand, but it goes much farther than mere moralism. The Lord has gone before us. He has already done what we have to do. He has opened a way that we ourselves could not have pioneered, because our powers do not extend to building a bridge to God. He himself became that bridge. And now the challenge is to allow ourselves to be taken up into his being "for" mankind, to let ourselves be embraced by his opened arms, which draw us to himself. He, the Holy One, hallows us with the holiness that none of us could ever give ourselves. We are incorporated into the great historical process by which the world moves toward the fulfillment of God being "all in all"... Christian liturgy is no longer replacement worship but the coming of the representative Redeemer to us, an entry into his representation that is an entry into reality itself... The liturgy is the means by which earthly time is inserted into the time of Jesus Christ and into its present. It is the turning point in the process of redemption. The Shepherd takes the lost sheep onto his shoulders and carries it home.

September

This is My Body

*I*n the language of the Bible the word "body" — "This is my Body" — does not mean just a body, in contradistinction to the spirit, for instance. Body, in the language of the Bible, denotes rather the whole person, in whom body and spirit are indivisibly one. "This is my Body" therefore means: This is my whole person, existent in bodily form. What the nature of this person is, however, we learn from what is said next: "which is given up for you." That means: This person is: existing-for-others. It is in its most intimate being a sharing with others. But that is why, since it is a matter of this person and because it is from its heart an opening up, a self-giving person, it can then be shared out... The body is the boundary that separates us from each other; and it thus involves our being somehow strangers to each other. We cannot look inside the other person; corporeal existence hides his inner self... We cannot even see into ourselves, into our own depths. That is one thing, then: The body is a boundary that makes us opaque, impermeable for each other, which sets us beside each other and prevents our being able to see or to touch each other's intimate selves. But there is a second thing: The body is also a bridge. For we meet each other through the body; through it we communicate in the common material of creation; through it we can see ourselves, feel ourselves, come close to one another. In the gestures of the body are revealed who and what the other person is. We see ourselves in the way the body sees, looks, acts, offers itself; it leads us to each other: it is both boundary and means of communion in one.

When the Body Ceases to be a Limit

*B*odily existence can also be lived as opening oneself up, as the developing freedom of a person who shares himself. We all know that this happens, too; that transcending the limits we touch one another intimately, are close to each other. What people call telepathy is only an extreme case of what to a lesser extent happens among us all: a hidden movement from the heart, being close to each other even at a distance. Resurrection means quite simply that the body ceases to be a limit and that its capacity for communion remains. Jesus could rise from the dead, and did rise from the dead, because he had become, as the Son and as the One who loved on the cross, the One who shares himself wholly with others. To have risen from the dead means to be communicable; it signifies being the one who is open, who gives himself. And on that basis we can understand that Jesus, in the speech about the Eucharist that John has handed down to us, puts the Resurrection and the Eucharist together and that the Fathers say that the Eucharist is the medicine of immortality. Receiving Communion means entering into communion with Jesus Christ; it signifies moving into the open through him who alone could overcome the limits and thus, with him and on the basis of his existence, becoming capable of Resurrection oneself.

A New Dimension of Being

hrist's death was an act of love. At the Last Supper he anticipated death and transformed it into self-giving. His existential communion with God was concretely an existential communion with God's love, and this love is the real power against death, it is stronger than death. The Resurrection was like an explosion of light, an explosion of love which dissolved the hitherto indissoluble compenetration of "dying and becoming." It ushered in a new dimension of being, a new dimension of life in which, in a transformed way, matter too was integrated and through which a new world emerges. It is clear that this event is not just some miracle from the past, the occurrence of which could be ultimately a matter of indifference to us. It is a qualitative leap in the history of "evolution" and of life in general towards a new future life, towards a new world which, starting from Christ, already continuously permeates this world of ours, transforms it and draws it to itself. But how does this happen? How can this event effectively reach me and draw my life upwards towards itself? The answer, perhaps surprising at first but totally real, is: this event comes to me through faith and Baptism. Baptism means precisely this, that we are not dealing with an event in the past, but that a qualitative leap in world history comes to me, seizing hold of me in order to draw me on. Baptism is something quite different from a complicated rite. It is also more than a simple washing, more than a kind of purification and beautification of the soul. It is truly death and Resurrection, rebirth, transformation to a new life.

SEPTEMBER 4

The Liberation of Our "I"

At Baptism, my "I" is taken away from me and is incorporated into a new and greater subject. This means that my "I" is back again, but now transformed, broken up, opened through incorporation into the other, in whom it acquires its new breadth of existence. Christ alone carries within himself the whole "promise." But what then happens with us? Paul answers: You have become one in Christ (cf. Gal 3: 28). Not just one thing, but one, one only, one single new subject. This liberation of our "I" from its isolation, this finding oneself in a new subject means finding oneself within the vastness of God and being drawn into a life which has now moved out of the context of "dying and becoming." The great explosion of the Resurrection has seized us in Baptism so as to draw us on. Thus we are associated with a new dimension of life into which, amid the tribulations of our day, we are already in some way introduced. To live one's own life as a continual entry into this open space: this is the meaning of being Christian. The Resurrection is not a thing of the past, the Resurrection has reached us and seized us. We grasp hold of it, we grasp hold of the risen Lord, and we know that he holds us firmly even when our hands grow weak. We grasp hold of his hand, and thus we also hold on to one another's hands, and we become one single subject, not just one thing. *I, but no longer I*: this is the formula of Christian life rooted in Baptism, the formula of the Resurrection within time. *I, but no longer I*: if we live in this way, we transform the world. It is a program opposed to corruption and to the desire for possession.

God Descends

God loves his creature, man; he even loves him in his fall and does not leave him to himself. He loves him to the end. He is impelled with his love to the very end, to the extreme: he came down from his divine glory. He came down to the extreme lowliness of our fall. He kneels before us and carries out for us the service of a slave: he washes our dirty feet so that we might be admitted to God's banquet and be made worthy to take our place at his. God is not a remote God, too distant or too great to be bothered with our trifles. Since God is great, he can also be concerned with small things. Since he is great, the soul of man, the same man, created through eternal love, is not a small thing but great, and worthy of God's love. God's holiness is not merely an incandescent power before which we are obliged to withdraw, terrified. It is a power of love and therefore a purifying and healing power. God descends and becomes a slave. In this, the entire mystery of Jesus Christ is expressed. In this, what redemption means becomes visible. The basin in which he washes us is his love, ready to face death. Only love has that purifying power which washes the grime from us and elevates us to God's heights. The basin that purifies us is God himself, who gives himself to us without reserve — to the very depths of his suffering and his death. He is continually on his knees at our feet and carries out for us the service of a slave, the service of purification, making us capable of God. His love is inexhaustible, it truly goes to the very end.

Saying No to Self-Sufficiency

"*ou are clean, but not all of you*," the Lord says (Jn 13: 10). This sentence reveals the great gift of purification that he offers to us, because he wants to be at table together with us, to become our food. *"But not all of you"* — the obscure mystery of rejection exists, which becomes apparent with Judas' act. The Lord's love knows no bounds, but man can put a limit on it. What is it that makes man unclean? It is the rejection of love, not wanting to be loved, not loving. It is pride that believes it has no need of any purification, that is closed to God's saving goodness. It is pride that does not want to admit or recognize that we are in need of purification. In Judas we see the nature of this rejection even more clearly. He evaluated Jesus in accordance with the criteria of power and success. For him, power and success alone were real; love did not count. And he was greedy: money was more important than communion with Jesus, more important than God and his love. He thus also became a liar who played a double game and broke with the truth; one who lived in deceit and so lost his sense of the supreme truth, of God. In this way, he became hard of heart and incapable of conversion, of the trusting return of the Prodigal Son, and he disposed of the life destroyed. Today, the Lord alerts us to the self-sufficiency that puts a limit on his unlimited love. He invites us to imitate his humility, to entrust ourselves to it, to let ourselves be "infected" by it. He invites us — however lost we may feel — to return home, to let his purifying goodness uplift us and enable us to sit at table with him, with God himself.

The Hands of a Priest

*J*esus Christ is always the One who gives, who draws us to himself. He alone can say: "This is my Body... this is my Blood." The mystery of the priesthood of the Church lies in the fact that we, miserable human beings, by virtue of the sacrament, can speak with his "I": *in persona Christi.* He wishes to exercise *his* priesthood through us. At the center of the sacrament is the very ancient rite of the imposition of hands, with which he took possession of me, saying to me: "You belong to me." However, in saying this he also said: "You are under the protection of my hands. You are under the protection of my heart. You are kept safely in the palm of my hands, and this is precisely how you find yourself in the immensity of my love. Stay in my hands, and give me yours." The Lord has laid his hands upon us and he now wants our hands so that they may become his own in the world. He no longer wants them to be instruments for taking things, people, or the world for ourselves, to reduce them to being our possession, but instead, by putting ourselves at the service of his love, they can pass on his divine touch. He wants our hands to be instruments of service, hence, an expression of the mission of the whole person who vouches for him and brings him to men and women. If human hands symbolically represent human faculties, then anointed hands must be a sign of the human capacity for giving, for creativity in shaping the world with love. Christ is giving the world a new kingship, a new priesthood, a new way of being a prophet who does not seek himself but lives for the One with a view to whom the world was created.

The Birthday of Mary

*M*ary's birthday is exceptional among the feasts in which honor is paid to saints, in that the Church usually does not celebrate the day of birth. The Church's practice was quite different here from that of pagan Greece or Rome, where the birthday of a great man — a Caesar or an Augustus, for example — was celebrated with great pomp as a day of redemption. The Church always argued that it was premature to celebrate a birthday because the rest of the life of the person born on that day was subject to such ambiguity. It was, in other words, impossible to predict the answers to certain questions simply on the basis of a person's birthday. Would his life really be a reason for celebration? Would the person who was born really be able to be glad about the day that he came into the world? Would the world be glad that this person had been born or would it curse the day that he was born?... No, the Church has always celebrated the day of death, believing that it is only possible to celebrate a person's life when he has passed beyond that life into death and judgment... Mary was the gate through which he came into the world and not simply the external gateway. She had already conceived Jesus in her heart before she became his mother according to the body, as Augustine so meaningfully said. Her soul was the space from which God was able to gain access into humanity. Unlike the great and mighty ones of this earth, Mary, the believer who bore the light of God in her heart, was able to play her vital part in changing the very foundation of the world. The world can be truly changed only by the power of the soul.

Bread for the Journey

The Son of God, becoming flesh, could become bread and in this way be the nourishment of his people journeying toward the promised land of heaven. We need this bread to cope with the toil and exhaustion of the journey... The Sunday precept is not a simple duty imposed from outside. To participate in the Sunday celebration and to be nourished with the eucharistic bread is a need of a Christian, who in this way can find the necessary energy for the journey to be undertaken... The way that God indicates through his law goes in the direction inscribed in the very essence of man. To follow the way means man's own fulfillment; to lose it, is to lose himself. The Lord does not leave us alone on this journey. He is with us; he wishes to share our destiny by absorbing us... In the Eucharist, Christ is really present among us. His presence is a dynamic presence, which makes us his; he assimilates us to himself... In the Eucharist the center is Christ who attracts us to himself; he makes us come out of ourselves to make us one with him. In this way, he introduces us into the community of brothers... This means that we can only encounter him together with all others. We can only receive him in unity... We cannot commune with the Lord if we do not commune among ourselves. If we wish to present ourselves to him, we must go out to meet one another... We must not allow the destructive larva of resentment to take hold of our spirit, but open our heart to the magnanimity of listening to the other, of understanding, of the possible acceptance of his apologies, of the generous offering of our own.

The Full Splendor of the Church

*S*aint Paul confessed: "I will all the more gladly boast of my weaknesses, that the power of Christ may rest upon me" (2 Cor 12: 9). In the mystery of the Church, the mystical Body of Christ, the divine power of love changes the heart of man, making him able to communicate the love of God to his brothers and sisters. Throughout the centuries many men and women, transformed by divine love, have consecrated their lives to the cause of the kingdom. Already on the shores of the Sea of Galilee, many allowed themselves to be won by Jesus: they were in search of healing in body or spirit, and they were touched by the power of his grace. Others were chosen personally by him and became his Apostles. We also find some, like Mary Magdalene and others, who followed him on their own initiative, simply out of love. Like the disciple John, they too found a special place in his heart. These men and women, who knew the mystery of the love of the Father through Jesus, represent the variety of vocations which have always been present in the Church. The model of one called to give witness in a particular manner to the love of God is Mary, the Mother of Jesus, who in her pilgrimage of faith is directly associated with the mystery of the Incarnation and Redemption. In Christ, the Head of the Church, which is his Body, all Christians form "a chosen race, a royal priesthood, a holy nation, God's own people, that you may declare the wonderful deeds of him" (1 Pt 2: 9). The Church is holy, even if her members need to be purified, in order that holiness, which is a gift of God, can shine forth from them with its full splendor.

God Penetrates Human Events

*H*istory is not in the hands of the powers of darkness, chance, or human decisions alone. When evil energy that we see is unleashed, when Satan vehemently bursts in, when a multitude of scourges and ills surface, the Lord, the supreme arbiter of historical events, arises. He leads history wisely towards the dawn of the new heavens and the new earth... There is consequently a desire to reaffirm that God is not indifferent to human events but penetrates them, creating his own "ways" or, in other words, his effective plans and "deeds"... The nations must learn to "read" God's message in history. The adventure of humanity is not confused and meaningless, nor is it doomed, never to be appealed against or to be abused by the overbearing and the perverse... This attitude of faith leads men and women to recognize the power of God who works in history and thus to open themselves to feeling awe for the name of the Lord. In biblical language, in fact, this "fear" is not fright. It is recognition of the mystery of divine transcendence. Thus, it is at the root of faith and is interwoven with love... As Saint Hilary of Poitiers, a fourth-century bishop, said: "All our fear is in love."

The Never-Ending Event of the Cross

The crucifixion of Christ, his death on the cross, and, in another way, the act of his Resurrection from the grave, which bestows incorruptibility on the corruptible, are historical events that happen just once and as such belong to the past... However, the exterior act of being crucified is accompanied by an interior act of self-giving (the Body is "given for you"). "No one takes my life from me," says the Lord in Saint John's Gospel, "but I lay it down of my own accord" (10: 18). This act of giving is in no way just a spiritual occurrence. It is a spiritual act that takes up the bodily into itself, that embraces the whole man; indeed, it is at the same time an act of the Son. As Saint Maximus the Confessor showed so splendidly, the obedience of Jesus' human will is inserted into the everlasting Yes of the Son to the Father. This "giving" on the part of the Lord, in the passivity of his being crucified, draws the passion of human existence into the action of love, and so it embraces all the dimensions of reality — Body, Soul, Spirit, Logos. Just as the pain of the body is drawn into the pathos of the mind and becomes the Yes of obedience, so time is drawn into what reaches beyond time. The real interior act, though it does not exist without the exterior, transcends time, but since it comes from time, time can again and again be brought into it. That is how we can become contemporary with the past events of salvation. Saint Bernard of Clairvaux has this in mind when he says that the true *semel* ("once") bears within itself the *semper* ("always"). What is perpetual takes place in what happens only once.

Peace and Truth

eace convicts us of our lies. It brings us out of our comfortable indifference into the struggle and the pain of the truth. And it is only thus that true peace can come into being, in place of the apparent peace, beneath which lie hidden hypocrisy and all kinds of conflict... Truth is worth pain and even conflict. I may not just accept a lie in order to have quiet. For it is not the first duty of a citizen, or of a Christian, to seek quiet; but rather it is that standing fast by what is noble and great, which is what Christ has given us and which can reach as far as suffering, as far as a struggle that ends in martyrdom — and exactly in that way bring peace... Christ embodies the great and undiluted loving-kindness of God... He comes to help us bear the load. He does not do this by simply taking away from us the burden of being human; that remains heavy enough. But we are no longer carrying it on our own; he is carrying it with us. Christ has nothing to do with comfort, with banality, yet we find in him that inner calm which comes from knowing that we are being supported by an ultimate kindness and an ultimate security. We see that the entire structure of the message of Jesus is full of tension; it is an enormous challenge. Its nature is such that it always has to do with the cross. Anyone who is not ready to get burned, who is not at least willing for it to happen, will not come near. But we can always be sure that it is there that we will meet true loving-kindness, which helps us, which accepts us — and which does not merely mean well toward us but will in fact ensure that things go well for us.

The Triumph of the Cross

*I*n one respect the cross does have a terrible aspect that we ought not to remove… To see that the purest of men, who was more than a man, was executed in such a grisly way can make us frightened of ourselves. But we also need to be frightened of ourselves and out of our self-complacency. Here, I think, Luther was right when he said that man must first be frightened of himself so that he can then find the right way. However, the cross doesn't stop at being a horror; it is not merely a horror, because the one who looks down at us from the cross is not a failure, a desperate man, not one of the horrible victims of humanity. For this crucified man says something different from Spartacus and his failed adherents, because, after all, what looks down at us from the cross is a goodness that enables a new beginning in the midst of life's horror. The goodness of God himself looks on us, God who surrenders himself into our hands, delivers himself to us, and bears the whole horror of history with us. Looked at more deeply this sign, which forces us to look at the dangerousness of man and all his heinous deeds, at the same time makes us look upon God, who is stronger, stronger in his weakness, and upon the fact that we are loved by God. It is in this sense a sign of forgiveness that also brings hope into the abysses of history… God is crucified and says to us that this God who is apparently so weak is the God who incomprehensibly forgives us and who in his seeming absence is stronger.

Mary under the Cross

*M*arian piety is, to be sure, primarily incarnational and focused on the Lord who has come. It tries to learn with Mary to stay in his presence. But the feast of Mary's Assumption into heaven, which gained in significance thanks to the dogma of 1950, accentuates the eschatological transcendence of the Incarnation. Mary's path includes the experience of rejection (Mk 3: 31-35; Jn 2: 4). When she is given away under the cross (Jn 19: 26), this experience becomes a participation in the rejection that Jesus himself had to endure on the Mount of Olives (Mk 14: 34) and on the cross (Mk 15: 34). Only in this rejection can the new come to pass; only in a going away can the true coming take place (Jn 16: 7). Marian piety is thus necessarily a Passion-centered piety. In the prophecy of the aged Simeon, who foretold that a sword would pierce Mary's heart (Lk 2: 35), Luke interweaves from the very outset the Incarnation and the Passion, the joyful and the sorrowful mysteries. In the Church's piety, Mary appears, so to speak, as the living Veronica's veil, as an icon of Christ that brings him into the present of man's heart, translates Christ's image into the heart's vision, and thus makes it intelligible.

The Sign of the Cross

*T*he most basic Christian gesture in prayer is and always will be the sign of the cross. It is a way of confessing Christ crucified with one's very body... To seal oneself with the sign of the cross is a visible and public Yes to him who suffered for us; to him who in the body has made God's love visible, even to the utmost; to the God who reigns not by destruction but by the humility of suffering and love, which is stronger than all the power of the world and wiser than all the calculating intelligence of men. The sign of the cross is a confession of faith: I believe in him who suffered for me and rose again; in him who has transformed the sign of shame into a sign of hope and of the love of God that is present with us. The confession of faith is a confession of hope: I believe in him who in his weakness is the Almighty; in him who can and will save me even in apparent absence and impotence. By signing ourselves with the cross, we place ourselves under the protection of the cross, hold it in front of us like a shield that will guard us in all the distress of daily life and give us the courage to go on. We accept it as a signpost that we follow... The cross shows us the road of life — the imitation of Christ... Whenever we make the sign of the cross, we accept our Baptism anew; Christ from the cross draws us, so to speak, to himself... We make the sign of the cross on ourselves and thus enter the power of the blessing of Jesus Christ. We make the sign over people to whom we wish a blessing... Through the cross, we can become sources of blessing for one another.

The Success of the Cross

On the cross, Christ saw love through to the end. For all the differences there may be between the accounts in the various Gospels, there is one point in common: Jesus died praying, and in the abyss of death he upheld the First Commandment and held on to the presence of God. Out of such a death springs this sacrament, the Eucharist... Did Jesus fail?... Success is definitely not one of the names of God and it is not Christian to have an eye to outward success or numbers. God's paths are other than that. His success comes about through the cross and is always found under that sign. The true witnesses to his authenticity, down through the centuries, are those who have accepted this sign as their emblem... What strengthens our faith, what remains constant, what gives us hope, is the Church of the suffering. She stands, to the present day, as a sign that God exists and that man is not just a cesspit, but that he can be saved... The Church of the suffering gives credibility to Christ: she is God's success in the world; the sign that gives us hope and courage; the sign from which still flows the power of life, which reaches beyond mere thoughts of success and which thereby purifies men and opens up for God a door into this world. So let us be ready to hear the call of Jesus Christ, who achieved the great success of God on the cross; he who, as the grain of wheat that died, has become fruitful down through all the centuries; the Tree of Life, in whom even today men may put their hope.

The Trust of Abraham

*L*ook back to the beginning of the history of faith. Abraham, in the end, does not sacrifice anything he has prepared himself but offers the ram (the lamb) that has been offered to him by God. Thus, through this original sacrifice of Abraham, a perspective opens up down the millennia; this lamb in the brambles that God gives him, so that he may offer it, is the first herald of that Lamb, Jesus Christ, who carries the crown of thorns of our guilt, who has come into the thorn bush of world history in order to give us something that we may give… Even when Abraham was still on his way, and as yet knew nothing of the mystery of the ram, he was able to say to Isaac, with trust in his heart: God will take care of us. Because he knew this God, therefore, even in the dark night of his incomprehension he knew that he is a loving God; therefore, even then, when he found he could understand nothing, he could put his trust in him and could know that the very one who seemed to be oppressing him truly loved him even then. Only in thus going onward, so that his heart was opened up, so that he entered the abyss of trust and, in the dark night of the uncomprehended God, dared keep company with him, did he thereby become capable of accepting the ram, of understanding the God who gives to us that we may give… The more we trust in him in the dark night of the uncomprehended God, the more we will become aware that that very God who seems to be tormenting us is the one who truly loves us, the one we can trust without reserve… God gives that we may give. This is the essence of the Eucharistic Sacrifice, of the sacrifice of Jesus Christ.

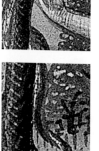

Trusting in Truth

*I*t was foretold that the struggle between humanity and the serpent, that is, between man and the forces of evil and death, would continue throughout history. It was also foretold, however, that the "offspring" of a woman would one day triumph and would crush the head of the serpent to death; it was foretold that the offspring of the woman — and in this offspring the woman and the mother herself — would be victorious and that thus through man, God would triumph. The human being does not trust God. Tempted by the serpent, he harbors the suspicion that, in the end, God takes something away from his life, that God is a rival who curtails our freedom and that we will be fully human only when we have cast him aside; in brief, that only in this way can we fully achieve our freedom. The human being lives in the suspicion that God's love creates a dependence and that he must rid himself of this dependency if he is to be fully himself. Man does not want to receive his existence and the fullness of his life from God. He himself wants to obtain from the tree of knowledge the power to shape the world, to make himself a god, raising himself to God's level, and to overcome death and darkness with his own efforts. He does not want to rely on love that to him seems untrustworthy; he relies solely on his own knowledge since it confers power upon him. Rather than on love, he sets his sights on power, with which he desires to take his own life autonomously in hand. And in doing so, he trusts in deceit rather than in truth and thereby sinks with his life into emptiness, into death.

Living in Accordance with the Truth of our Being

*L*ove is not dependence but a gift that makes us live. The freedom of a human being is the freedom of a limited being, and therefore is itself limited. We can possess it only as a shared freedom, in the communion of freedom: only if we live in the right way, with one another and for one another, can freedom develop. We live in the right way if we live in accordance with the truth of our being, and that is, in accordance with God's will. For God's will is not a law for the human being imposed from the outside and that constrains him, but the intrinsic measure of his nature, a measure that is engraved within him and makes him the image of God, hence, a free creature. If we live in opposition to love and against the truth— in opposition to God — then we destroy one another and destroy the world. Then we do not find life but act in the interests of death. If we sincerely reflect about ourselves and our history, we have to say that we all carry within us a drop of the poison of that way of thinking. We call this drop of poison "original sin." We have a lurking suspicion that a person who does not sin must really be basically boring and that something is missing from his life: the dramatic dimension of being autonomous; that the freedom to say no, to descend into the shadows of sin and to want to do things on one's own, is part of being truly human; that only then can we make the most of all the vastness and depth of our being men and women, of being truly ourselves; that we should put this freedom to the test, even in opposition to God, in order to become, in reality, fully ourselves.

Abandoning Ourselves to God

*I*n a word, we think that evil is basically good, we think that we need it, at least a little, in order to experience the fullness of being. We think that a little bargaining with evil, keeping for oneself a little freedom against God, is basically a good thing, perhaps even necessary. The person who abandons himself totally in God's hands does not become God's puppet, a boring "yes man." Only the person who entrusts himself totally to God finds true freedom, the great, creative immensity of the freedom of good. The person who turns to God does not become smaller but greater, for through God and with God he becomes great, he becomes divine, he becomes truly himself. The person who puts himself in God's hands does not distance himself from others, withdrawing into his private salvation; on the contrary, it is only then that his heart truly awakens and he becomes a sensitive, hence, benevolent and open person. The closer a person is to God, the closer he is to people. We see this in Mary. The fact that she is totally with God is the reason why she is so close to human beings. For this reason she can be the Mother of every consolation and every help, a Mother whom anyone can dare to address in any kind of need in weakness and in sin, for she has understanding for everything and is for everyone the open power of creative goodness. Thus, we see that the image of the Sorrowful Virgin, of the Mother who shares her suffering and her love, is also a true image of the Immaculate Conception. Her heart was enlarged by being and feeling together with God. In her, God's goodness came very close to us.

Fascinated by the Beauty of God

*I*n the Eucharist we contemplate the sacrament of the living synthesis of the law: Christ offers to us, in himself, the complete fulfillment of love for God and love for our brothers and sisters. He communicates his love to us when we are nourished by his Body and Blood. In this way, Saint Paul's words to the Thessalonians are brought to completion in us: "You turned to God from idols, to serve him who is the living and true God" (1 Thes 1: 9). This conversion is the beginning of the walk of holiness that the Christian is called to achieve in his own life. The saint is the person who is so fascinated by the beauty of God and by his perfect truth as to be progressively transformed by it. Because of this beauty and truth, he is ready to renounce everything, even himself. Love of God is enough for him, experienced in humble and disinterested service to one's neighbor, especially towards those who cannot give back in return. Like the disciples of Emmaus, whose hearts were kindled by the words of the Risen One and enlightened by his living presence recognized in the breaking of the bread, who hurriedly returned to Jerusalem and became messengers of Christ's Resurrection, we too must take up the path again, enlivened by the fervent desire to witness to the mystery of this love that gives hope to the world.

Holy Matrimony

he basic way in which any society is buil depends on marriage... We must pa attention to this: Wherever two peopl give themselves to each other and, between them, giv life to children, this touches the holiness, the myster of human existence, which goes beyond the realm c what I can control and dispose of. I simply do nc belong to myself alone. There is a divine mystery with in each and every person. That is why the associatio of husband and wife is regarded within the religiou realm, within the sphere of the sacred, of bein answerable before God. Being answerable before Go is a necessity — and in the sacrament this is plante deep and given its proper foundation... Only if I giv myself entirely, without keeping any part of me bac or being involved just until further notice, until, so to speak, I find some thing better, does this fully correspond to human dignity. Human life i not an experiment. This is not a commercial contract, but a surrender c myself to another person. Only in the form of a love that is entire an unreserved is the self-giving of one person to another commensurat with the essence of man.

Human Capacity for God

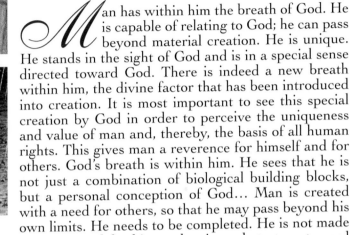

Man has within him the breath of God. He is capable of relating to God; he can pass beyond material creation. He is unique. He stands in the sight of God and is in a special sense directed toward God. There is indeed a new breath within him, the divine factor that has been introduced into creation. It is most important to see this special creation by God in order to perceive the uniqueness and value of man and, thereby, the basis of all human rights. This gives man a reverence for himself and for others. God's breath is within him. He sees that he is not just a combination of biological building blocks, but a personal conception of God... Man is created with a need for others, so that he may pass beyond his own limits. He needs to be completed. He is not made to be alone — that is not good for him — but is made to turn toward someone else. He must look for himself in the other person and find himself in him. In a text from Genesis there follows the prophetic declaration that the man will on this account leave his father and his mother and will become one flesh with the woman. They will be one flesh with each other, one united human being. The entire drama of the two sexes' need for each other, of their being turned toward each other, is contained within this declaration. In addition it is also said that they are there in order to give themselves each to the other, so as to make the gift of new life in doing so, and then finally to devote themselves to this new life. In this sense, the mystery of marriage is contained within it, and basically the family is likewise envisaged.

The Bond of Marriage

he question of the right relationship between man and woman sinks its roots in the most profound essence of the human being, and can only find its answer in the latter. It cannot be separated from the always ancient and always new question of man about himself: Who am I? Does God exist? And, who is God? What is his face really like? The Bible's answer to these questions is unitary and consequential: Man is created in the image of God, and God himself is love. For this reason, the vocation to love is what makes man the authentic image of God: He becomes like God in the measure that he becomes someone who loves. From this fundamental bond between God and man another is derived: The indissoluble bond between spirit and body. Man is, in fact, soul that expresses itself in the body and [the] body that is vivified by an immortal spirit. Also, the body of man and of woman has, therefore, so to speak, a theological character, it is not simply body, and what is biological in man is not only biological, but an expression and fulfillment of our humanity… In this way, from the two bonds, that of man with God and — in man — that of the body with the spirit, arises a third bond: the one that exists between person and institution. The totality of man includes the dimension of time, and man's "yes" goes beyond the present moment: In his totality, the "yes" means "always," it constitutes the area of fidelity. Only in his interior can this faith grow which gives a future and allows the children, the fruit of love, to believe in man and in his future in difficult times.

The Truth of Marriage

he truth of marriage and the family, which sinks its roots in the truth of man, has found its application in the history of salvation, at whose center is the word: "God loves his people." In fact, biblical revelation is above all the expression of a history of love, the history of God's covenant with men. For this reason, God has been able to assume the history of love and of the union of a man and a woman in the covenant of marriage, as symbol of the history of salvation... In the New Testament, God radicalizes his love until he becomes himself, through his Son, flesh of our flesh, authentic man. Thus, God's union with man has assumed its supreme, irreversible and definitive form. And in this way, the definitive form of human love is also drawn, that reciprocal "yes" that cannot be revoked. It does not alienate man, but liberates him from the alienations of history to return him to the truth of creation. The sacramental character that marriage assumes in Christ means, therefore, that the gift of creation has been raised to the grace of redemption. Christ's grace is not superimposed from outside of man's nature, it does not violate it, but liberates and restores it, by raising it beyond its frontiers. And just as the Incarnation of the Son of God reveals its true meaning in the cross, so also authentic human love is surrender of oneself; it cannot exist if it avoids the cross.

The Yes of Christian Families

*I*n the procreation of children, marriage reflects its divine model, the love of God for man. In man and woman, paternity and maternity, as happens with the body and with love, the biological aspect is not circumscribed: life is only given totally when, with birth, love and meaning are also given, which make it possible to say yes to this life. Precisely because of this, it is clear to what point the systematic closing of the union itself to the gift of life and, even more, the suppression or manipulation of unborn life is contrary to human love, to the profound vocation of man and woman. However, no man and no woman, on their own and by their own strength, can give love and the meaning of life adequately to their children. To be able to say to someone: "your life is good, even if I don't know your future," needs a superior authority and credibility which the individual cannot give himself on his own. The Christian knows that that authority is conferred to that larger family that God, through his Son, Jesus Christ, and the gift of the Holy Spirit, has created in the history of men, namely, to the Church. It acknowledges the action of that eternal and indestructible love that assures to the life of each one of us a permanent meaning, even if we do not know the future. For this reason, the building of each of the Christian families is framed in the context of the great family of the Church, which supports and accompanies it, and guarantees that there is a meaning and that in the future there will be the "yes" of the Creator.

Love as Suffering

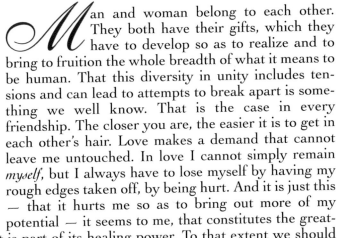

Man and woman belong to each other. They both have their gifts, which they have to develop so as to realize and to bring to fruition the whole breadth of what it means to be human. That this diversity in unity includes tensions and can lead to attempts to break apart is something we well know. That is the case in every friendship. The closer you are, the easier it is to get in each other's hair. Love makes a demand that cannot leave me untouched. In love I cannot simply remain *myself*, but I always have to lose myself by having my rough edges taken off, by being hurt. And it is just this — that it hurts me so as to bring out more of my potential — it seems to me, that constitutes the greatness of love, that is part of its healing power. To that extent we should not think of love just as romantic love, so that, so to speak, heaven comes down to earth for the two lovers when they find each other, and they then live happily ever after. We must think of love as suffering. Only if we are ready to endure it as suffering and thus ever again to accept each other and once again to take the other to ourselves, only then can a lifelong partnership develop. If, on the contrary, we say when we get to the critical point, I want to avoid that, and we separate, then what we are really renouncing is the true opportunity that is to be found in man and woman being turned toward each other and in the reality of love.

Becoming Like the Angels

*F*aith gives joy. When God is not there, the world becomes desolate, and everything becomes boring, and everything is completely unsatisfactory. It's easy to see today how a world empty of God is also increasingly consuming itself, how it has become a wholly joyless world. The great joy comes from the fact that there is this great love, and that is the essential message of faith. You are unswervingly loved. This also explains why Christianity spread first predominantly among the weak and suffering. To that extent it can be said that the basic element of Christianity is joy... It is joy in the proper sense. A joy that exists together with a difficult life and also makes this life liveable... Faith also makes man light. To believe means that we become like angels. We can fly, because we no longer weigh so heavy in our own estimation. To become a believer means to become light, to escape our own gravity, which drags us down, and thus to enter the weightlessness of faith... Catholics are not promised an "exterior" happiness but rather a deep interior security through communion with the Lord. That *he* is an ultimate light of happiness in one's life is in fact a part of all this... We are so alienated from God's voice that we simply do not recognize it immediately as his. But I would still say that everyone who is in some sense attentive can experience and sense for himself that now *he* is speaking to me. And it is a chance for me to get to know him. Precisely in catastrophic situations he can suddenly break in, if I am awake and if someone helps me decipher the message.

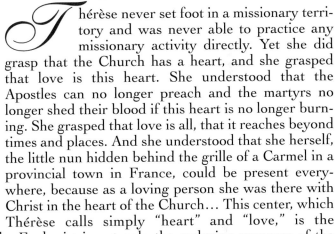

The Heart of the Missionary Impulse

Thérèse never set foot in a missionary territory and was never able to practice any missionary activity directly. Yet she did grasp that the Church has a heart, and she grasped that love is this heart. She understood that the Apostles can no longer preach and the martyrs no longer shed their blood if this heart is no longer burning. She grasped that love is all, that it reaches beyond times and places. And she understood that she herself, the little nun hidden behind the grille of a Carmel in a provincial town in France, could be present everywhere, because as a loving person she was there with Christ in the heart of the Church... This center, which Thérèse calls simply "heart" and "love," is the Eucharist. For the Eucharist is not only the enduring presence of the divine and human love of Jesus Christ, which is always the source and origin of the Church and without which she would founder, would be overcome by the gates of hell. As the presence of the divine and human love of Christ, it is also always the channel open from the man Jesus to the people who are his "members," themselves becoming a Eucharist and thereby themselves a "heart" and a "love" for the Church... The heart must remain the heart, that through the heart the other organs may serve aright. It is at that point, when the Eucharist is being celebrated aright.

October

The Theology of Littleness

The theology of littleness is a basic category of Christianity. After all, the tenor of our faith is that God's distinctive greatness is revealed precisely in powerlessness. That in the long run, the strength of history is precisely in those who love, which is to say, in a strength that, properly speaking, cannot be measured according to categories of power. So in order to show who he is, God consciously revealed himself in the powerlessness of Nazareth and Golgotha. Thus, it is not the one who can destroy the most who is the most powerful — in the world, of course, destructive capacity is still the real proof of power — but, on the contrary, the least power of love is already greater than the greatest power of destruction... The essence of religion is the relation of man beyond himself to the unknown reality that faith calls God. It is man's capacity to go beyond all tangible, measurable reality and to enter into this primordial relation. Man lives in relationships, and the ultimate goodness of his life depends on the rightness of his essential relationships... But none of these relationships can be right if the first relationship, the relationship with God, is not right. This relationship itself, I would say, is, properly speaking, the content of religion.

God is Waiting for Us

*I*n Sacred Scripture, bread represents all that human beings need for their daily life. Water makes the earth fertile: it is the fundamental gift that makes life possible. Wine, on the other hand, expresses the excellence of creation and gives us the feast in which we go beyond the limits of our daily routine: wine, the Psalm says, "gladdens the heart." So it is that wine and with it the vine have also become images of the gift of love in which we can taste the savor of the Divine. God created a vineyard for himself — this is an image of the history of love for humanity, of his love for Israel which he chose. God instilled in men and women, created in his image, the capacity for love, hence also the capacity for loving him, their Creator. With the Prophet Isaiah's canticle of love God wants to speak to the hearts of his people — and to each one of us. "I have created you in my image and likeness," he says to us. "I myself am love and you are my image to the extent that the splendor of love shines out in you, to the extent that you respond lovingly to me." God is waiting for us. He wants us to love him: should not our hearts be moved by this appeal? He comes to meet us, he comes to meet me. Will he find a response? Or will what happened to the vine of which God says in Isaiah: "He waited for it to produce grapes but it yielded wild grapes" also happen to us? Is not our Christian life often far more like vinegar than wine? Self-pity, conflict, indifference?

The World's Need for Transformation

he holy mystery of God, the mustard seed of the Gospel, cannot be identified with the world but is rather destined to permeate the whole world. That is why we must find again the courage to embrace what is sacred, the courage to distinguish what is Christian — not in order to segregate it, but in order to transform it — the courage to be truly dynamic. In an interview in 1975, Eugene Ionesco, one of the founders of the theater of the absurd, expressed this with all the passion of seeking and searching that characterizes the person of our age. I quote here a few sentences from that interview: "The Church does not want to lose her current clientele; but she does want to gain new members. The result is a kind of secularization that is truly pitiful. The world is losing its way; the Church is losing herself in the world... I once heard a priest say in church: 'Let us be happy; let us shake hands... Jesus is pleased to wish you a pleasant good day!' Before long they will be setting up a bar in Church for the Communion of bread and wine and offering sandwiches and Beaujolais... Nothing is left to us; nothing solid. Everything is in flux. But what we need is a rock." It seems to me that if we listen to the voices of our age, of people who are consciously living, suffering, and loving in the world today, we will realize that we cannot serve this world with a kind of banal officiousness. It has no need of confirmation but rather of transformation, of the radicalism of the Gospel.

OCTOBER 4

Respect for Creator and Creation

There is a story that goes as follows: Francis told the brother responsible for the garden never to plant the whole area with vegetables but to leave part of the garden for flowers, so that at every season of the year it may produce our sisters, the flowers, out of love for her who is called "the flower of the field and the lily of the valley" (Song 2: 1). In the same way he wanted there always to be a particularly beautiful flower bed, so that, at all times, people would be moved by the sight of flowers to praise God, "for every creature calls to us: God has made me for thy sake, O man" (*Mirror of Perfection* 11: 118). We cannot take this story and simply leave the religious element to one side as a relic of a bygone age, while accepting its refusal of mean utility and its appreciation of the wealth of species. This would in no way correspond to what Francis did and intended... When man himself is out of joint and can no longer affirm himself, nature cannot flourish. On the contrary: man must first be in harmony with himself; only then can he enter into harmony with creation and it with him. And this is only possible if he is in harmony with the Creator who designed both nature and us. Respect for man and respect for nature go together, but ultimately both can only flourish and find their true measure if, in man and nature, we respect the Creator and his creation. The two only harmonize in relationship with the Creator. We shall assuredly never find the lost equilibrium if we refuse to press forward and discover this relationship. Let Francis of Assisi, then, make us reflect; let him set us on the right path.

The Parable of the Talents

*E*ach life has its own calling. It has its own code and its own path. None is just an imitation, stamped-out along with a mass of other identical ones. And each one requires the creative courage to live one's own life, and not just to turn oneself into a copy of someone else. If you look at the parable of the lazy servant, who buried his talent so that nothing could happen to it, that expresses what I am trying to say. Here is someone who will not take the risk of living his life in its proper originality and letting it develop; or of exposing it to the dangers that necessarily arise with that… Each individual person tries to find someone who can explain things to him, whom he can ask, how did *you* do it; how did *he* do it; how can *I* do it? How can I get to know myself and learn my own capabilities? We are convinced that the fundamental, authoritative source of information is Christ. On one hand, he gives us the broad common outlines, and, on the other, he comes into such a close relationship with us that with him and in the community of the believers we can come to know our own originality — and can then reconcile community and originality.

OCTOBER 6

Image of God

The human being is created in God's image and likeness (Gn 1: 26-27). In the human being heaven and earth touch one another. In the human being God enters into his creation; the human being is directly related to God. The human being is called by him. God's words in the Old Testament are valid for every individual human being: "I call you by name and you are mine." Each human being is known by God and loved by him. Each is willed by God, and each is God's image. Precisely in this consists the deeper and greater unity of humankind — that each of us, each individual human being, realizes the *one* project of God and has his or her origin in the same creative idea of God. Hence the Bible says that whoever violates a human being violates God's property (Gn 9: 5). Human life stands under God's special protection, because each human being, however wretched or exalted he or she may be, however sick or suffering, however good-for-nothing or important, whether born or unborn, whether incurably ill or radiant with health — each one bears God's breath in himself or herself, each one is God's image. This is the deepest reason for the inviolability of human dignity, and upon it is founded ultimately every civilization. When the human person is no longer seen as standing under God's protection and bearing God's breath, then the human being begins to be viewed in utilitarian fashion. It is then that the barbarity appears that tramples upon human dignity. And vice versa: When this is seen, then a high degree of spirituality and morality is plainly evident.

The Rosary

The historical origin of the rosary lies in the Middle Ages. People looked for some kind of psalter for them and found the prayers to Mary with the mysteries of the life of Jesus Christ strung out like beads on a necklace. They touch you in a meditative way, so that the repetition allows the soul to settle into tranquility and, holding fast to the Word, above all to the figure of Mary and to the images of Christ that pass you by, make your soul calm and free and grant it a vision of God. The rosary does in fact provide a link for us with this primitive knowledge that repetition is a part of prayer, of meditation, that repetition is a way of settling oneself into the rhythm of tranquility. It's a matter of allowing myself to be carried away by the calm of repetition and of steady rhythm. So much the more so, since this text does not lack content. It brings great images and visions and above all the figure of Mary — and through her the figure of Jesus — before my eyes. These people had needed a prayer to bring them calm, to take them out of themselves, away from their troubles, and set before them consolation and healing. This basic experience in the history of religion, of repetition, of rhythm, of words in unison, of singing together, which carries me and soothes me and fills my space, which does not torment me, but lets me be still and comforts me and sets me free, has here become fully Christian in that people pray quite simply in the Marian context and in that of the appearance of Christ to men, and yet at the same time let this prayer be internalized in them — where the soul becomes one with the words.

The Parables

*J*esus taught consistently in the form of parables... Jesus states explicitly that the parable is the way in which knowledge of the faith is to be realized in this world (Jn 16: 25)... The parables have two principal functions. On the one hand, they transcend the realm of creation in order, by this transcendence, to draw it above itself to the Creator. On the other hand, they accept the past historical experience of faith, that is, they prolong the parables that have grown up with the history of Israel. We should add here a third point: they also interpret the simple world of everyday life in order to *show* how a transcendence to what is more than just human stereotype occurs in it. On the one hand, the content of faith reveals itself only in parables, but, on the other hand, the parable makes clear the core of reality itself. This is possible because reality itself is a parable. Hence, it is only by way of parable that the nature of the world and of man himself is made known to us... The parable does not approach our experience of the world from without; on the contrary, it is the parable that gives this experience its proper depth and reveals what is hidden in things themselves. Reality is self-transcendence, and when man is led to transcend it, he not only comprehends God but, for the first time, also understands reality and enables himself and creation to be what they were meant to be. Only because creation *is* parable can it *become* the *word* of parable.

The Challenge of Mission

The Christian faith, which carries within itself the great heritage of the religions and which opens up this heritage to the Logos, to true reason, could offer a new basis to them at the deepest level and could at the same time make possible a real synthesis of technological rationality and religion, something that can only come about, not by a flight into the irrational, but by opening up reason to its true height and breadth. Here lie the great tasks of our contemporary historical moment. Christian mission will doubtless have to understand other religions far more profoundly and accept them at a deeper level than has been the case hitherto, but these religions, on the other hand, in order for their best elements to survive, need to recognize their own adventual character, the way they point forward to Christ. If in this sense we proceed on an intercultural search for traces of a path toward a common truth, then something unexpected will appear: Christianity has more in common with the ancient cultures of mankind than with the relativistic and rationalistic world... For the knowledge that man must turn toward God, and toward what is eternal, is found right across all the cultures; the knowledge about sin, repentance, and forgiveness; the knowledge concerning communion with God and eternal life; and finally the knowledge of the basic rules of morality, as they are found in the form of the Ten Commandments.

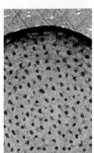

The God of Israel

*I*n the normal way of things, a God who loses his land, who leaves his people defeated, and is unable to protect his sanctuary, is a God who has been overthrown. He has no more say in things. He vanishes from history. When Israel went into exile, quite astonishingly, the opposite happened. The stature of this God, the way he was completely different from the other divinities in the religions of the world, was now apparent, and the faith of Israel at last took on its true form and stature. This God could afford to let others have his land because he was not tied down to any country. He could allow his people to be defeated so as to awaken it thereby from its false religious dream. He was not dependent on this people, yet nevertheless he did not abandon them in their hour of defeat... Thus, together with a more profound concept of God, a new idea of worship developed. Certainly, since the time of Solomon the personal God of the Fathers had been identified with the high god, the Creator, who is known to all religions, but in general this latter had been excluded from worship, as not being responsible for one's individual needs. This identification, which had been made in principle, although it had probably hitherto impinged little upon people's consciousness, now became the driving force for survival of the faith: Israel has no particular God at all but simply worships the one single God. This God spoke to Abraham and chose Israel, but he is in reality the God of all peoples, the universal God who guides the course of all history... The true sacrifice is the man who has become worthy of God.

OCTOBER 11

The Force of Truth

aith has a fundamental importance in the life of the Church, because the gift that God makes of himself in revelation is fundamental and God's gift of himself is accepted through faith… If the truth of the faith is placed simply and decisively at the heart of Christian existence, human life is innovated and revived by a love that knows no bounds. Charity moves from God's Heart to the Heart of Jesus Christ, and through his Spirit across the world. This love is born from the encounter with Christ in faith… Jesus Christ is the Personified Truth who attracts the world to himself. The light that shines out from Jesus is the splendor of the truth. Every other truth is a fragment of the Truth that he is, and refers to him… Without the knowledge of the truth, freedom degenerates, becomes isolated, and is reduced to sterile arbitration. With him, freedom is rediscovered, it is recognized to have been created for our good and is expressed in charitable actions and behavior. Therefore, Jesus gives men and women total familiarity with the truth and continuously invites them to live in it. It is truth offered as a reality that restores the human being and at the same time surpasses him and towers above him, as a Mystery that embraces and at the same time exceeds the impulse of his intelligence. Nothing succeeds as well as love for the truth in impelling the human mind towards unexplored horizons. Jesus Christ draws to himself the heart of each person, enlarges it and fills it with joy that moves and attracts the human person to free adoration, to bow with heartfelt respect before the Truth he has encountered.

God Becomes Our Richness

*T*he poverty that Jesus means — that the prophets mean — presupposes above all inner freedom from the greed for possession and the mania for power. This is a greater reality than merely a different distribution of possessions, which would still be in the material domain and thereby make hearts even harder. It is first and foremost a matter of purification of heart, through which one recognizes possession as responsibility, as a duty towards others, placing oneself under God's gaze and letting oneself be guided by Christ, who from being rich became poor for our sake (cf. 2 Cor 8: 9). Inner freedom is the prerequisite for overcoming the corruption and greed that devastate the world today. This freedom can only be found if God becomes our richness; it can only be found in the patience of daily sacrifices, in which, as it were, true freedom develops. It is the King who points out to us the way to this goal: Jesus, whom we acclaim on Palm Sunday, whom we ask to take us with him on his way... He comes in all cultures and all parts of the world, everywhere, in wretched huts and in poor rural areas as well as in the splendor of cathedrals. He is the same everywhere, the One, and thus all those gathered with him in prayer and communion are also united in one body. Christ rules by making himself our Bread and giving himself to us. It is in this way that he builds his kingdom.

Mary and Christ are Inseparable

*N*ot only does Mary have a unique relationship with Christ, the Son of God who, as man, chose to become her Son. Since she was totally united to Christ, she also totally belongs to us. Yes, we can say that Mary is close to us as no other human being is, because Christ becomes man for all men and women and his entire being is "being here for us." Christ, as the Head, is inseparable from his Body which is the Church, forming with her, so to speak, a single living subject. The Mother of the Head is also the Mother of all the Church; she is, so to speak, totally emptied of herself; she has given herself entirely to Christ and with him is given as a gift to us all. Indeed, the more the human person gives himself, the more he finds himself. Mary is so interwoven in the great mystery of the Church that she and the Church are inseparable, just as she and Christ are inseparable. Mary mirrors the Church, anticipates the Church in her person, and in all the turbulence that affects the suffering, struggling Church she always remains the Star of salvation. In her lies the true center in which we trust, even if its peripheries very often weigh on our soul. In Mary, the Immaculate, we find the essence of the Church without distortion. We ourselves must learn from her to become "ecclesial souls" so that we too may be able, in accordance with Saint Paul's words, to present ourselves "blameless" in the sight of the Lord, as he wanted us from the very beginning (cf. Col 1: 21-22; Eph 1: 4). Mary is holy Israel: she says "yes" to the Lord, she puts herself totally at his disposal and thus becomes the living temple of God.

The Truth About Lying

Whenever there is a loss of fidelity to the transcendent order, and a loss of respect for that "grammar" of dialogue which is the universal moral law written on human hearts, whenever the integral development of the person and the protection of his fundamental rights are hindered or denied, whenever countless people are forced to endure intolerable injustices and inequalities, how can we hope that the good of peace will be realized? The essential elements which make up the truth of that good are missing. Saint Augustine described peace as the tranquility of order. By this, he meant a situation which ultimately enables the truth about man to be fully respected and realized. Who and what, then, can prevent the coming of peace? Sacred Scripture, in the book of Genesis, points to the lie told at the very beginning of history by the animal with a forked tongue, whom the Evangelist John calls "the father of lies" (Jn 8: 44). Lying is linked to the tragedy of sin and its perverse consequences, which continue to have devastating effects on the lives of individuals and nations. We need but think of the events of the past century, when aberrant ideological and political systems willfully twisted the truth and brought about the exploitation and murder of an appalling number of men and women, wiping out entire families and communities. How can we fail to be seriously concerned about lies in our own time? Any authentic search for peace must begin with the realization that the problem of truth and untruth is the concern of every man and woman; it is decisive for the peaceful future of our planet.

OCTOBER 15

The Truth Who Gives Peace

Peace is an irrepressible yearning present in the heart of each person. All people are members of one and the same family. An extreme exaltation of differences clashes with this fundamental truth. We need to regain an awareness that we share a common destiny which is ultimately transcendent, so as to maximize our historical and cultural differences, not in opposition to, but in cooperation with, people belonging to other cultures. These simple truths are what make peace possible; they are easily understood whenever we listen to our own hearts with pure intentions. Peace thus comes to be seen in a new light: not as the mere absence of war, but as a harmonious coexistence of individual citizens within a society governed by justice, one in which the good is also achieved, to the extent possible, for each of them. The truth of peace calls upon everyone to cultivate productive and sincere relationships; it encourages them to seek out and to follow the paths of forgiveness and reconciliation, to be transparent in their dealings with others, and to be faithful to their word. In a particular way, the followers of Christ, recognizing the insidious presence of evil and the need for that liberation brought by the divine Master, look to him with confidence, in the knowledge that "he committed no sin; no guile was found on his lips" (1 Pt 2: 22). Jesus defined himself as the Truth in person. He has disclosed the full truth about humanity and about human history. The power of his grace makes it possible to live "in" and "by" truth, since he alone is completely true and faithful. Jesus is the truth which gives us peace.

The Duty to Proclaim the Gospel of Peace

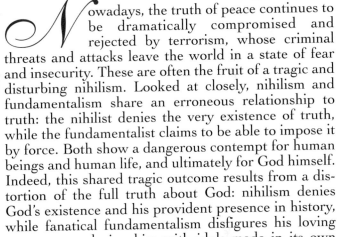

Nowadays, the truth of peace continues to be dramatically compromised and rejected by terrorism, whose criminal threats and attacks leave the world in a state of fear and insecurity. These are often the fruit of a tragic and disturbing nihilism. Looked at closely, nihilism and fundamentalism share an erroneous relationship to truth: the nihilist denies the very existence of truth, while the fundamentalist claims to be able to impose it by force. Both show a dangerous contempt for human beings and human life, and ultimately for God himself. Indeed, this shared tragic outcome results from a distortion of the full truth about God: nihilism denies God's existence and his provident presence in history, while fanatical fundamentalism disfigures his loving and merciful countenance, replacing him with idols made in its own image. In analyzing the causes of the contemporary phenomenon of terrorism, consideration should be given to its deeper cultural, religious, and ideological motivations. All Catholics in every part of the world have a duty to proclaim and embody ever more fully the "Gospel of Peace," and to show that acknowledgment of the full truth of God is the first, indispensable condition for consolidating the truth of peace. God is Love which saves, a loving Father who wants to see his children look upon one another as brothers and sisters, working responsibly to place their various talents at the service of the common good of the human family. God is the unfailing source of the hope which gives meaning to personal and community life. God, and God alone, brings to fulfillment every work of good and of peace.

Safeguarding the Good of Peace

*H*istory has amply demonstrated that declaring war on God in order to eradicate him from human hearts only leads a fearful and impoverished humanity toward decisions which are ultimately futile. This realization must impel believers in Christ to become convincing witnesses of the God who is inseparably truth and love, placing themselves at the service of peace in broad cooperation with other Christians, the followers of other religions, and with all men and women of good will. The truth of peace requires that all agree to strive for a progressive and concerted nuclear disarmament. The resources which would be saved could then be employed in projects of development capable of benefiting all their people, especially the poor. It can only be hoped that the international community will find the wisdom and courage to take up once more, jointly and with renewed conviction, the process of disarmament, and thus concretely ensure the right to peace enjoyed by every individual and every people. By their commitment to safeguarding the good of peace, the various agencies of the international community will regain the authority needed to make their initiatives credible and effective. With confidence and filial abandonment let us lift up our eyes to Mary, Mother of the Prince of Peace. Let us ask her to help all God's People to work for peace and to be guided by the light of the truth that sets man free (cf. Jn 8: 32). Through Mary's intercession, may all mankind grow in esteem for this fundamental good and strive to make it ever more present in our world.

A New Heart

To renew man, the Lord... recognized with Ezekiel that, to live this vocation, we need a new heart; instead of a heart of stone — as Ezekiel said — we need a heart of flesh, a heart that is truly human. And the Lord "implants" this new heart in us at Baptism, through faith. It is not a physical transplant, but perhaps we can make this comparison. After a transplant, the organism needs treatment, requires the necessary medicines to be able to live with the new heart, so that it becomes "one's own heart" and not the "heart of another." This is especially so in this "spiritual transplant" when the Lord implants within us a new heart, a heart open to the Creator, to God's call. To be able to live with this new heart, adequate treatment is necessary; one must have recourse to the appropriate medicines so that it can really become "our heart"... The Lord gives us a new heart and we must live with this new heart, using the appropriate therapies to ensure that it is really "our own." In this way we live with all that the Creator has given us and this creates a truly happy life... Life itself is like this. Becoming men and women according to Jesus' plan demands sacrifices, but these are by no means negative; on the contrary, they are a help in living as people with new hearts, in living a truly human and happy life. Since a consumer culture exists that wants to prevent us from living in accordance with the Creator's plan, we must have the courage to create islands, oases, and then great stretches of land of Catholic culture where the Creator's design is lived out.

Making God Present in Society

*W*e all ask ourselves what the Lord expects of us… There is a desire to reduce God to the private sphere, to a sentiment… As a result, everyone makes his or her own plan of life. But this vision, presented as though it were scientific, accepts as valid only what can be proven. With a God who is not available for immediate experimentation, this vision ends by also injuring society. The result is in fact that each one makes his own plan and in the end finds himself opposed to the other. As can be seen, this is definitely an unliveable situation. We must make God present again in our society. This is the first essential element: that God be once again present in our lives, that we do not live as though we were autonomous, authorized to invent what freedom and life are. We must realize that we are creatures, aware that there is a God who has created us and that living in accordance with his will is not dependence but a gift of love that makes us alive. Therefore, the first point is to know God, to know him better and better, to recognize that God is in my life, and that God has a place… The second point, therefore, is recognizing God who has shown us his face in Jesus, who suffered for us, who loved us to the point of dying, and thus overcame violence. It is necessary to make the living God present in our "own" lives first of all… a God only thought of, but a God who has shown himself, who has shown his being and his face. Only in this way do our lives become true, authentically human; hence, the criteria of true humanism emerge in society.

Christianity as Revelation

We can say of the Christian faith, in line with the faith of Abraham, that no one simply finds it there as his possession. It never comes out of what we have ourselves. It breaks in from outside. That is still always the way. Nobody is born a Christian, not even in a Christian world and of Christian parents. Being Christian can only ever happen as a new birth. Being a Christian begins with Baptism, which is death and Resurrection (Rom 6), not with biological birth… The Christian faith is not the product of our own experiences; rather, it is an event that comes to us from without. Faith is based on our meeting something (or someone) for which our capacity for experiencing things is inadequate. It is not our experience that is widened or deepened…but something happens. The categories of "encounter," "otherness," "event," describe the inner origins of the Christian faith and indicate the limitations of the concept of "experience." Certainly, what touches us there effects an experience in us, but experience as the result of an event, not of reaching deeper into ourselves. This is exactly what is meant by the concept of revelation: something not ours, not to be found in what we have, comes to me and takes me out of myself, above myself, creates something new. That also determines the historical nature of Christianity, which is based on events and not on becoming aware of the depths of one's own inner self, what is called "illumination." The Trinity is not the object of our experience but is something that has to be uttered from outside, that comes to me from outside as "revelation."

The Missionary Nature of the Church

The person who has trust and participates in the faith of the Church wants to believe with the Church. This seems like our life-long pilgrimage: to arrive with our entire life at the communion of faith. We can offer this to everyone, so that little by little one can identify and especially take this step over and over again to trust in the faith of the Church, to insert themselves in this pilgrimage of faith, so as to receive the light of faith... The essence of Christianity is not an idea but a Person. Great theologians have tried to describe the essential ideas that make up Christianity. But in the end, the Christianity that they constructed was not convincing, because Christianity is in the first place an Event, a Person. And thus in the Person we discover the richness of what is contained... How can one's personal authenticity be discovered if in reality, in the depth of our hearts, there is the expectation of Jesus, and the genuine authenticity of each person is found exactly in communion with Christ and not without Christ? If we have found the Lord and if he is the light and joy of our lives, are we sure that for someone else who has not found Christ he is not lacking something essential and that it is our duty to offer him this essential reality?... If we are convinced and we have experienced the fact that without Christ life is incomplete, is missing a reality, the fundamental reality, we must also be convinced that we do harm to no one if we show them Christ and we offer them in this way too the possibility to discover, the joy of having discovered life.

What Evangelizing Means

hat does "evangelizing" actually mean? What is happening when you do it? What is this Gospel?... Word and sign are indivisible. Whenever the signs are regarded as simple miracles, without the word that is within them, Jesus breaks off his activity. Nor, however, does he countenance his preaching being regarded as a merely intellectual matter, as material for discussion: his word demands a decision; it creates reality. In this sense it is an "incarnate" word; the relation of word and sign to each other shows a "sacramental" structure. We still have to go a step farther. Jesus does not communicate any contents that are independent of his own person, as a teacher or a storyteller would usually do. He is more, and something other, than a rabbi. As his preaching continues, it becomes ever clearer that in his parables he is talking about himself, that the "Kingdom" and his own person belong together, that the Kingdom is coming in his own person. The decision he demands is a decision on how one stands in relation to him... Thus we now understand that Jesus' preaching should be termed "sacramental" in a still more profound sense than we could previously have seen: his message carries within it the concrete reality of the Incarnation and the theme of cross and Resurrection. It is in this most profound sense a verbal action. And thus, for the Church, it points forward to the mutual relationship of preaching and the Eucharist and yet also that between preaching and a witness lived out in suffering... Christian preaching is a matter, not of words, but of *the* Word.

Preaching as a Giving Away of Self

hrist's "I" is totally open to the "Thou" of the Father; it does not remain in itself, but takes us inside the very life of the Trinity. This means that the Christian preacher will not speak about himself, but will become Christ's own voice, by making way for the Logos, and leading, through communion with the Man Jesus, to communion with the living God... The ministry of the Word demands that the priest divest himself profoundly of his own self... The ministry of the Word requires that the priest share in the *kenosis* of Christ, in his "increasing and decreasing." The fact that the priest does not speak about himself, but bears the message of another, certainly does not mean that he is not personally involved, but precisely the opposite: it is a giving-away-of-the-self in Christ that takes up the path of his Easter mystery, and leads to a true finding-of-the-self, and communion with him who is the Word of God in person. This Paschal structure of the "not-self" that turns out to be the "true self" after all, shows, in the last analysis, that the ministry of the Word reaches beyond all "functions" to penetrate the priest's very being and presupposes that the priesthood is a sacrament.

OCTOBER 24

Mission and Losing Self

The encounter with the Word is a gift for us, too, which was given to us so that we might give it to others, freely, as we have received it. God made a choice... and we can only acknowledge in humility that we are unworthy messengers who do not proclaim ourselves but rather speak with a holy fear about something that is not ours but that comes from God. Only in this way can the missionary task be understood... The model for the missions is clearly prescribed in the way of the Apostles and of the early Church, especially in the commissioning discourses of Jesus. Missionary work requires, first and foremost, being prepared for martyrdom, a willingness to lose oneself for the sake of the truth and for the sake of others. Only in this way does it become believable; again and again this has been the situation with the missions, and so it will always be. For only then do Christians raise the standard of the primacy of the truth... The truth can and must have no other weapon but itself. Someone who believes has found in the truth the pearl for which he is ready to give everything, even himself. For he knows that he finds himself by losing himself, that only the grain of wheat that has died bears much fruit. Someone who can both believe and say, "We have found Love," has to pass this gift on. He knows that in doing so he does no one violence, does not destroy anyone's identity, does not disrupt cultures, but rather sets them free to realize their own great potential; he knows that he is fulfilling a responsibility.

The Law as the Visibility of the Truth

he law is the visibility of the truth, the visibility of God's countenance, and so it gives us the possibility of right living. Are not these our questions: Who am I? Where am I going? What shall I do to put my life in order? The hymn to God's word that we find in Psalm 119 expresses this joy of being delivered, the joy of knowing God's will. For his will is our truth and therefore our way; it is what all men are looking for... It is characteristic of the Messiah — he who is "greater than Moses" — that he brings the definitive interpretation of the Torah, in which the Torah is itself renewed, because now its true essence appears in all its purity and its character as grace becomes undistorted reality... The Torah of the Messiah is the Messiah, Jesus, himself. It is to him that the command, "Listen to him," refers. In this way the "Law" becomes universal; it is grace, constituting a people which becomes such by hearing the word and undergoing conversion. In this Torah, which is Jesus himself, the abiding essence of what was inscribed on the stone tablets at Sinai is now written in living flesh, namely, the twofold command of love. This is set forth in Philippians 2: 5 as "the mind of Christ." To imitate him, to follow him in discipleship, is therefore to keep the Torah, which has been fulfilled in him once and for all. Thus the Sinai covenant is indeed superseded. But once what was provisional in it has been swept away, we see what is truly definitive in it.

The Character of the Covenant

*I*t belongs to God's nature to love what he has created; so it belongs to his nature to bind himself and, in doing so, to go all the way to the cross. Thus, as the Bible sees it, the unconditional nature of God's action results in a genuine two-sidedness: the testament becomes a covenant. The Church Fathers described this novel two-sidedness, which arises from faith in Christ as the fulfiller of the promises, as the "incarnation of God" and the "divinization of man." God binds himself by giving Scripture as the binding word of promise, but he goes beyond this by binding himself, in his own existence, to the human creature by assuming human nature. Conversely, this means that man's primal dream comes true, and man becomes "like God": in this exchange of natures, the unconditional nature of the divine covenant has become a definitively two-sided relationship... When we say that man is the image of God, it means that he is a being designed for relationship; it means that, in and through all his relationships, he seeks that relation which is the ground of his existence. In this context, covenant would be the response to man's imaging of God; it would show us who we are and who God is. And for God, since he is entirely relationship, covenant would not be something external in history, apart from his being, but the manifestation of his self, the "radiance of his countenance."

The Certitude behind Mission

he final word of the Risen Lord to his disciples is a word of mission to the ends of the earth: "Go therefore and make disciples of all nations, baptizing them... [and] teaching them to observe all that I have commanded you" (Mt 28: 19f.; cf. Acts 1: 8). Christianity entered the world in the consciousness of a universal commission. The believers in Jesus Christ knew, from the first moment on, that they had the duty of handing on their faith to all men; they saw in their faith something that did not belong to them alone, something to which, rather, everyone could lay claim. It would have been utterly faithless not to carry what they had received to the farthest corner of the earth. It was not the drive to power that launched Christian universalism but the certitude of having received the saving knowledge and the redeeming love to which all people have a claim and for which, in the inmost depths of their being, they are waiting. The mission was regarded, not as the acquisition of people for their own sphere of domination, but as the passing on, as a matter of obligation, of something meant for everyone and of which everyone stood in need.

Witness to a Person

The Gospels agree in mentioning that the call of the Apostles marked the first steps of Jesus' ministry. They were men who were waiting for the kingdom of God, anxious to know the Messiah whose coming had been proclaimed as imminent. It was enough for John the Baptist to point out Jesus to them as the Lamb of God (cf. Jn 1: 36) to inspire in them the desire for a personal encounter with the Teacher. This is how the Apostles' adventure began, as an encounter of people who are open to one another. For the disciples, it was the beginning of a direct acquaintance with the Teacher, seeing where he was staying and starting to get to know him. Indeed, they were not to proclaim an idea, but to witness to a person. Before being sent out to preach, they had to "be" with Jesus (cf. Mk 3: 14), establishing a personal relationship with him. On this basis, evangelization was to be no more than the proclamation of what they felt and an invitation to enter into the mystery of communion with Christ (cf. 1 Jn 1: 1-3). Thus, the Twelve, taken on to share in the same mission as Jesus, cooperate with the Pastor of the last times, also seeking out the lost sheep of the house of Israel, that is, addressing the people of the promise whose reunion is the sign of salvation for all peoples, the beginning of the universalization of the Covenant. The Lord's command to gather the peoples together in the unity of his love still continues. This is our hope and also our mandate: to contribute to this universality, to this true unity in the riches of cultures, in communion with our true Lord Jesus Christ.

The Truth of Scripture

To interpret Scripture theologically means not only to listen to the historical authors whom it juxtaposes, even opposes, but to seek the one voice of the whole, to seek the inner identity that sustains the whole and binds it together. A purely historical method attempts to distill the historical moment of genesis, thereby setting it apart from all others and fixing it. Theological exegesis, while not displacing such a historical approach from its proper terrain, nonetheless does transcend it. The moment does not exist in isolation. It is part of a whole, and I do not really understand even this part until I understand it together with the whole… Scripture is interpreted by Scripture… The reading of Scripture as a unity thus logically entails a second principle. It means reading it as something present, not only in order to learn about what was once the case or what people once thought, but to learn what is true. This, too, is an aim that a strictly historical exegesis cannot directly pursue. Such an exegesis focuses, after all, on the past moment of the genesis of the text and therefore necessarily reads it in relation to its prior history… The question of truth is a naive, unscientific question. And yet, it is the real question of the Bible as such… The question is meaningful only if the Bible itself is something present, if a subject that is present speaks out of it, and if this subject stands apart from all other living historical subjects because it is bound up with the truth and, therefore, can convey knowledge of the truth in human speech.

OCTOBER 30

The Creating Reason is Love

*I*t is important to be attentive to the Lord's gestures on our journey. He speaks to us through events, through people, through encounters; it is necessary to be attentive to all of this. It is necessary to enter into real friendship with Jesus in a personal relationship with him and not to know who Jesus is only from others or from books, but to live an ever deeper personal relationship with Jesus, where we can begin to understand what he is asking of us… The more we can delve into the world with our intelligence, the more clearly the plan of creation appears. In the end to reach the definitive question I would say: God exists or he does not exist. There are only two options. Either one recognizes the priority of reason, of creative Reason that is at the beginning of all things and is the principle of all things — the priority of reason is also the priority of freedom — or one holds the priority of the irrational, inasmuch as everything that functions on our earth and in our lives would be only accidental, marginal, an irrational result — reason would be a product of irrationality. One cannot ultimately "prove" either project, but the great option of Christianity is the option for rationality and for the priority of reason. This seems to me to be an excellent option, which shows us that behind everything is a great Intelligence to which we can entrust ourselves… Therefore, we can confidently work out a vision of the world based on this priority of reason, on this trust that the creating Reason is love and that this love is God.

What Hell is Like

The path we follow toward genuine loving leads by way of losing oneself and through all the affliction of an exodus. Thus along the way lie all those temptations to get there more quickly, to accept substitutes. Only later do we realize that these substitutes bring only enormous disappointment and will plunge us afterward into unbearable loneliness, into the frustration of an absolutely empty existence. They are in fact images of hell. For if we ask ourselves what *being damned* really means, it is this: taking no pleasure in anything any more, liking nothing and no one, and being liked by no one. Being robbed of any capacity for loving and excluded from the sphere in which loving is possible — that is absolute emptiness, in which a person exists in contradiction to his own nature, and his life is totally ruined. If, then, the essential characteristic of man is his likeness to God, his capacity for love, then humanity as a whole and each of us individually can only survive where there is love and where we are taught the way to this love. We come back to Christ: the saving act of Christ consists of making comprehensible to us the fact that God loves us. He brings this home to each of us, and by his way of the cross he accompanies each of us along the path of losing ourselves. And by transforming the law of love into the gift of love, he overcomes that greatest loneliness of all, the state of being unredeemed.

November

The Saints as Constellations

*T*he great feasts that structure the year of faith are feasts of Christ and precisely as such are ordered toward the one God who revealed himself to Moses in the burning bush and chose Israel as the confessor of faith in his uniqueness. In addition to the sun, which is the image of Christ, there is the moon, which has no light of its own but shines with a brightness that comes from the sun. This is a sign to us that we men are in constant need of a "little" light, whose hidden light helps us to know and love the light of the Creator, God one and triune. That is why the feasts of the saints from earliest times have formed part of the Christian year. We have already encountered Mary, whose person is so closely interwoven with the mystery of Christ that the development of the Christmas cycle inevitably introduced a Marian note into the Church's year. The Marian dimension of the christological feasts was made visible. Then, in addition, come the commemorations of the Apostles and martyrs and, finally, the memorials of the saints of every century. One might say that the saints are, so to speak, new Christian constellations, in which the richness of God's goodness is reflected. Their light, coming from God, enables us to know better the interior richness of God's great light, which we cannot comprehend in the refulgence of its glory.

The Role of Purgatory

With regard to turning out right, which is what we all hope for despite all our failures, purgatory plays an important part here. There will be few people whose lives are pure and fulfilled in all respects. And, we would hope, there will be few people whose lives have become an irredeemable and total No. For the most part, the longing for good has remained, despite many breakdowns, in some sense determinative. God can pick up the broken pieces and make something of them. In any case, we need a final cleansing, a cleansing by fire, to be exact, in which the gaze of Christ, so to say, burns us free from everything, and only under this purifying gaze are we, as it were, fit to be with God and able, then, to make our home with him… I think it is something very human. I would go so far as to say that if there was no purgatory, then we would have to invent it, for who would dare say of himself that he was able to stand directly before God. And yet we don't want to be, to use an image from Scripture, "a pot that turned out wrong," that has to be thrown away; we want to be able to be put right. Purgatory basically means that God can put the pieces back together again. That he can cleanse us in such a way that we are able to be with him and can stand there in the fullness of life. Purgatory strips off from one person what is unbearable and from another the inability to bear certain things, so that in each of them a pure heart is revealed, and we can see that we all belong together in one enormous symphony of being.

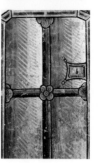

What Heaven Means

*I*f heaven means being in Christ, then it also means co-being with all those who together form the one Body of Christ. There is no isolation in heaven. It is the open society of the saints and, consequently, also the fulfillment of all human togetherness, not in competition with the Beatific Vision, but rather in consequence thereof. Christian veneration of the saints depends on this knowledge, not on a mythical omniscience about the saints, but simply on the inviolable openness of every member of the whole Body of Christ to every other member, which presumes the unlimited closeness of love and is sure of finding God in everyone and everyone in God. There results from this an anthropological component. The integration of the I into the Body of Christ, its being at the disposal of the Lord and of everyone else, is not a dissolution of the I but its purification, which, at the same time, fulfills its highest potential. That is why heaven is different for each individual. Everyone sees God in his own way; everyone receives the love of the whole Body in his own unalterable uniqueness.

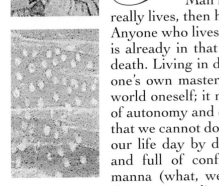

The Meaning of the Manna

he manna in the desert was to show that man can live only in dependence on God. Man is to learn to live by God, for then he really lives, then he has eternal life, for God is eternal. Anyone who lives with him and in dependence on him is already in that real life which reaches out beyond death. Living in dependence on God means not being one's own master, not wanting to take charge of the world oneself; it means saying good-bye to the dream of autonomy and of being one's own boss, recognizing that we cannot do it on our own and learning to accept our life day by day from his hands, without anxiety and full of confidence. This core meaning of the manna (what, we might say, it actually *is*), namely, that we are to live in dependence on God, not on ourselves, becomes utterly concrete. We can live by God because God now lives for us. We can live by God because he has made himself one of us, because he himself, as it were, has become our bread. We can live by God because he gives himself to us, not only as the Word, but as the Body that is given up for us and is given to us, ever new, in the sacrament... Living by God means first of all believing, it means being in touch with him, entering into an inner harmony with him... Believing means living by the God whose Body is in the Church; it means being nourished by this embodied God who encounters us in the sacraments and who has ultimately become so incarnate that in the Eucharist he gives himself to us as Body, so that we can enter into his life: just as he lives for us, so we live by him and for him.

Christian Experience

hristian experience begins in the everyday world of communal experience. Today, the interior space in which Church is experienced is, for many, a foreign world. Nevertheless, this world continues to be a possibility, and it will be the task of religious education to open doors on the experiential space — Church — and to encourage people to take an interest in this kind of experience. When people share the same faith, when they pray, celebrate rejoice, suffer, and live together, Church becomes "community" and thus a real living space that enables humanity to experience faith as a life-bringing force in daily life and in the crises of existence. One who truly believes, who opens himself to the maturing effects of faith, begins to be a light for others; he becomes a bulwark where others can find help. The saints, as the living models of a faith that has been tried and found steadfast, of transcendence that has been experienced and confirmed, are, so to speak, themselves the living spaces into which one can turn, in which faith as experience is simultaneously stored up, anthropologically conditioned, and approximated to our life. Specifically Christian experience, in the intrinsic meaning of the word, can ultimately grow by its gradually maturing and deepening participation in such experiences — this is what the language of the Psalms and of the New Testament calls "tasting the heavenly gifts" (Ps 34: 9; 1 Pt 2: 3; Heb 6: 4). By it one touches reality itself and is no longer merely a "second-hand" believer.

The Church as Sacrament

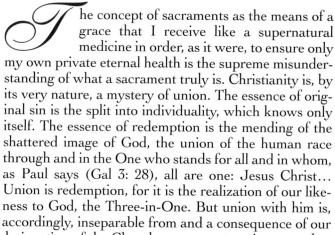

he concept of sacraments as the means of a grace that I receive like a supernatural medicine in order, as it were, to ensure only my own private eternal health is the supreme misunderstanding of what a sacrament truly is. Christianity is, by its very nature, a mystery of union. The essence of original sin is the split into individuality, which knows only itself. The essence of redemption is the mending of the shattered image of God, the union of the human race through and in the One who stands for all and in whom, as Paul says (Gal 3: 28), all are one: Jesus Christ... Union is redemption, for it is the realization of our likeness to God, the Three-in-One. But union with him is, accordingly, inseparable from and a consequence of our own unity... The designation of the Church as a sacrament is opposed to an individualistic understanding of the sacraments as a means of grace; it teaches us to understand the sacraments as the fulfillment of the life of the Church; in doing so, it enriches the teaching about grace: grace is always the beginning of union... The designation of the Church as a sacrament thus deepens and clarifies the concept of Church and offers a response to contemporary man's search for the unity of mankind: the Church is not merely an external society of believers; by her nature, she is a liturgical community; she is most truly Church when she celebrates the Eucharist and makes present the redemptive love of Jesus Christ, which, as love, frees men from their loneliness and leads them to one another by leading them to God.

Why the Church is There

Where God is, there is heaven: there, even in the tribulations of our daily living, life becomes bright. Christianity is not a complicated philosophy that has in the meanwhile also become obsolete, not a package of dogmas and rules beyond being grasped as a whole. Christian faith is being touched by God and witnessing to him. That is why Paul, on the Areopagos, described his task and his intention as wishing to make known to the Athenians, whom he addressed as representative of the peoples of the world, the unknown God — the God who had emerged from his hiddenness, who had made himself known, and who could therefore be proclaimed by him (Acts 17: 16-34). The reference to the expression "the unknown god" presupposes that man, in not knowing, still does know about God in some way; it responds to the situation of the agnostic, who does not know God personally and yet cannot exclude him. It presupposes that man is in some sense waiting for God and yet cannot of his own resources reach him, so that he is in need of preaching, of the hand that helps him over into the sphere of his presence. Thus we can say: the Church is there so that God, the living God, may be made known — so that man may learn to live with God, live in his sight and in fellowship with him. The Church is there to prevent the advance of hell upon earth and to make the earth fit to live in through the light of God. On the basis of God's presence, and only through him, is it humanized.

The Primacy of God Alive in the Church

*K*nowledge of God may be compared to the knowledge of someone in love: it concerns me as a whole; it also demands my will; and it comes to nothing if it does not attain this all-embracing assent... The Church is not there for her own sake. She cannot be like an association that, in difficult circumstances, is simply trying to keep its head above water. She has a task to perform for the world, for mankind. The only reason she has to survive is because her disappearance would drag humanity into the whirlpool of the eclipse of God and, thus, into the eclipse, indeed the destruction, of all that is human. We are not fighting for our own survival; we know that we have been entrusted with a mission that lays upon us a responsibility for everyone. That is why the Church has to measure herself, and be measured by others, by the extent to which the presence of God, the knowledge of him, and the acceptance of his will are alive within her. A church that was merely an organization pursuing its own ends would be the caricature of a Church. To the extent to which she is revolving around herself and looks only to the aims necessary for maintaining herself, she is rendering herself redundant and is in decline, even if she disposes of considerable means and skillful management. She can live and be fruitful only if the primacy of God is alive within her. The Church is there, not for her own sake, but for mankind. She is there so that the world may become a sphere for God's presence, the sphere of the covenant between God and men.

The Church as Pilgrim Fellowship

*G*od has come to meet man. He has shown him his face, opened up his heart to him... The Church has to make him more widely known; she has to bring men to Christ and Christ to men, so as to bring God to them and them to God. Christ is not just some great man or other with a significant religious experience; he is God, God who became man to establish a bridge between man and God and so that man may become truly himself. Anyone who sees Christ only as a great religious person is not truly seeing him. The path from Christ and to Christ has to arrive at the point at which the Gospel of Mark ends up, at the confession of the Roman centurion before the Crucified One: "Truly this man was the Son of God!" (15: 39). It has to arrive at the point where the Gospel of John ends up, in the confession of Thomas: "My Lord and my God!" (20: 28). It has to stride along the great arch that the Gospel of Matthew sets up from the Annunciation story to the missionary speech of the Risen One. In the story of the Annunciation, Jesus is heralded as the "God with us" (1: 23). And the final saying in the Gospel takes up this message: "Behold, I am with you always, to the close of the age" (28: 20). In order to know Christ, we have to join in following the path along which the Gospels lead us. The great and central task of the Church today is, as it ever was, to show people this path and to offer a pilgrim fellowship in walking it. We know God, not simply with our understanding, but also with our will and with our heart. Therefore the knowledge of God, the knowledge of Christ, is a path that demands the involvement of the whole of our being.

The Rationality of Faith and the Church

*W*ithout God, the world cannot be bright, and the Church is serving the world by the fact that God lives within her and that she is transparent for him and carries him to mankind. And thereby we come at last to the quite practical question: How does that happen? How can we ourselves recognize God, and how can we bring him to other people? I think that for this purpose, several different ways must be interwoven. First there is the way that Paul adopted on the Areopagos — the reference to the capacity to know God that is buried within men, appealing to reason… That is one task the Church has today: to revive the argument about the rationality of belief or unbelief. Belief is not an opponent of reason, but the advocate of its true stature… The struggle for the new presence of the rationality of faith is what I regard as an urgent task for the Church in our century. Faith should not withdraw into its own shell, behind a decision for which it gives no further reason; it should not shrink into being no more than a kind of system of symbols, in which people can make themselves at home but which would ultimately remain a random choice among other visions of life and the world. It needs the wide realm of open reason; it needs the confession of faith in the Creator God… The appeal to reason is a great task for the Church, especially today, for whenever faith and reason part company, both become diseased.

Beholding the Lamb

We climb up the mountain of time, bearing with us the instruments of our own death. At first the goal is far distant. We do not think of it; the present is enough… But the longer it grows, the more unavoidable the question becomes: Where is it going? What does it all mean? We look with apprehension at the signs of death which, up to now, we had not noticed, and the fear rises within us that perhaps the whole of life is only a variation of death; that we have been deceived, and that life is actually not a gift at all but an imposition. Then the strange reply, "God will provide," sounds more like an excuse than an explanation. Where this view predominates, where talk of "God" is no longer believable, humor dies. In such a case man has nothing to laugh about anymore; all that is left is a cruel sarcasm or that rage against God and the world with which we are all acquainted. But the person who has seen the Lamb— Christ on the cross — knows that God *has* provided… All we can see is — like Isaac — the Lamb, of whom the Apostle Peter says that he was destined before the foundation of the world (1 Pt 1: 20). But this sight of the Lamb — the crucified Christ — is in fact our glimpse of heaven, of what God has eternally provided for us. In this Lamb we actually do glimpse heaven, and we see God's gentleness, which is neither indifference nor weakness but power of the highest order. It is in this way, and only thus, that we see the mysteries of creation and catch a little of the song of the angels… Since we see the Lamb, we can laugh and give thanks; we too see from him what worship is.

Church and Society

$\mathscr{T}$he Church must accept her responsibility for society in various ways, not least by attempting to make herself comprehensible; she must give insight into what belongs to God and into the moral sphere that results from this. She must convince, for it is only by convincing that she opens up space for what has been entrusted to her; and this can be made accessible only along the path of freedom, which means via reason, will, and emotion. The Church must be ready to suffer. She must prepare space for the divine, not through power but through spirit, not through institutional strength but through witness, through love, life, and suffering: and in this way she must help society to find its moral identity. History is marked by the confrontation between love and the inability to love, that devastation of the soul that comes when the only values man is able to recognize at all as values and realities are quantifiable values. The capacity to love, that is, the capacity to wait in patience for what is not under one's own control and to let oneself receive this as a gift, is suffocated by the speedy fulfillments in which I am dependent on no one but in which I am never obliged to emerge from my own self and thus never find the path into my own self. This destruction of the capacity to love gives birth to lethal boredom. It is the poisoning of man. If he were to have his way, man would be destroyed, and the world with him. In this drama, we should not hesitate to oppose the omnipotence of the quantitative and to take up our position on the side of love. This is the decision that the present hour demands of us.

The Church is Alive

The Church is alive — she is alive because Christ is alive, because he is truly risen... It is not a matter of indifference that so many people are living in the desert. And there are so many kinds of desert... The Church as a whole and all her pastors, like Christ, must set out to lead people out of the desert, towards the place of life, towards friendship with the Son of God, towards the One who gives us life, and life in abundance... It is really so: the purpose of our lives is to reveal God to men. And only where God is seen does life truly begin. Only when we meet the living God in Christ do we know what life is. We are not some casual and meaningless product of evolution. Each of us is the result of a thought of God. Each of us is willed, each of us is loved, each of us is necessary. There is nothing more beautiful than to be surprised by the Gospel, by the encounter with Christ. There is nothing more beautiful than to know him and to speak to others of our friendship with him... If we let Christ enter fully into our lives, if we open ourselves totally to him, are we not afraid that he might take something away from us? Are we not perhaps afraid to give up something significant, something unique, something that makes life so beautiful? Do we not then risk ending up diminished and deprived of our freedom? No! If we let Christ into our lives, we lose nothing, nothing, absolutely nothing of what makes life free, beautiful and great. No!... Only in this friendship is the great potential of human existence truly revealed. Only in this friendship do we experience beauty and liberation.

The Church is God's People

kklesia means *called out*, those who are called
out. The word in its technical sense refers to
the "assembly," and in the Greek-speaking area
people thought of the democratic assemblies of that
time. But in Christian usage its reference was to the
assembly at Sinai, the assembly of the people of Israel.
In that way it refers to "those called together by God,"
those who have gathered together with him, who
belong to God and who know that he is in their midst.
The underlying notion is that the Church has been
appropriated by God to be his particular possession in
the world, something that especially belongs to him,
the living temple. The Christians took quite seriously
the idea that God does not live in stone but is alive.
Those people in whom he is alive and who belong to him, accordingly,
form his true temple. The expression *people of God* also signifies belonging to God in a special way — and living on the basis of being owned by
him.

God Comes to People through People

*P*art of the essence of Christianity — and this is included in the concept of the Church — is that our relationship to God is not just an inner one, one made up of my "I" and his "Thou," but is also a matter of being spoken to, of being led. A meeting is part of every path to conversion. The Church is there so that people who have searched for the door and found it can be in her. Among all the variety of temperaments, there will always be someone who suits me and who has the right word to say to me. As human beings we are there so that God can come to people by way of other people. He always comes to people through people. So we, too, always come to him through other people who are being led by him, in whom he himself meets us and opens us up to him. If we could lift ourselves up to the ultimate degree simply by reading Holy Scripture, then this would be just another philosophical movement, without this element of community that is such a vital element in faith.

Eucharistic Fellowship

The eucharistic fellowship of the Church is not a collectivity, in which fellowship is achieved by leveling down to the lowest common denominator, but fellowship is created precisely by our each being ourself. It does not rest on the suppression of the self, on collectivization, but arises through our truly setting out, with our whole self, and entering into this new fellowship of the Lord. That is the only way that something other than collectivization can come about; the only way that a true attitude of turning toward each other, one that reaches down to the roots and into the heart and up to the highest level of a person, can develop... What we receive is a person. But this Person is the Lord Jesus Christ, both God and man... We are in danger of only seeing the man Jesus and forgetting that in him, as he gives himself to us in bodily form, we are at the same time coming into contact with the living God. Yet because this is so, Communion is therefore always simultaneously adoration.

Communion and Adoration

*I*n any genuine human love there is an element of bowing down before the God-given dignity of the other person, who is in the image of God. Even genuine human love cannot mean that we have the other person all to ourselves and possess him; it includes our reverential recognition of something sublime and unique in this other person, whom we can never entirely possess, our bowing down and thus becoming one with him. In our Communion with Jesus Christ this attains a new level, since it inevitably goes beyond any human partnership. The Word of the Lord as our "partner" explains a great deal but leaves much else undisclosed. We are not on the same footing. He is the wholly other; it is the majesty of the living God that comes to us with him. Uniting ourselves with him means submitting and opening ourselves up to his greatness... Augustine says in one place, in a sermon to his new communicants: No one can receive Communion without first adoring... What we are told about the monks of Cluny, around the year one thousand, is particularly striking. Whenever they went to receive Communion, they took their shoes off. They knew that the burning bush was here, the mystery before which Moses, in the desert, sank to his knees. The form may change, but what has to remain is the spirit of adoration, which signifies a genuine act of stepping outside ourselves, communication, freeing ourselves from our own selves and thereby in fact discovering human fellowship.

The Paralysis of Sin

The paralyzed man is the image of every human being whom sin prevents from moving about freely, from walking on the path of good and from giving the best of himself. Indeed, by taking root in the soul, evil binds the person with the ties of falsehood, anger, envy, and other sins and gradually paralyzes him. Jesus, therefore, scandalizing the scribes who were present, first said: "…your sins are forgiven." Only later, to demonstrate the authority to forgive sins that God had conferred upon him, did he add: "Stand up! Pick up your mat and go home" (Mk 2: 11), and heals the man completely. The message is clear: human beings, paralyzed by sin, need God's mercy which Christ came to give to them so that, their hearts healed, their whole life might flourish anew. Today too, humanity is marked by sin which prevents it from rapidly progressing in those values of brotherhood, justice, and peace that with solemn declarations it had resolved to practice. Why? What is blocking it? What is paralyzing this integral development? We know well that there are many historical reasons for this and that the problem is complex. But the Word of God invites us to have a gaze of faith and to trust, like the people who were carrying the paralytic, that Jesus alone is capable of true healing… Only God's love can renew the human heart, and only if he heals the heart of paralyzed humanity can it get up and walk. The love of God is the true force that renews the world.

The Communion of the Church

The Church, a community gathered by the Son of God who came in the flesh, will live on through the passing times, building up and nourishing the communion in Christ and in the Holy Spirit to which all are called and in which they can experience the salvation given by the Father. This life of fellowship with God and with one another is the proper goal of Gospel proclamation, the goal of conversion to Christianity. Wherever communion with God, which is communion with the Father, the Son, and the Holy Spirit, is destroyed, the root and source of our communion with one another is destroyed. And wherever we do not live communion among ourselves, communion with the Trinitarian God is not alive and true either. Communion is also a gift with very real consequences. It lifts us from our loneliness, from being closed in on ourselves, and makes us sharers in the love that unites us to God and to one another. It is easy to understand how great this gift is if we only think of the fragmentation and conflicts that afflict relations between individuals, groups, and entire peoples. "Communion" is truly the Good News, the remedy given to us by the Lord to fight the loneliness that threatens everyone today, the precious gift that makes us feel welcomed and beloved by God, in the unity of his People gathered in the name of the Trinity. Thus, the Church, despite all the human frailties that mark her historical profile, is revealed as a marvelous creation of love, brought into being to bring Christ close to every man and every woman who truly desire to meet him, until the end of time.

The Profound Meaning of Being a Priest

*F*aith in Jesus, Son of the living God, is the means through which, time and again, we can take hold of Jesus' hand and in which he takes our hands and guides us. The Lord makes us priests his friends; he entrusts everything to us; he entrusts himself to us, so that we can speak with him himself — *in persona Christi capitis*. What trust! He has truly delivered himself into our hands. I no longer call you servants but friends. This is the profound meaning of being a priest: becoming the friend of Jesus Christ. For this friendship we must daily recommit ourselves. This means that we should know Jesus in an increasingly personal way, listening to him, living together with him, staying with him. The core of the priesthood is being friends of Jesus Christ. Only in this way can we truly speak *in persona Christi*, even if our inner remoteness from Christ cannot jeopardize the validity of the Sacrament. Being a friend of Jesus, being a priest, means being a man of prayer. In this way we recognize him and emerge from the ignorance of simple servants. We thus learn to live, suffer and act with him and for him. Being a priest means becoming an ever closer friend of Jesus Christ with the whole of our existence. The world needs God — the God of Jesus Christ, the God who made himself flesh and blood, who loved us to the point of dying for us, who rose and created within himself room for man. This God must live in us and we in him. This is our priestly call: only in this way can our action as priests bear fruit. Jesus assumed our flesh; let us give him our own. In this way he can come into the world and transform it.

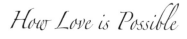

How Love is Possible

*L*ove of neighbor is thus shown to be possible in the way proclaimed by the Bible, by Jesus. It consists in the very fact that, in God and with God, I love even the person whom I do not like or even know. This can only take place on the basis of an intimate encounter with God, an encounter which has become a communion of will, even affecting my feelings. Then I learn to look on this other person not simply with my eyes and my feelings, but from the perspective of Jesus Christ. His friend is my friend. Going beyond exterior appearances, I perceive in others an interior desire for a sign of love, of concern. This I can offer them not only through the organizations intended for such purposes, accepting it perhaps as a political necessity. Seeing with the eyes of Christ, I can give to others much more than their outward necessities; I can give them the look of love which they crave… If I have no contact whatsoever with God in my life, then I cannot see in the other anything more than the other, and I am incapable of seeing in him the image of God. But if in my life I fail completely to heed others, solely out of a desire to be "devout" and to perform my "religious duties," then my relationship with God will also grow arid. It becomes merely "proper," but loveless. Only my readiness to encounter my neighbor and to show him love makes me sensitive to God as well. Only if I serve my neighbor can my eyes be opened to what God does for me and how much he loves me.

Praise and Music

homas says that through the praise of God man ascends to God. Praise itself is a movement, a path; it is more than understanding, knowing, and doing — it is an "ascent," a way of reaching him who dwells amid the praises of the angels. Thomas mentioned another factor: this ascent draws man away from what is opposed to God. Anyone who has ever experienced the transforming power of great liturgy, great art, great music, will know this. Thomas adds that the sound of musical praise leads us and others to a sense of reverence. It awakens the inner man, as Augustine had discovered in Milan. With Augustine the academic, a man who had come to appreciate Christianity as a philosophy but was uneasy about the Church herself, which seemed to have a lot of vulgarity about her, it was the singing Church which gave him a shattering experience, penetrating the whole man, and which led him forward on the way to the Church. From this point of view, the other, pedagogical aspect, the "stimulating of others to praise God," becomes meaningful and intelligible, particularly when we recall what "pedagogy" meant for the ancients, namely, a leading to one's real nature, a process of redemption and liberation.

Judgment and Hope

*I*t is not simply — as one might expect — God, the infinite, the unknown, the eternal, who judges. On the contrary, he has handed the judgment over to one who, as man, is our brother. It is not a stranger who judges us but he whom we know in faith. The judge will not advance to meet us as the other, but as one of us, who knows human existence from inside and has suffered. Thus over the judgment glows the dawn of hope; it is not only the day of wrath but also the second coming of our Lord. One is reminded of the mighty vision of Christ with which the Book of Revelation begins (1: 9-19): the seer sinks down as though dead before this being full of sinister power. But the Lord lays his hand on him and says to him as once in the days when they were crossing the Lake of Gennesaret in wind and storm: "Fear not, it is I" (1: 17). The Lord of all power is the Jesus whose comrade the visionary had once been in faith. The Creed's article about the judgment transfers this very idea to our meeting with the judge of the world. On that day of fear the Christian will be allowed to see in happy wonder that he "to whom all power is given in heaven and on earth" (Mt 28: 18) was the companion in faith of his days on earth, and it is as if through the words of the Creed Jesus were already laying his hands on him and saying: Be without fear, it is I. Perhaps the problem of the intertwining of justice and mercy can be answered in no more beautiful way than that it is the idea that stands in the background of our Creed.

Christ's Gaze upon the World

*E*ven now, the compassionate "gaze" of Christ continues to fall upon individuals and peoples. He watches them, knowing that the divine "plan" includes their call to salvation. Jesus knows the perils that put this plan at risk, and he is moved with pity for the crowds. He chooses to defend them from the wolves even at the cost of his own life. The gaze of Jesus embraces individuals and multitudes, and he brings them all before the Father, offering himself as a sacrifice of expiation. Enlightened by this Paschal truth, the Church knows that if we are to promote development in its fullness, our own "gaze" upon mankind has to be measured against that of Christ. In fact, it is quite impossible to separate the response to people's material and social needs from the fulfillment of the profound desires of their hearts. This has to be emphasized all the more in today's rapidly changing world, in which our responsibility towards the poor emerges with ever greater clarity and urgency. Thus, the "gaze" of Christ upon the crowd impels us to affirm the true content of this "complete humanism" that consists in the fully-rounded development of the whole man and of all men. For this reason, the primary contribution that the Church offers to the development of mankind and peoples does not consist merely in material means or technical solutions. Rather, it involves the proclamation of the truth of Christ, who educates consciences and teaches the authentic dignity of the person and of work; it means the promotion of a culture that truly responds to all the questions of humanity.

Christ the King

What is really remarkable is that God consented to Israel's desire for a king and even provided an opportunity for that kingship to be renewed and fulfilled. Jesus was himself the son of David, the king. God entered mankind in him and espoused the cause of mankind in him. If we look more closely at this question, we can see that it is the fundamental form of God's activity with mankind. He has no rigid plan that he has at all costs to carry out. On the contrary, he has many different ways of seeking man out and finding him. He even makes man's devious and wrong ways into ways leading to him. This is clear, for example, in the case of Adam, whose very sin was made a happy sin in the second Adam, Christ, and it is clear in all the twisted ways of human history. This, then, is God's kingship — a rule of love that seeks and finds man in ways that are always new. For us, this means a trust that cannot be shaken. God rules as king over us still and, what is more, he rules over each one of us. None of us should be afraid and none should capitulate. God can always be found. The pattern of our own lives should also be like this — we should always be available, never write anyone off, and try again and again to find others in the openness of our hearts. Our most important task is not to assert ourselves, but always to be ready to set off on the way to God and to each other. The feast of Christ the King is therefore not a feast of those who are subjugated, but a feast of those who know that they are in the hands of the one who writes straight on crooked lines.

Followers of the King

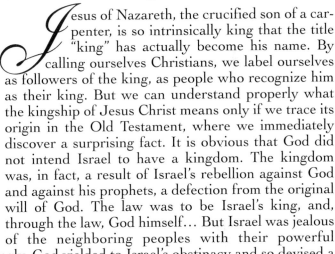

Jesus of Nazareth, the crucified son of a carpenter, is so intrinsically king that the title "king" has actually become his name. By calling ourselves Christians, we label ourselves as followers of the king, as people who recognize him as their king. But we can understand properly what the kingship of Jesus Christ means only if we trace its origin in the Old Testament, where we immediately discover a surprising fact. It is obvious that God did not intend Israel to have a kingdom. The kingdom was, in fact, a result of Israel's rebellion against God and against his prophets, a defection from the original will of God. The law was to be Israel's king, and, through the law, God himself... But Israel was jealous of the neighboring peoples with their powerful kings... Surprisingly, God yielded to Israel's obstinacy and so devised a new kind of kingship for them. The son of David, the king, is Jesus; in him God entered humanity and espoused it to himself... God does not have a fixed plan that he must carry out; on the contrary, he has many different ways of finding man and even of turning his wrong ways into right ways. We can see that, for instance, in the case of Adam, whose fault became a happy fault, and we see it again in all the twisted ways of history. This, then, is God's kingship — a love that is impregnable and an inventiveness that finds man by ways that are always new... God's kingship means that we must have an unshakeable confidence... No one has reason to fear or to capitulate. God can always be found.

NOVEMBER 27

Salvation and the Unity of the Good

*H*eaven begins on earth. Salvation in the world to come presumes a righteous life in this world. Thus one cannot simply ask who will get to heaven and suppose that this disposes of the matter of heaven. We have to ask what heaven is and how it comes upon earth. Future salvation must make its mark in a way of life that makes a person "human" here and thus capable of relating to God… Salvation begins with man becoming righteous in this world — something that always includes the twin poles of the individual and society. There are kinds of behavior that can never serve man's growth in righteousness and others that are always a part of man's righteousness. That means that salvation does not lie in religions as such, but it is connected to them, inasmuch as, and to the extent that, they lead man toward the one good, toward the search for God, for truth, and for love. The question of salvation therefore always carries within it an element of the criticism of religion, just as, contrariwise, it can build a positive relationship to religions. It has in any case to do with the unity of the good, with the unity of what is true — with the unity of God and man.

Eternal Life

Eternal life is not simply what comes afterward, something about which we can form no notion at all. Because it is a new quality of existence, it can be already present in the midst of this earthly life and its fleeting temporality as something new and different and greater, albeit in an imperfect and fragmentary fashion. But the dividing line between eternal and temporal life is by no means simply of a chronological order: so that the years before death would be temporal life; the endless time afterward would be eternal life — as we generally think. But because eternity is not just endless time but another level of being, such a merely chronological distinction cannot be right. Eternal life is there, in the midst of time, wherever we come face to face with God; through the contemplation of the living God, it can become something like the firm base of our soul. Like a great love, it can no longer be taken from us by any change or chance; rather, it is an indestructible heart from which spring the courage and the joy to go on, even when exterior things are painful and hard... When God touches his soul man learns to see aright... "This is eternal life, that they know you the only true God, and Jesus Christ whom you have sent," says the Lord in the Gospel of John (17: 3)... Wherever such an encounter takes place, there is eternal life. The dividing line between temporal life and eternal life runs right through the midst of our temporal life.

How to Make Sense of Eternity

ternal life is that mode of living, in the midst of our present earthly life, which is untouched by death because it reaches out beyond death. Eternal life in the midst of time. If we live in this way, then the hope of eternal fellowship with God will become the expectation that characterizes our existence, because some conception of its reality develops for us, and the beauty of it transforms us from within. Thus it becomes apparent that there is in this face-to-face encounter with God nothing selfish, no withdrawal into a merely private realm, but that very liberation from the self which alone makes any sense of eternity. An endless succession of moments would be unbearable; when our existence is gathered up into the single gaze of the love of God, this not only transforms endlessness into eternity, into God's today; at the same time it means fellowship with all those who have been accepted by that same love. In the kingdom of the Son of his love, as John Chrysostom once expressed it, there are no more "cold words [like] 'mine' and 'yours.'" Because we all share in God's love, we belong to each other. Where God is all in all, we are all in everyone and all in ourselves, are in one Body, in the Body of Christ, in which the joy of one member is the joy of all other members, as the suffering of one member was the suffering of all members… Eternal life, which takes its beginning in communion with God here and now, seizes this here and now and takes it up within the great expanse of true reality, which is no longer fragmented by the stream of time.

God Surrounds Us from Above

*L*ife shared with God, eternal life within temporal life, is possible because of God's living with us: Christ is God being here with us. In him God has time for us; he is God's time for us and thus at the same time the opening of time into eternity. God is no longer the distant and indeterminate God to whom no bridge will reach; he is the God at hand: the Body of the Son is the bridge for our souls. Through him, each single person's relationship with God has been blended together in his one relationship with God, so that turning one's gaze toward God is no longer a matter of turning one's gaze away from others and from the world, but a uniting of our gaze and of our being with the single gaze and the one being of the Son. Because he has descended right to the depths of the earth (Eph 4: 9f.), God is no longer merely a God up there, but God surrounds us from above, from below, and from within: he is all in all, and therefore all in all belongs to us: "All that is mine is yours." God's being "all in all" began with Christ's renunciation on the cross of what was properly his. It will be complete when the Son finally hands over to the Father the Kingdom, that is, in-gathered humanity and the creation that is carried with them (1 Cor 15: 28). That is why the purely private existence of the isolated self no longer exists, but "all that is mine is yours."

December

Advent Presence

"*A*dvent" does not mean "expectation," as some may think. It is a translation of the Greek word *parousia* which means "presence" or, more, accurately, "arrival," i.e., the beginning of a presence. In antiquity the word was a technical term for the presence of a king or ruler and also of the god being worshiped, who bestows his *parousia* on his devotees for a time. "Advent," then, means a presence begun, the presence being that of God. Advent reminds us, therefore, of two things: first, that God's presence in the world has already begun, that he is present though in a hidden manner; second, that his presence has only *begun* and is not yet full and complete, that it is in a state of development, of becoming and progressing toward its full form. His presence has already begun, and we, the faithful, are the ones through whom he wishes to be present in the world. Through our faith, hope, and love he wants his light to shine over and over again in the night of the world… That night is "today" whenever the "Word" again becomes "flesh" or genuine human reality. "The Christ child comes" in a real sense whenever human beings act out of authentic love for the Lord.

Advent Means Presence

"*A*dvent" is a Latin word that can be translated as "presence" or "coming." In the ancient world, it was a technical term, denoting the arrival of a person in office such as a king or an emperor. It could also indicate the coming of the deity, in which case the god's advent was his emerging from concealment and making his presence known in power or else having it solemnly celebrated in an act of worship. Christians took over this word in order to express their particular relationship with Jesus Christ. For them, he was and is the king who has entered this wretched province, the earth, and enables it to celebrate his visit. What Christians mean in general by this word "Advent," then, is: God is there. He has not withdrawn from the world. He has not left us alone. Even though we cannot see him or touch him as we can the things that surround us, he is still there and, what is more, he comes to us in many different ways. We have mentioned the word "visit" in this context. This word can be used in its happy, original, and almost literal sense of "going to see" a person, persons, or a place. It is, however, also used in the less pleasant sense of afflicting or punishing, when it is associated with such concepts as trouble, famine, plague, or illness. This word should there-fore enable us to see that something of the beauty of Advent can be found even in difficulty. Illness and suffering can therefore, like a great joy, also be a personal Advent — a visit by God who wants to enter my life and turn toward me.

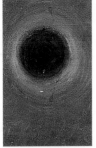

DECEMBER 3

Living as if There is God

*I*n his writings while in prison, Bonhoeffer once remarked that even the Christian must live today *quasi Deus non daretur* — as if there were no God. He must not involve God in the perplexities of his everyday life, but must assume responsibility himself for the course of that life. Personally, I would prefer to state this thought in exactly the opposite way: in practice, even one for whom the existence of God, the world of faith, has grown dim, should live today *quasi Deus esset* — *as if* God really exists. He should live subject to the reality of truth, which is not our creation, but our mistress. He should live under the standard of justice, which is not just a product of our own minds, but the norm by which we ourselves are measured. He should live subject to the love that awaits us and that loves even us. He should live under the challenge of eternity. In fact, one who consciously lets himself be formed by this concept will see that it is the only way that the human race can be saved. God — and he alone — is our salvation. This unprecedented truth, which we so long regarded as a scarcely tenable theory, has become the most practical formula for our present history. And one who — even if perhaps at first only hesitantly — entrusts himself to this difficult yet inescapable *as if*, who lives *as if* there were a God, will become ever more aware that this *as if* is the only reality. He will perceive its justification, its inner strength. And he will know profoundly and indelibly why Christianity is still necessary today as the genuinely Good News by which we are redeemed.

Togetherness with God

God is understood by some in the manner of Arius who thought that God cannot have any relationship outside of himself because only he is completely himself. Humans want to be such a god, one to whom everything flows and who gives nothing himself. This is why the true God is the real enemy, the competitor of those who have become inwardly blind in such a way. This is the real heart of their disease, for they then live a lie and are turned away from love, which is, also in the Trinity, an unconditional self-giving without limits… Today we are generally no longer capable of seeing that the matter of God is something most real, indeed, the true key to our deepest human needs… Indeed, there will be no cure if God is not recognized as the structural core of our whole existence. Only in togetherness with God, being with God, does human life become real life. Without him it remains below its threshold and destroys itself. Redemptive togetherness or union with God, however, is possible only in the one whom he sent and through whom he himself is a God-with-us. We cannot "construct" this togetherness. Christ is the life because he leads us into this union with God.

DECEMBER 5

Advent Waiting

One aspect of Advent is a waiting that is full of hope. In this, Advent enables us to understand the content and meaning of Christian time and of history as such... Man is always waiting in his life... Mankind has never been able to cease hoping for better times. Christians have always hoped that the Lord will always be present in history and that he will gather up all our tears and all our troubles so that everything will be explained and fulfilled in his kingdom. It becomes especially clear during a time of illness that man is always waiting. Every day we are waiting for a sign of improvement and in the end for a complete cure. At the same time, however, we discover how many different ways there are of waiting. When time itself is not filled with a present that is meaningful, waiting becomes unbearable. If we have to look forward to something that is not there now — if, in other words, we have nothing here and now and the present is completely empty, every second of our life seems too long. Waiting itself becomes too heavy a burden to bear, when we cannot be sure whether we really have anything at all to wait for. When, on the other hand, time itself is meaningful and every moment contains something especially valuable, our joyful anticipation of the greater experience that is still to come makes what we have in the present even more precious and we are carried by an invisible power beyond the present moment. Advent helps us to wait with precisely this kind of waiting. It is the essentially Christian form of waiting and hoping.

The Marks of Original Sin

The human being does not trust God. Tempted by the serpent, he harbors the suspicion that in the end, God takes something away from his life, that God is a rival who curtails our freedom and that we will be fully human only when we have cast him aside… The human being lives in the suspicion that God's love creates a dependence and that he must rid himself of this dependency if he is to be fully himself. Man does not want to receive his existence and the fullness of his life from God. He himself wants to obtain from the tree of knowledge the power to shape the world, to make himself a god, raising himself to God's level, and to overcome death and darkness with his own efforts. He does not want to rely on love that to him seems untrustworthy; he relies solely on his own knowledge since it confers power upon him. Rather than on love, he sets his sights on power, with which he desires to take his own life autonomously in hand. And in doing so, he trusts in deceit rather than in truth and thereby sinks with his life into emptiness, into death. Love is not dependence but a gift that makes us live… We live in the right way if we live in accordance with the truth of our being, and that is, in accordance with God's will. For God's will is not a law for the human being imposed from the outside and that constrains him, but the intrinsic measure of his nature, a measure that is engraved within him and makes him the image of God, hence, a free creature.

Preparing for the Immaculate Conception

*I*f we look at the world that surrounds us we can see that evil is always poisonous, does not uplift human beings but degrades and humiliates them. It does not make them any the greater, purer, or wealthier, but harms and belittles them. This is something we should indeed learn on the day of the Immaculate Conception: The person who abandons himself totally in God's hands does not become God's puppet, a boring "yes man"; he does not lose his freedom. Only the person who entrusts himself totally to God finds true freedom, the great, creative immensity of the freedom of good. The person who turns to God does not become smaller but greater, for through God and with God he becomes great, he becomes divine, he becomes truly himself. The person who puts himself in God's hands does not distance himself from others, withdrawing into his private salvation; on the contrary, it is only then that his heart truly awakens and he becomes a sensitive, hence, benevolent and open person. The closer a person is to God, the closer he is to people. We see this in Mary. The fact that she is totally with God is the reason why she is so close to human beings. For this reason she can be the Mother of every consolation and every help, a Mother whom anyone can dare to address in any kind of need in weakness and in sin, for she has understanding for everything and is for everyone the open power of creative goodness. In her, God has impressed his own image.

The Doctrine of the "Immaculata"

his contradiction between God's "is" and man's "is not" is lacking in the case of Mary, and consequently God's judgment about her is pure "Yes," just as she herself stands before him as a pure "Yes." This correspondence of God's "Yes" with Mary's being as "Yes" is the freedom from original sin. Preservation from original sin, therefore, signifies no exceptional proficiency, no exceptional achievement; on the contrary, it signifies that Mary reserves no area of being, life, or will for herself as a private possession: instead, precisely in the total dispossession of self, in giving herself to God, she comes to the true possession of self. Grace as dispossession becomes response as appropriation. Thus from another viewpoint the mystery of barren fruitfulness, the paradox of the barren mother, the mystery of virginity, becomes intelligible once more: dispossession as belonging, as the locus of new life. Thus the doctrine of the *Immaculata* reflects ultimately faith's certitude that there really is a holy Church — as a person and in a person. In this sense it expresses the Church's certitude of salvation. Included therein is the knowledge that God's covenant in Israel did not fail but produced a shoot out of which emerged the blossom, the Savior. The doctrine of the *Immaculata* testifies accordingly that God's grace was powerful enough to awaken a response, that grace and freedom, grace and being oneself, renunciation and fulfillment are only apparent contradictories; in reality one conditions the other and grants it its very existence.

John the Baptist in Advent

*L*et us gaze on John the Baptist. Challenging and active he stands before us, a "type" of the manly vocation. In harsh terms he demands *metanoia*, a radical transformation of attitudes. Those who would be Christians must be "transformed" ever again. Our natural disposition, indeed, finds us always ready to assert ourselves to pay like with like, to put ourselves at the center. Those who want to find God need, again and again, that inner conversion, that new direction. And this applies also to the total outlook on life. Day by day we encounter the world of visible things. It assaults us through billboards, broadcasts, traffic, and all the activities of daily life, to such an enormous extent that we are tempted to assume there is nothing else but this. Yet the truth is that what is invisible is greater and much more valuable than anything visible. One single soul, in Pascal's beautiful words, is worth more than the entire visible universe. But in order to have a living awareness of this, we need conversion, we need to turn around inside, as it were, to overcome the illusion of what is visible, and to develop the feeling, the ears and the eyes, for what is invisible. This has to be more important than anything that bombards us day after day with such exaggerated urgency. *Metanoeite*: change your attitude, so that God may dwell in you and, through you, in the world. John himself was not spared this painful process of change, of turning around.

The Witness of John the Baptist

*J*ohn appears in the wilderness as a man dedicated to God. First of all he preaches repentance, purification, and the gathering together of the people for the coming of God. In a sense this proclamation summarizes the whole of prophecy at the very moment when history is reaching its goal. His mission is to open the door for God, so that Israel is ready to welcome him and to prepare for his hour in history. The important things are first his call to repentance, which continues what all the prophets said, and second his witness to Christ, which again makes prophecy concrete in the image of the lamb, which is the Lamb of God. Let us recall the stories of Abraham, the stories of Isaac, the sacrifices that involve a lamb, especially the paschal sacrifice, in which a lamb is sacrificed. These substitutes now find their fulfillment. Basically, the Paschal Lamb stands in place of us men. Now Christ is sent by God to become the Paschal Lamb, and he shares our fate and thereby transforms it... John says that Christ is not just some historical personage, but is the one who goes before us all, who comes forth from the eternity of God and is an intimate part of that eternity.

The Genealogy of Jesus

*T*he New Testament begins with man, just as the Old Testament had begun with the incalculably mysterious soliloquy of the Creator: "Let us make man in our image, after our likeness." A man stands at the beginning of the New Testament and reminds us of the nocturnal vision in which Daniel sees four beasts coming up from the sea: images, these, of the forces and powers of this world, the kingdoms that share dominion over this world and determine the course of history. Then, in counterbalance to the emergence of the beasts from the sea, he sees a man descending from heaven: an image, this, of the holy people, of the holy power of the human amid the inhuman powers that rise from the deep. The man Jesus stands at the beginning of the New Testament, but as one who emerges from the history of mankind. In his genealogy, Matthew carefully plots the transition from the long and bewildering history set down in the Old Testament to the new reality that has begun with Jesus Christ. He sums up, as it were, this entire history in three sets of fourteen names and brings it down to him for whose sake alone, in the last analysis, it had existed. He shows that as it traveled its many ways and byways this history was, in a hidden manner, already bringing forth Christ; that during those centuries it was already, and at every point, one and the same God who was visiting his people and who now, in Jesus Christ, had become a brother to the human race. He brings out the inherent finality of history, which in the last analysis had no higher purpose than to produce this man Jesus.

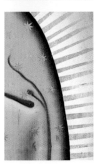

Our Lady of Guadalupe

Christianity established a continuity with regard to places of worship, while at the same time renewing other cults through its own contributions. The most impressive example of such continuity within change is the picture of Our Lady of Guadalupe. The veneration of the tilma began at the place where once had stood a distinguished image of "our venerable mother, Lady Snake," an important native goddess. It is significant, though, that she wears no mask and that her face is visible… In the figures and symbols with which she appears, the entire wealth of the previous religions is taken up and unified around a new center, which descends from new heights. She stands above the religions, so to speak, but does not trample them. Thus Our Lady of Guadalupe is in many respects an image of the relationship between Christianity and the religions of the world: all of these streams flow together into it, are purified and renewed, but are not destroyed. It is also an image of the relationship of the truth of Jesus Christ to the truths of those religions: the truth does not destroy; it purifies and unites.

The History of which Jesus Becomes a Part

The history of which Jesus becomes a part is a very ordinary history, marked by all the scandals and infamies to be found among human beings, all the advances and good beginnings, but also all the sinfulness and vileness — an utterly human history! The only four women named in the genealogy are all four of them witnesses to human sinfulness: Among them is Rahab the harlot who delivered Jericho into the hands of the migrating Israelites. Among them, too, is the wife of Uriah, the woman whom David got for himself through adultery and murder. Nor are the males in the genealogy any different. Neither Abraham nor Isaac nor Jacob is an ideal human being; David certainly is not, nor is Solomon; and finally we meet such abhorrent rulers as Ahaz and Manasseh, whose thrones are sticky with the blood of innocent victims. It is a somber history that leads to Jesus; it is not without its moments of light, its hopes, and advances, but on the whole it is a history of shabbiness, sin, and failure... All this is a sign for us. It tells us that the Incarnation of God does not result from an ascent on the part of the human race but from the descent of God. The ascent of man, the attempt to bring forth God by his own efforts and to attain the status of superman — this attempt failed wretchedly back in Paradise. The person who tries to become God by his own efforts, who highhandedly reaches for the stars, always ends up by destroying himself. Thus the wretched course of Israelite history is a sign for us that it is not through arrogance and self-exaltation that human beings are delivered, but through humility, self-surrender, and service.

DECEMBER 14

The Fidelity of God in History

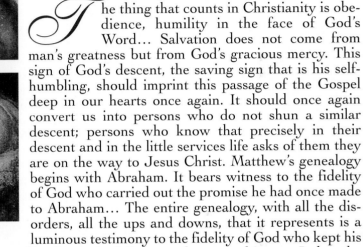

he thing that counts in Christianity is obedience, humility in the face of God's Word... Salvation does not come from man's greatness but from God's gracious mercy. This sign of God's descent, the saving sign that is his self-humbling, should imprint this passage of the Gospel deep in our hearts once again. It should once again convert us into persons who do not shun a similar descent; persons who know that precisely in their descent and in the little services life asks of them they are on the way to Jesus Christ. Matthew's genealogy begins with Abraham. It bears witness to the fidelity of God who carried out the promise he had once made to Abraham... The entire genealogy, with all the disorders, all the ups and downs, that it represents is a luminous testimony to the fidelity of God who kept his word despite all of man's failure and unworthiness. Luke the Evangelist... traces the Lord's ancestry back not simply to Abraham but to Adam and the hands of God that formed man. He thus makes it clear that the community Jesus has established is not simply a new Israel, a people whom God gathers for himself in this world, but that the mission of Jesus embraces instead the whole of the human race. His mission is not aimed at salvation for one group, one set of people alone, but is directed to the whole race, the entire world. In Jesus Christ the creation of man first attains its true goal; in him the Creator's conception of man finds its full expression; in him the beast that lurks in all of us is overcome for the first time, and the human in its fullness comes on the stage of history.

377

God Waits for Us

od has become man. He has become a child. Thus he fulfills the great and mysterious promise to be Emmanuel: God-with us. Now he is no longer unreachable for anybody. God is Emmanuel. By becoming a child, he offers us the possibility of being on familiar terms with him. I am reminded here of a rabbinical tale recorded by Elie Wiesel. He tells of Jehel, a little boy, who comes running into the room of his grandfather, the famous Rabbi Baruch. Big tears are rolling down his cheeks. And he cries, "My friend has totally given up on me. He is very unfair and very mean to me." "Well, could you explain this a little more?" asks the master. "Okay," responds the little boy. "We were playing hide and seek. I was hiding so well that he could not find me. But then he simply gave up and went home. Isn't that mean?" The most exciting hiding place has lost its excitement because the other stops playing. The master caresses the boy's face. He himself now has tears in his eyes. And he says, "Yes, this is not nice. But look, it is the same way with God. He is in hiding, and we do not seek him. Just imagine! God is hiding, and we people do not even look for him." In this little story a Christian is able to find the key to the ancient mystery of Christmas. God is in hiding. He waits for his creation to set out toward him, he waits for a new and willing Yes to come about, for love to arise as a new reality out of his creation. He waits for man.

DECEMBER 16

Joy and Harmony

The root of man's joy is the harmony he enjoys with himself. He lives in this affirmation. And only one who can accept himself can also accept the *you*, can accept the world. The reason why an individual cannot accept the *you*, cannot come to terms with him, is that he does not like his own *I* and, for that reason, cannot accept a *you*. Something strange happens here. We have seen that the inability to accept one's *I* leads to the inability to accept a *you*. But how does one go about affirming, assenting to, one's *I*? The answer may perhaps be unexpected: We cannot do so by our own efforts alone. Of ourselves, we cannot come to terms with ourselves. Our *I* becomes acceptable to us only if it has first become acceptable to another *I*. We can love ourselves only if we have first been loved by someone else. The life a mother gives to her child is not just physical life; she gives total life when she takes the child's tears and turns them into smiles. It is only when life has been accepted and is perceived as accepted that it becomes also acceptable. Man is that strange creature that needs not just physical birth but also appreciation if he is to subsist... If an individual is to accept himself, someone must say to him: "It is good that you exist" — must say it, not with words, but with that act of the entire being that we call love. For it is the way of love to will the other's existence and, at the same time, to bring that existence forth again. The key to the *I* lies with the *you*; the way to the *you* leads through the *I*.

DECEMBER 17

The Genealogy

*M*atthew's genealogy presents Jesus as a son of Abraham, yet primarily it characterizes him as the true David, who fulfills the sign of hope which David had become for his people. Luke proceeds further; he follows Jesus' path back to Adam, "who came from God" (3: 38). Adam is purely and simply "man," the human being. The genealogy extending back to Adam answers the question about human nature, which in the course of its wanderings and gropings is searching for itself. Jesus is the man for all men, the man in whom man's divine destination, his divine origin, finds its goal. In him man's fragmented nature is unified and preserved in unity with the God from whom it derives and whom, in its forlorn state, it seeks. Both genealogies are concerned with the historical and human context of Jesus' life... Jesus' origin is from below, yet simultaneously from above — and this is no contradiction. He is entirely man precisely because he does not have his origin only in this earth. Matthew points this out insofar as the pattern of his genealogy, which joins one member to another through the phrase "he begot," is broken in the final statement: Joseph, the husband of Mary, *from whom was born* Jesus, called the Christ (1: 16). Luke makes the same point when Jesus does not figure as the son of Joseph, but is assigned his legitimate place in the series as the one who "was considered to be Joseph's son" (3: 23).

The Genealogy and Christ the King

he face of Jesus Christ shows us clearly what God is, and it also makes visible what man is. God is the faithful and gracious One who pursues man even amid his confused wanderings, seeks him out with everlasting pity, and takes human nature, like a lost sheep, on his own shoulders in order to bring it back to its source. Man, on the other hand, is the one who, when all is said and done, is unable, despite all his cleverness and greatness, to find any better place for God than a stable or to offer him anything but a history full of filth and inhumanity... In the last analysis Matthew's genealogy is also Good News about Christ the King. The genealogy is made up of three series of fourteen names. Now if we write the number fourteen in Hebrew letters we have the three consonants that make up the name David. Thus the number fourteen, which dominates the genealogy, is a symbol of kingship. It turns the genealogy into a royal genealogy in which not only is the promise to Abraham fulfilled but the promise as well that accompanies the name of David. The meaning is that the One who is coming is the true King of the world. He is indeed the merciful God, but even in his mercy he remains the Lord God, the King to whose commands we are subject, the King who summons us and has a claim upon our obedience. Thus the genealogy at the beginning of the Gospel is at the same time a flourish of trumpets, as it were, for the King. It calls us into the presence of Jesus Christ. It calls us to a holy obedience to God's Word, and to the service of the Lord Jesus, whom to serve is to reign.

Genuine Joy

*I*t is in fact true, is it not, that all joy which arises independently of Christ or contrary to his will proves insufficient and only thrusts the person back down into a confusion in which, when all is said and done, he can find no lasting joy? Only with Christ has authentic joy made its appearance and the only thing of ultimate importance in our lives is to learn to see and know Christ, the God of grace, the light and joy of the world. Our joy will be genuine only when it no longer depends on things that can be stripped from us and destroyed and when it has its basis rather in those innermost depths of our existence which no worldly power can take from us. Every external loss should turn us back to these innermost depths and better dispose us for our true life... To celebrate Advent means to bring to life within ourselves the hidden Presence of God. It takes place to the extent that we travel the path of conversion and change our cast of mind by turning from the visible to the invisible. As we travel this path, we learn to see the miracle of grace; we learn that there can be no more luminous source of joy for human beings and the world than the grace that has appeared in Christ. The world is not a futile confusion of drudgery and pain, for all the distress the world contains is supported in the arms of merciful love; it is caught up in the forgiving and saving graciousness of our God.

The Weakness of the Baby Jesus

*A*t the heart of the mystery is the paradox that the glorious God decided to manifest himself... in the helplessness of a child who is overlooked by adult society and comes into the world in a stable. The powerlessness of a child has become the proper expression of God's all-subduing power, for the only force he employs is the silent force of truth and love. It was, then, in the defenseless weakness of a child that God wanted us to have our first encounter with saving mercy. And, in fact, how comforting it is, amid all the self-assertiveness of this world's powers, to see the peaceful tranquility of God and thus to experience the security emanating from a power that in the end will be stronger than any other force and will outlast all the loud triumphal cries of the world... Once again, it is unfortunately all too true that for many people religion has been transmuted into a sentiment which no longer has any reality to support it... Yet in many respects another attitude is perhaps even more dangerous: the attitude of those who regard themselves as religious but limit religion to the realm of feeling and allow it no contact with a sober rationalism of daily life in which they seek naught but personal gain... The unparalleled realism of the divine love of which Christmas speaks, and the action of the God who is not satisfied with words but takes on himself the wretched burden of human life — these should challenge us anew, year after year, to examine the realism of our faith and to strive for something more than the sentimentality of mere feeling.

The Real Point of Christmas

*W*hy do we really celebrate Christmas despite the wretchedness, turmoil, and isolation that are still man's lot and are if anything intensifying rather than lessening? What is the real point of Christmas?… Is it not consoling to see how, despite all the misunderstandings, the message of Jesus of Nazareth is heard? It is not only conflict that the message has produced but also and ever more the miracle of understanding, so that across ages and cultures, and even across the boundaries between religions, human beings find one another in his name. Distance vanishes and people are drawn together when this name is spoken… For Christmas says to us, amid all our doubts and bewilderment: God exists. Not as an infinitely distant power that can at best terrify us; not as being's ultimate ground that is not conscious of itself. Rather he exists as One who can be concerned about us; he is such that everything we are and do lies open to his gaze. But that gaze is the gaze of Love. For anyone who accepts this in faith and knows it by faith, there is no longer any ultimate isolation. *He* is here. The light that one man became in history and for history is not an accident or something powerless, but Light from Light. The hope and encouragement that emanate from this light thus acquire a wholly new depth. But precisely because it is an entirely divine hope, we can and should accept it as also an entirely human hope and pass it on to others.

The Method of the Incarnation

*T*he Incarnation of the Word means that God does not merely want to come to the spirit of man, through the Spirit, but that he is seeking him through and in the material world, that he also in fact wants to encounter him as a social and historical being. God wants to come to men through men. God has approached men in such a way that through him, and on account of him, they can find their way to one another. Thus the Incarnation includes the communal and historical aspects of faith. Taking the way of the body means that the time, as a reality, and the social nature of man become features of man's relationship with God, features that are in turn based upon God's existing relationship with man. God's action brings into being "the People of God," and "the People of God," on the basis of Christ, become "the body of Christ"... The ultimate goal for us all is that of becoming happy. Yet happiness exists only in company with each other, and we can keep company only in the infinity of love. There is happiness only in the removal of the barriers of the self in moving into divinity, in becoming divine.

plena

dominus

You will Prepare the Way

Saint Augustine tried to make clear, for himself and his faithful, the nature of priestly service. It came to him from meditation on the figure of John the Baptist, in whom he finds a prefiguring of the role of the priest. He points out that in the New Testament John is described, with a saying borrowed from Isaiah, as a "voice," while Christ appears in the Gospel of John as "the Word." The relation of "voice" (*vox*) to "word" (*verbum*) helps to make clear the mutual relationship between Christ and the priest. The word exists in someone's heart before it is ever perceptible to the senses through the voice. Through the mediation of the voice, it then enters into the perception of the other person and is then present likewise in his heart, without the speaker's having thereby in any sense lost the word. Thus, voice that carries the word from one person to the other (or others) passes away. The word remains. Ultimately, the task of the priest is quite simply to be a voice for the word: "He must increase, but I must decrease" — the voice has no other purpose than to pass on the word; it then once more effaces itself. On this basis the stature and the humbleness of priestly service are both equally clear: the priest is, like John the Baptist, purely a forerunner, a servant of the Word. It is not he who matters, but the other. Yet he is, with his entire existence, *vox*; it is his mission to be a voice for the Word, and thus, precisely in his being radically referred to, dependent upon, someone else, he takes a share in the stature of the mission of the Baptist and in the mission of the Logos himself.

DECEMBER 24

God the Living God

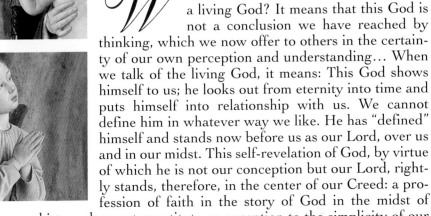

What does it mean when we call this God a living God? It means that this God is not a conclusion we have reached by thinking, which we now offer to others in the certainty of our own perception and understanding... When we talk of the living God, it means: This God shows himself to us; he looks out from eternity into time and puts himself into relationship with us. We cannot define him in whatever way we like. He has "defined" himself and stands now before us as our Lord, over us and in our midst. This self-revelation of God, by virtue of which he is not our conception but our Lord, rightly stands, therefore, in the center of our Creed: a profession of faith in the story of God in the midst of human history does not constitute an exception to the simplicity of our profession of faith in God but is the essential condition at its heart. That is why the heart of all our creeds is our Yes to Jesus Christ: "By the power of the Holy Spirit he was born of the Virgin Mary." We genuflect at this clause, because at this point the heavens, the veil behind which God is secluded, are swept aside, and the mystery touches us directly. *The distant God becomes our God, becomes "Emmanuel" — "God with us"* (Mt 1: 23)... But because it was the Word that became flesh, we must ever again strive, nonetheless, to translate into our human words this first creative Word, which "was with God" and which "is God" (Jn 1: 1), so that in those words we may hear *the* Word.

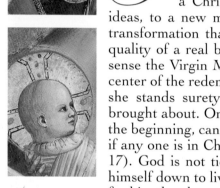

New Beginning, New Creation

To become a Christian means to be brought in to share in a new beginning. Becoming a Christian is more than turning to new ideas, to a new morality, to a new community. The transformation that happens here has all the drastic quality of a real birth, of a new creation. But in this sense the Virgin Mother is once more standing at the center of the redemption event. With her whole being, she stands surety for the new thing that God has brought about. Only if her story is true, and stands at the beginning, can what Paul says be true: "Therefore, if any one is in Christ, he is a new creation" (2 Cor 5: 17). God is not tied down to stones, but he does tie himself down to living people. The Yes of Mary opens for him the place where he can pitch his tent. She herself becomes a tent for him, and thus she is the beginning of the Holy Church, which in her turn points forward to the New Jerusalem, in which there is no temple any more, because God himself dwells in her midst. The faith in Christ that we confess in the Creed of the baptized people thus becomes a spiritualization and a purification of everything that was ever said or hoped, in the history of religions, about God's dwelling in the world. Yet it is at the same time an embodiment of God's being with men, which renders this concrete and particular, going far beyond anything that might have been hoped for. "God is in the flesh" — this indissoluble association of God with his creature, in particular, is what constitutes the heart of the Christian faith.

Incarnate Love

This divine activity now takes on dramatic form when, in Jesus Christ, it is God himself who goes in search of the "stray sheep," a suffering and lost humanity. When Jesus speaks in his parables of the shepherd who goes after the lost sheep, of the woman who looks for the lost coin, of the father who goes to meet and embrace his prodigal son, these are no mere words: they constitute an explanation of his very being and activity. His death on the cross is the culmination of that turning of God against himself in which he gives himself in order to raise man up and save him. This is love in its most radical form. By contemplating the pierced side of Christ (cf. Jn 19: 37), we can understand the starting-point of this Encyclical Letter: "God is love" (1 Jn 4: 8). It is there that this truth can be contemplated. It is from there that our definition of love must begin. In this contemplation the Christian discovers the path along which his life and love must move. Jesus gave this act of oblation an enduring presence through his institution of the Eucharist at the Last Supper. He anticipated his death and Resurrection by giving his disciples, in the bread and wine, his very self, his body and blood as the new manna (cf. Jn 6: 31-33). The ancient world had dimly perceived that man's real food — what truly nourishes him as man — is ultimately the Logos, eternal wisdom: this same Logos now truly becomes food for us — as love. The Eucharist draws us into Jesus' act of self-oblation. More than just statically receiving the incarnate Logos, we enter into the very dynamic of his self-giving.

Union with Christ

*U*nion with Christ is also union with all those to whom he gives himself. I cannot possess Christ just for myself; I can belong to him only in union with all those who have become, or who will become, his own. Communion draws me out of myself towards him, and thus also towards unity with all Christians. We become "one body," completely joined in a single existence. Love of God and love of neighbor are now truly united: God incarnate draws us all to himself. In the Eucharist, God's own *agape* comes to us bodily in order to continue his work in us and through us... The transition which he makes from the Law and the Prophets to the twofold commandment of love of God and of neighbor, and his grounding the whole life of faith on this central precept, is not simply a matter of morality — something that could exist apart from and alongside faith in Christ and its sacramental re-actualization. Faith, worship and *ethos* are interwoven as a single reality which takes shape in our encounter with God's *agape*. Here the usual contraposition between worship and ethics simply falls apart. "Worship" itself, eucharistic communion, includes the reality both of being loved and of loving others in turn. A Eucharist which does not pass over into the concrete practice of love is intrinsically fragmented. Conversely, ... the "commandment" of love is only possible because it is more than a requirement. Love can be "commanded" because it has first been given.

Mature Love

*I*t is characteristic of mature love that it calls into play all man's potentialities; it engages the whole man, so to speak. Contact with the visible manifestations of God's love can awaken within us a feeling of joy born of the experience of being loved. But this encounter also engages our will and our intellect. Acknowledgment of the living God is one path towards love, and the "yes" of our will to his will unites our intellect, will, and sentiments in the all-embracing act of love. But this process is always open-ended; love is never "finished" and complete; throughout life, it changes and matures, and thus remains faithful to itself... The love-story between God and man consists in the very fact that this communion of will increases in a communion of thought and sentiment, and thus our will and God's will increasingly coincide: God's will is no longer for me an alien will, something imposed on me from without by the commandments, but it is now my own will, based on the realization that God is in fact more deeply present to me than I am to myself. Then self-abandonment to God increases and God becomes our joy (cf. Ps 73 [72]: 23-28).

Glory and Justice

his was the new joy Christians discovered: that now, beginning with Christ, they understood how God ought to be glorified and how precisely through this the world would become just. That these two things should go together — how God is glorified and how justice comes — the angels had proclaimed on the holy night: "Glory to God in the highest, and peace on earth, goodwill toward men," they had said (Lk 2: 14). God's glory and peace on earth are inseparable. Where God is excluded, there is a breakdown of peace in the world; without God, no orthopraxis can save us. In fact, there does not exist an orthopraxis which is simply just, detached from a knowledge of what is good. The will without knowledge is blind, and so action, orthopraxis, without knowledge is blind and leads to the abyss. But if we do not know in what direction to change the world, if we do not understand its meaning and its inner purpose, then change alone becomes destruction — as we have seen and continue to see. But the inverse is also true: doctrine alone, which does not become life and action, becomes idle chatter and so is equally empty. The truth is concrete. Knowledge and action are closely united, as are faith and life.

Passover and Family

*I*n the course of a year, a people is always in danger of disintegrating, not only through external causes, but also interiorly, and of losing hold of the inner motivation which sustains it. It needs to return to its fundamental origin... We experience the primal, chaotic powers rising up from the very midst of a progressive society — which seems to know everything and to be able to do anything — and attacking the very progress of which it is so proud. We see how, in the midst of prosperity, technological achievement, and the scientific domination of the world, a nation can be destroyed from within; we see how the creation can be threatened by the chaotic powers which lurk in the depths of the human heart. We realize that neither money nor technology nor organizational ability alone can banish chaos. Only the real protective wall given to us by the Lord, the new family he has created for us, can do this... Passover is a summons, urgently reminding us that the family is the living home in which humanity is nurtured, which banishes chaos and futility, and which must be protected as such... The individual family cannot survive; it will disintegrate unless it is kept safe within the larger family which guarantees it and gives it security. So this night needs to be the night in which we set out once again on our twin paths: we set out on the path to the new city, the new family, the Church, and dedicate ourselves irrevocably to her, to our heart's true home; and then, on the basis of this family of Jesus Christ, we can proceed to grasp what is meant by the human family and by the humanity which sustains and protects us.

In the Beginning Was the Word

n the beginning was the Word" — this venerable and ancient sentence, which we have heard so often, is no longer really meaningful for us. Goethe has his Faust say: "I cannot value the word so highly," whereupon he translates the sentence: "In the beginning was the deed." Physicists tell us: "In the beginning was the 'big bang.'" But when we think about it, neither of these variations is satisfying to us. And so we turn again to the biblical "Word." To understand it, we must read the whole sentence, which says: "In the beginning was the Word, and the Word was with God, and the Word was God." That means that God existed already in the beginning, God is the beginning, God is the origin. All things come from the Creator Spirit, from the Creator God. And if he is called "the Word," that means that in the beginning there was a God who is mind. In the beginning was the creative mind who called the world into being; and this mind is, so to speak, the firm foundation that supports the universe, the source from whom we come, in whom we exist, in whom we can put our trust. But when the Bible says: "In the beginning was the Word," it says much more as well. It is not just a mind that, as it were, governs the universe like an idea in higher mathematics, while remaining itself untouchable and uninvocable; this God, who is truth, spirit, mind, is likewise Word, that is, he is also gift. He is for us the constant new beginning, and thus also a new hope and a new way.

The Heart of a Shepherd

Reverend Brian Mulcahy, O.P.

"*A*men, amen, I say to you, when you were younger, you used to dress yourself and go where you wanted; but when you grow old, you will stretch out your hands, and someone else will dress you and lead you where you do not want to go" (Jn 21: 18).

These words of the Risen Lord to Simon Peter along the shores of the Sea of Tiberias came to my mind after I got over my initial shock and disbelief on April 19, 2005, when Cardinal Camerlengo announced *urbi et orbi* the election of Cardinal Joseph Ratzinger as Pope Benedict XVI. While I was overjoyed for the Church at the choice of the College of Cardinals, I felt sad personally for the man whom God had chosen to lead his flock here on earth, the man for whom I had the privilege of working for a little more than two years back in the early 1990s. From July 1992 through November 1994, I served on the staff of the doctrinal section of the Congregation for the Doctrine of the Faith under the leadership of the then Cardinal Joseph Ratzinger. I knew from personal conversations with His Eminence that there was nothing more he *humanly* desired than to be relieved of his administrative duties so that he could once again devote himself to his theological studies and writing. This is why our Lord's words to Simon Peter in the twenty-first chapter of Saint John's Gospel came to my mind.

"Follow Me!"

In remarks to a group of German pilgrims who came to Rome for his installation Mass as Successor of Saint Peter, Pope Benedict alluded to this passage from Saint John's Gospel, in speaking of how he felt as it became clear to him that the College of Cardinals was coalescing around him as their choice as the next Roman Pontiff. This is how our Holy Father described his own thoughts and feelings at the time to this group of his fellow Germans:

"When, little by little, the trend of the voting led me to understand that, to say it simply, the axe was going to fall on me, my head began to spin. I was convinced that I had already carried out my life's work and could look forward to ending my days peacefully. With profound conviction I said to the Lord: Do not do this to me! You have younger and better people at your disposal, who can face this great responsibility with greater dynamism and greater strength.

"I was then very touched by a brief note written to me by a brother cardinal. He reminded me that on the occasion of the Mass for John Paul II, I had based my homily, starting from the Gospel, on the Lord's words to Peter by the Lake of Gennesaret: 'Follow me!' I spoke of how again and again, Karol Wojtyla received this call from the Lord, and how each time he had to renounce much and to simply say: Yes, I will follow you, even if you lead me where I never wanted to go. This brother cardinal wrote to me: Were the Lord to say to you now, 'Follow me,' then remember what you preached. Do not refuse! Be obedient in the same way that you described the great Pope, who has returned to the house of the Father. This deeply moved me. The ways of the Lord are not easy, but we were not created for an easy life, but for great things, for goodness.

"Thus, in the end I had to say 'yes.' I trust in the Lord and I trust in you, dear friends."

The Church is the Lord's

"The ways of the Lord are not easy, but we were not created for an easy life, but for great things, for goodness." These very personal and touching words of Pope Benedict XVI, a few days after his elevation to the See of Peter, reveal to us the paternal and pastoral heart of this remarkable man and servant of God and his holy Church. So it has been with great admiration and affection and fervent prayers for his intentions that I have watched, from a distance, our Holy Father, Pope Benedict XVI, take upon his shoulders the ministry of Vicar of Christ on earth, of Chief Shepherd of the flock, during these intervening months since his election.

While I served on the staff of the Congregation for the Doctrine of the Faith under Cardinal Ratzinger, I was a very recently ordained priest, and the Cardinal took a paternal interest in how I was adjusting to my new duties. I fondly recall that when he would see me, he would usually make two comments to me: first, he would always remark on how beautiful our Dominican habit is (I fully agree!), and then secondly, he would playfully say to me, "You know, I'm not a Thomist." And I would smile and say, deferentially, "*Si, Eminenza. Lo so!*" (Yes, your Eminence, I know that!)

One last personal recollection: during my time on his staff, I had the opportunity to sit in on an interview that Cardinal Ratzinger gave to a major American news magazine. After all the formal questions had been asked, there was a period of informal chat and questions with the three reporters from the magazine. One of them remarked to the cardinal, "How do you sleep at night, with all the problems in the Church and the world?" I'll never forget the cardinal's response. He laughed and said (I'm paraphrasing), "I sleep very well, thank you! And I'm sure if you asked the Holy Father the same question, he would tell you the same thing. You see, we know that the Church belongs to the Lord; he is in charge. We are merely his servants, who have been given a task to fulfill for the time being, but the Church is the Lord's!"

"*Sogni d'oro, Santo Padre!*" Sweet dreams, Holy Father!

Father Brian M. Mulcahy, O.P. , is currently pastor of Saint Thomas Aquinas
University Parish in Charlottesville, VA,
serving the University of Virginia.

Bibliographical Information

BOOKS BY JOSEPH RATZINGER/POPE BENEDICT XVI:

A New Song for the Lord, Martha M. Matesich, Tr. © 1996, The Crossroad Publishing Company, New York, NY. Used with permission.

A Turning Point For Europe? Brian McNeil, C.R.V., Tr. © 1994, Ignatius Press, San Francisco, CA. Used with permission.

Behold The Pierced One, An Approach to a Spiritual Christology, Graham Harrison, Tr. © 1986, Ignatius Press, San Francisco, CA. Used with permission.

Called to Communion, Understanding the Church Today, Adrian Walker, Tr. © 1996, Ignatius Press, San Francisco, CA. Used with permission.

Co-Workers of the Truth. © 1992, Ignatius Press, San Francisco, CA. Used with permission.

Daughter Zion, Meditations on the Church's Marian Belief, John, M. McDermott, S.J. Tr. © 1983, Ignatius Press, San Francisco, CA. Used with permission.

Dogma and Preaching, Matthew J. O'Connell, Tr. © 1985, Franciscan Herald Press, Chicago, IL. Used with permission.

The Feast of Faith, Approaches to a Theology of the Liturgy. © 1986, Ignatius Press, San Francisco, CA. Used with permission.

God and the World, A Conversation with Peter Seewald, Henry Taylor, Tr. © 2002, Ignatius Press, San Francisco, CA. Used with permission.

God Is Love, Deus Caritas Est, Encyclical Letter of Pope Benedict XVI, Vatican Translation, USCCB, Washington, DC, February 2006. Reprinted by permission of the Libreria Editrice Vaticana.

God Is Near Us, The Eucharist, the Heart of Life, Stephan Otto Horn, Ed., Vinzen Pfnür, Ed., Henry Taylor, Tr. © 2003, Ignatius Press, San Francisco, CA. Used with permission.

Gospel, Catechesis, Catechism. © 1997, Ignatius Press, San Francisco, CA. Used with permission.

In the Beginning… A Catholic Understanding of the Story of Creation and the Fall, Boniface Ramsey, O.P., Tr. © 1995, William B. Eerdmans Publishing Co., Grand Rapids, MI. Used with permission.

Introduction to Christianity, J. R. Foster, Tr. © 1990, Ignatius Press, San Francisco, CA. Used with permission.

Many Religions — One Covenant, Israel, the Church and the World, Graham Harrison, Tr. © 1999, Ignatius Press, San Francisco, CA. Used with permission.

Mary, The Church at the Source, Adrian Walker, Tr. © 2005, Ignatius Press, San Francisco, CA. Used with permission.

The Nature and Mission of Theology, Adrian Walker, Tr. © 1995, Ignatius Press, San Francisco, CA. Used with permission.

On The Way To Jesus Christ. © 2005, Ignatius Press, San Francisco, CA. Used with permission.

Pilgrim Fellowship of Faith, The Church as Communion, Stephan Otto Horn, Ed., Vinzen Pfnür, Ed., Henry Taylor, Tr. © 2005, Ignatius Press, San Francisco, CA. Used with permission.

Principles of Catholic Theology, Sr. Mary Frances McCarthy, S.N.D., Tr. © 1987, Ignatius Press, San Francisco, CA. Used with permission.

Salt of the Earth, The Church at the End of the Millennium, Adrian Walker, Tr. © 1997, Ignatius Press, San Francisco, CA. Used with permission.

Seek That Which Is Above. © 1986, Ignatius Press, San Francisco, CA. Used with permission.

Seeking God's Face, David Smith and Robert Cunningham, Tr. © 1982, Franciscan Herald Press, Chicago, IL. Used with permission.

The Spirit of the Liturgy, John Saward, Tr. © 2000, Ignatius Press, San Francisco, CA. Used with permission.
Truth and Tolerance, Christian Belief and World Religions, Henry Taylor, Tr. © 2004, Ignatius Press, San Francisco, CA. Used with permission.

PERIODICALS:

30 Days in the Church and in the World, Year XVI, Number 10, 1998. Reprinted by permission of the Libreria Editrice Vaticana.
Homiletic & Pastoral Review, Vol. XCVII, August-September 1997, (No. 11/12). www.ignatiusinsight.com. Used with permission.

L'OSSERVATORE ROMANO:

May 8, 2002, N. 19 (1742), Presentation, Apostolic Letter – *Misericordia Dei*, May 2, 2002. Reprinted by permission of the Libreria Editrice Vaticana.
November 13, 2002, N. 46 (1768), Lecture, Bishops Conference of the Region of Campania, June 2, 2002. Reprinted by permission of the Libreria Editrice Vaticana.
April 20, 2005, N. 16 (1890), Homily, Cappella Papale Mass, April 18, 2005. Reprinted by permission of the Libreria Editrice Vaticana.
May 18, 2005, N. 20 (1894), Address, General Audience, May 11, 2005. Reprinted by permission of the Libreria Editrice Vaticana.
June 1, 2005, N. 22 (1896), Homily, Pastoral Visit for the Closing of the 24th Italian National Eucharistic Congress, May 29, 2005. Reprinted by permission of the Libreria Editrice Vaticana.
August 3, 2005, N. 20 (1905), Address, Meeting with Diocesan Clergy of Aosta, July 25, 2005. Reprinted by permission of the Libreria Editrice Vaticana.
August 24, 2005, N. 34 (1907), Address, The XX World Youth Day, August 18, 2005. Reprinted by permission of the Libreria Editrice Vaticana.
February 22, 2006, N. 8 (1932), Address, Plenary Assembly of the Congregation of the Doctrine of the Faith, February 10, 2006. Reprinted by permission of the Libreria Editrice Vaticana.
February 22, 2006, N. 8 (1932), Address, Angelus, November 19, 2006. Reprinted by permission of the Libreria Editrice Vaticana.
April 12, 2006, N. 15 (1939), Message, Preparation of XXI World Youth Day, April 6, 2006. Reprinted by permission of the Libreria Editrice Vaticana.

VATICAN WEBSITE — www.vatican.va:

Address, Angelus, July 10, 2005. Reprinted by permission of the Libreria Editrice Vaticana.
General Audience, February 15, 2006. Reprinted by permission of the Libreria Editrice Vaticana.
General Audience, March 15, 2006. Reprinted by permission of the Libreria Editrice Vaticana.
General Audience, March 22, 2006. Reprinted by permission of the Libreria Editrice Vaticana.
General Audience, March 29, 2006. Reprinted by permission of the Libreria Editrice Vaticana.
General Audience, April 26, 2006. Reprinted by permission of the Libreria Editrice Vaticana.
General Audience, May 24, 2006. Reprinted by permission of the Libreria Editrice Vaticana.
Homily, Mass of Priestly Ordination, May 15, 2005. Reprinted by permission of the Libreria Editrice Vaticana.
Homily, Marienfield – Cologne, Germany, The XX World Youth Day Eucharistic Celebration, August 21, 2005. Reprinted by permission of the Libreria Editrice Vaticana.

Homily, Opening Mass of the 11th Ordinary General Assembly of the Synod of Bishops, October 2, 2005. Reprinted by permission of the Libreria Editrice Vaticana.

Homily, Conclusion of the 11th Ordinary General Assembly of the Synod of Bishops and Year of the Eucharist, World Mission Sunday, October 23, 2005. Reprinted by permission of the Libreria Editrice Vaticana.

Homily, 40th Anniversary of the Closure of the Second Vatican Council, December 8, 2005. Reprinted by permission of the Libreria Editrice Vaticana.

Homily, Celebration of Palm Sunday, April 9, 2006. Reprinted by permission of the Libreria Editrice Vaticana.

Homily, Chrism Mass, Holy Thursday, April 13, 2006. Reprinted by permission of the Libreria Editrice Vaticana.

Homily, Mass of the Lord's Supper, Holy Thursday, April 13, 2006. Reprinted by permission of the Libreria Editrice Vaticana.

Homily, Easter Vigil, Holy Saturday, April 15, 2006. Reprinted by permission of the Libreria Editrice Vaticana.

Message, Celebration of the World Day of Peace, January 1, 2006. Reprinted by permission of the Libreria Editrice Vaticana.

Message, Lent 2006. Reprinted by permission of the Libreria Editrice Vaticana.

Message, 43rd World Day of Prayer for Vocations, May 7, 2006. Reprinted by permission of the Libreria Editrice Vaticana.

ZENIT NEWS AGENCY — www.zenit.org:

ZE05042402, "Do Not Be Afraid of Christ! He Takes Nothing Away and Gives Everything", April 24, 2005. Used with permission.

ZE05050220, "The Feeling of Things, the Contemplation of Beauty", August 24-30, 2002. Used with permission.

ZE05050901, "Leader in the Profession of Faith in Christ" Part 1, May 7, 2005. Used with permission.

ZE05052023, "We Christians Must Be Ready to Explain Our Faith", May 13, 2005. Used with permission.

ZE05052904, "The Sacrament of Unity", May 29, 2005. Used with permission.

ZE05053020, "Jesus Goes Before Us to the Father", May 26, 2005. Used with permission.

ZE05060923, "Anthropological Foundation of the Family", June 6, 2005. Used with permission.

ZE05062904, "Catholicity and Unity Go Together", June 29, 2005. Used with permission.

ZE05081905, "If you abide in Christ, You Will Bear Much Fruit", August 19, 2005. Used with permission.

ZE05082005, "Only From God Does True Revolution Come", August 20, 2005. Used with permission.

ZE05082204, "Meeting for Friendship Among People", August 21-27, 2005. Used with permission.

ZE05082521, "We Have a Mother in Heaven", August 15, 2005. Used with permission.

ZE05100408, "The Lord is Close to Each One of Us", October 3, 2005. Used with permission.

ZE05121420, "Mary Turns to Us, Saying: 'Have the Courage to Dare with God'", December 8, 2005. Used with permission.

ZE06030103, "A Propitious Moment to Be Converted to Love", March 1, 2006. Used with permission.

ZE06031201, "No One Lives 'on Tabor' While on Earth", March 12, 2006. Used with permission.

Index of Meditations

JANUARY

1 (p. 14) *Daughter Zion*... pp. 77-78
2 (p. 15) *In the Beginning*... pp. 23-25
3 (p. 16) *In the Beginning*... pp. 48-49
4 (p. 17) *Seeking God's Face*, pp. 11-12, 13
5 (p. 18) *God Is Love*... pp. 1-2
6 (p. 19) ZENIT, ZE05082005
7 (p. 20) ZENIT, ZE05081905
8 (p. 21) *On The Way To Jesus Christ*, pp. 84-85
9 (p. 22) *L'Osservatore Romano*, (1907), p. 4
10 (p. 23) *A Turning Point*... pp. 104-105, 106
11 (p. 24) *God and the World*... pp. 23, 29, 31
12 (p. 25) *God and the World*... pp. 33, 35, 36
13 (p. 26) *God and the World*... pp. 46, 49
14 (p. 27) *Co-Workers of the Truth*, pp. 333-334
15 (p. 28) *God and the World*... pp. 96, 97
16 (p. 29) *God and the World*... pp. 240-241

17 (p. 30) *Pilgrim Fellowship of Faith*... pp. 296-297
18 (p. 31) *The Nature and Mission*... pp. 32-33, 34
19 (p. 32) *God and the World*... p. 251
20 (p. 33) *God and the World*... pp. 282-283
21 (p. 34) *God and the World*... pp. 320, 321
22 (p. 35) *Pilgrim Fellowship of Faith*... pp. 18-23
23 (p. 36) *Pilgrim Fellowship of Faith*... pp. 23-24
24 (p. 37) *Truth and Tolerance*... pp. 254-255
25 (p. 38) *The Nature and Mission*... pp. 51, 52
26 (p. 39) *The Nature and Mission*... pp. 58-59, 60
27 (p. 40) *A New Song*... pp. 20, 21-22
28 (p. 41) *Principles of Catholic*... pp. 51-52
29 (p. 42) *God and the World*... pp. 61-62
30 (p. 43) *Dogma and Preaching*, pp. 6-7
31 (p. 44) *God and the World*... pp. 219-221

FEBRUARY

1 (p. 46) *In the Beginning*... pp. 47-48
2 (p. 47) *The Spirit of the Liturgy*, pp. 43-44
3 (p. 48) *Principles of Catholic*... pp. 31-33
4 (p. 49) *In the Beginning*... pp. 30-31, 32
5 (p. 50) *Seeking God's Face*, pp. 27-28
6 (p. 51) *Seeking God's Face*, pp. 29-31
7 (p. 52) *In the Beginning*... pp. 56-58
8 (p. 53) *In the Beginning*... pp. 66-67
9 (p. 54) *In the Beginning*... pp. 69-71
10 (p. 55) *In the Beginning*... pp. 72-73
11 (p. 56) *In the Beginning*... pp. 73-74, 75-76
12 (p. 57) *In the Beginning*... pp. 98-99
13 (p. 58) *Seeking God's Face*, pp. 32-34
14 (p. 59) *Many Religions*... pp. 81, 82-83, 87
15 (p. 60) *Dogma and Preaching*, pp. 31-32

16 (p. 61) *Dogma and Preaching*, pp. 24, 27-28
17 (p. 62) *Called to Communion*... pp. 73-74
18 (p. 63) *A New Song*... pp. 54, 55
19 (p. 64) *The Nature and Mission*... p. 39
20 (p. 65) *The Nature and Mission*... p. 40
21 (p. 66) ZENIT, ZE06030103
22 (p. 67) ZENIT, ZE05050901
23 (p. 68) *Dogma and Preaching*, pp. 24-25
24 (p. 69) *Seeking God's Face*, pp. 16-17, 18-19
25 (p. 70) *30 Days*... pp. 31-32
26 (p. 71) *Co-Workers of the Truth*, pp. 63-64
27 (p. 72) *Co-Workers of the Truth*, pp. 82-83
28 (p. 73) *Co-Workers of the Truth*, p. 139
29 (p. 74) ZENIT, ZE05100408

MARCH

1 (p. 76) *Co-Workers of the Truth*, pp. 174-175
2 (p. 77) *L'Osservatore Romano*, (1890), p. 3
3 (p. 78) *The Nature and Mission*... p. 103

4 (p. 79) ZENIT, ZE06031201
5 (p. 80) *Principles of Catholic*... pp. 52, 53
6 (p. 81) *Behold The Pierced One*... pp. 125-126

7 (p. 82) *A Turning Point...* pp. 36, 38-39
8 (p. 83) *Behold The Pierced One...* pp. 33-34, 35
9 (p. 84) ZENIT, ZE05082204
10 (p. 85) *Principles of Catholic...* p. 81
11 (p. 86) *Principles of Catholic...* pp. 353-355
12 (p. 87) *Behold The Pierced One...* pp. 108-109
13 (p. 88) *God and the World...* pp. 26-27
14 (p. 89) *God and the World...* pp. 43, 44-45
15 (p. 90) *God and the World...* p. 51
16 (p. 91) *God and the World...* pp. 94, 95
17 (p. 92) *A New Song...* pp. 22-23, 25
18 (p. 93) *Co-Workers of the Truth,* pp. 97-98
19 (p. 94) *Dogma and Preaching,* pp. 35-36

20 (p. 95) *Introduction to Christianity,* pp. 201, 202-203
21 (p. 96) *Truth and Tolerance...* pp. 253-254
22 (p. 97) *God and the World...* pp. 184-185
23 (p. 98) *God and the World...* pp. 185-186
24 (p. 99) *A New Song...* pp. 42-43
25 (p. 100) *Dogma and Preaching,* pp. 78-79
26 (p. 101) *God and the World...* pp. 107, 108
27 (p. 102) *God and the World...* pp. 186-187
28 (p. 103) *God and the World...* p. 258
29 (p. 104) *God and the World...* pp. 322, 323
30 (p. 105) *God and the World...* pp. 222, 223
31 (p. 106) *L'Osservatore Romano,* (1742), p. 5

APRIL

1 (p. 108) *A New Song...* p. 41
2 (p. 109) *A New Song...* p. 19
3 (p. 110) *On The Way To Jesus Christ,* pp. 85, 86-87
4 (p. 111) *God Is Near Us...* pp. 31-32
5 (p. 112) *God and the World...* pp. 259-260
6 (p. 113) *Co-Workers of the Truth,* pp. 122-123
7 (p. 114) *Dogma and Preaching,* pp. 43-44
8 (p. 115) *Dogma and Preaching,* p. 42
9 (p. 116) *Seek That Which Is Above,* pp. 54-56
10 (p. 117) *A New Song...* pp. 63-64
11 (p. 118) *Pilgrim Fellowship of Faith...* pp. 293-294
12 (p. 119) *On The Way To Jesus Christ,* pp. 14-16, 26-27, 31
13 (p. 120) *The Spirit of the Liturgy,* pp. 102-103
14 (p. 121) *Dogma and Preaching,* pp. 50-51
15 (p. 122) *Seek That Which Is Above,* pp. 63, 64-65

16 (p. 123) *Seek That Which Is Above,* pp. 35-36
17 (p. 124) *Gospel, Catechesis, Catechism,* pp. 25-26
18 (p. 125) *God Is Near Us...* pp. 49-50
19 (p. 126) *Dogma and Preaching,* pp. 45-46
20 (p. 127) *Dogma and Preaching,* pp. 47-48
21 (p. 128) *Dogma and Preaching,* pp. 57, 58-59
22 (p. 129) *Dogma and Preaching,* pp. 59-60
23 (p. 130) *A New Song...* pp. 46-47
24 (p. 131) *God Is Near Us...* pp. 86-87
25 (p. 132) *God Is Near Us...* pp. 90-91
26 (p. 133) *Seek That Which Is Above,* pp. 38-40
27 (p. 134) Homily, May 15, 2005, www.vatican.va
28 (p. 135) *The Spirit of the Liturgy,* pp. 33-34
29 (p. 136) ZENIT, ZE05042402
30 (p. 137) Address, April 26, 2006, www.vatican.va

MAY

1 (p. 140) *Dogma and Preaching,* pp. 110-111
2 (p. 141) *Daughter Zion...* pp. 18-19
3 (p. 142) *Daughter Zion...* pp. 20-21, 22-23-24
4 (p. 143) *Daughter Zion...* pp. 26, 27-28
5 (p. 144) Address, February 15, 2006, www.vatican.va
6 (p. 145) *Mary, The Church at the Source,* pp. 14-15
7 (p. 146) *Mary, The Church at the Source,* pp. 15-17
8 (p. 147) *Mary, The Church at the Source,* pp. 29, 30
9 (p. 148) *Mary, The Church at the Source,* pp. 31-32, 33
10 (p. 149) *Mary, The Church at the Source,* pp. 35-36
11 (p. 150) *Mary, The Church at the Source,* pp. 49-50
12 (p. 151) *Mary, The Church at the Source,* pp. 64-65, 66

13 (p. 152) *Mary, The Church at the Source,* pp. 67-68
14 (p. 153) *Dogma and Preaching,* pp. 62-63, 65
15 (p. 154) *Co-Workers of the Truth,* pp. 235-236
16 (p. 155) ZENIT, ZE05050901
17 (p. 156) *Co-Workers of the Truth,* pp. 155-156
18 (p. 157) Address, May 24, 2006, www.vatican.va
19 (p. 158) *Principles of Catholic...* pp. 282-284
20 (p. 159) *The Feast of Faith...* pp. 94-95
21 (p. 160) *Pilgrim Fellowship of Faith...* pp. 161, 162
22 (p. 161) *Pilgrim Fellowship of Faith...* pp. 162-164
23 (p. 162) *God Is Near Us...* pp. 30-31
24 (p. 163) *The Spirit of the Liturgy,* pp. 171-173
25 (p. 164) *Pilgrim Fellowship of Faith...* pp. 47, 49

26 (p. 165) *Pilgrim Fellowship of Faith...* pp. 44-45
27 (p. 166) *Dogma and Preaching,* pp. 68, 69, 70, 71
28 (p. 167) *The Nature and Mission...* p. 55

29 (p. 168) *Principles of Catholic...* pp. 31-32
30 (p. 169) *Principles of Catholic...* p. 33
31 (p. 170) *Daughter Zion...* pp. 80-82

JUNE

1 (p. 172) *Behold The Pierced One...* pp. 126-127-128
2 (p. 173) *God and the World...* p. 400
3 (p. 174) *Seeking God's Face,* pp. 37-38, 39
4 (p. 175) *The Feast of Faith...* pp. 134-135
5 (p. 176) *God and the World...* pp. 188, 189
6 (p. 177) *Pilgrim Fellowship of Faith...* pp. 101-102
7 (p. 178) *God and the World...* pp. 246-247
8 (p. 179) *The Feast of Faith...* pp. 136-137
9 (p. 180) *The Feast of Faith...* pp. 130, 131
10 (p. 181) *The Feast of Faith...* pp. 128-129
11 (p. 182) *Introduction to Christianity,* pp. 214, 215
12 (p. 183) *Co-Workers of the Truth,* pp. 81-82
13 (p. 184) *L'Osservatore Romano,* (1768), p. 6
14 (p. 185) *God Is Near Us...* pp. 119, 120
15 (p. 186) *God Is Near Us...* pp. 104-105

16 (p. 187) *L'Osservatore Romano,* (1896), pp. 6, 7
17 (p. 188) *Pilgrim Fellowship of Faith...* pp. 204-205
18 (p. 189) ZENIT, ZE05053020
19 (p. 190) *On The Way To Jesus Christ,* pp. 104, 105
20 (p. 191) *Called to Communion...* pp. 28-29
21 (p. 192) *Called to Communion...* pp. 36-37
22 (p. 193) *Behold The Pierced One...* pp. 88-89, 90
23 (p. 194) Homily, August 21, 2005, www.vatican.va
24 (p. 195) *Dogma and Preaching,* p. 74
25 (p. 196) Address, March 15, 2006, www.vatican.va
26 (p. 197) Address, March 22, 2006, www.vatican.va
27 (p. 198) Address, March 29, 2006, www.vatican.va
28 (p. 199) *Called to Communion...* pp. 24-25
29 (p. 200) ZENIT, ZE05062904
30 (p. 201) *Called to Communion...* pp. 55-56

JULY

1 (p. 204) *Behold The Pierced One...* pp. 63, 67-68, 69
2 (p. 205) *Principles of Catholic...* p. 357
3 (p. 206) *L'Osservatore Romano,* (1905), p. 3
4 (p. 207) *A Turning Point...* pp. 39, 40
5 (p. 208) *L'Osservatore Romano,* (1905), p. 3
6 (p. 209) Homily, August 21, 2005, www.vatican.va
7 (p. 210) *God and the World...* pp. 397, 398
8 (p. 211) *God and the World...* pp. 402, 403
9 (p. 212) *God and the World...* pp. 421-422
10 (p. 213) *God and the World...* pp. 433-434
11 (p. 214) *Truth and Tolerance...* pp. 160-161
12 (p. 215) *The Feast of Faith...* pp. 148-149
13 (p. 216) *The Feast of Faith...* pp. 150-151
14 (p. 217) *God and the World...* pp. 392, 393
15 (p. 218) *Pilgrim Fellowship of Faith...* pp. 105-107
16 (p. 219) *Pilgrim Fellowship of Faith...* pp. 109-110

17 (p. 220) *Pilgrim Fellowship of Faith...* pp. 116, 117, 118
18 (p. 221) *On The Way To Jesus Christ,* pp. 48, 49
19 (p. 222) Address, July 10, 2005, www.vatican.va
20 (p. 223) *Dogma and Preaching,* pp. 98-99
21 (p. 224) *God Is Near Us...* pp. 29-30
22 (p. 225) *Truth and Tolerance...* pp. 60-61
23 (p. 226) *Truth and Tolerance...* pp. 61-62
24 (p. 227) *Truth and Tolerance...* pp. 67, 70-71
25 (p. 228) *Truth and Tolerance...* pp. 155-156
26 (p. 229) *Truth and Tolerance...* pp. 158, 159
27 (p. 230) *Truth and Tolerance...* pp. 191, 193, 195, 199
28 (p. 231) *God Is Love...* pp. 9-10
29 (p. 232) *God Is Love...* p. 11
30 (p. 233) Homily, October 2, 2005, www.vatican.va
31 (p. 234) Address, March 15, 2006, www.vatican.va

AUGUST

1 (p. 236) *Dogma and Preaching,* pp. 11-13
2 (p. 237) *Dogma and Preaching,* pp. 14, 15
3 (p. 238) *God Is Near Us...* pp. 126, 127-128
4 (p. 239) Homily, April 15, 2006, www.vatican.va
5 (p. 240) ZENIT, ZE05050220

6 (p. 241) *Behold The Pierced One...* pp. 17-18, 19-20
7 (p. 242) Message, May 7, 2006, www.vatican.va
8 (p. 243) *The Nature and Mission...* pp. 69-70, 71
9 (p. 244) *The Nature and Mission...* pp. 62, 63
10 (p. 245) *Behold The Pierced One...* pp. 25, 26

11 (p. 246) *Behold The Pierced One*... pp. 27-28, 29, 30
12 (p. 247) *The Feast of Faith*... pp. 25-26
13 (p. 248) *The Feast of Faith*... pp. 26-28
14 (p. 249) *The Feast of Faith*... pp. 64-65
15 (p. 250) *Daughter Zion*... pp. 78-79
16 (p. 251) *The Feast of Faith*... pp. 66, 67
17 (p. 252) ZENIT, ZE05082521
18 (p. 253) *God and the World*... pp. 40-41
19 (p. 254) *God and the World*... pp. 85. 111-112, 120-121, 142
20 (p. 255) *God and the World*... pp. 269-270-271

21 (p. 256) *God and the World*... pp. 272-273
22 (p. 257) *Seek That Which Is Above*, pp. 96-97, 100-101
23 (p. 258) *God and the World*... p. 275
24 (p. 259) *The Spirit of the Liturgy*, pp. 26, 27, 28
25 (p. 260) *The Spirit of the Liturgy*, pp. 173-174
26 (p. 261) *God Is Near Us*... p. 54
27 (p. 262) *On The Way To Jesus Christ*, pp. 66, 67
28 (p. 263) *The Nature and Mission*... pp. 57-58
29 (p. 264) *Dogma and Preaching*, pp. 76-77
30 (p. 265) *The Spirit of the Liturgy*, pp. 57-58
31 (p. 266) *The Spirit of the Liturgy*, pp. 59, 61

SEPTEMBER

1 (p. 268) *God Is Near Us*... pp. 79-80
2 (p. 269) *God Is Near Us*... pp. 80-81
3 (p. 270) Homily, April 15, 2006, www.vatican.va
4 (p. 271) Homily, April 15, 2006, www.vatican.va
5 (p. 272) Homily, April 13, 2006, www.vatican.va
6 (p. 273) Homily, April 13, 2006, www.vatican.va
7 (p. 274) Homily, April 13, 2006, www.vatican.va
8 (p. 275) *Seeking God's Face*, pp. 52, 53
9 (p. 276) ZENIT, ZE05052904
10 (p. 277) Message, May 7, 2006, www.vatican.va
11 (p. 278) *L'Osservatore Romano*, (1894), p. 11
12 (p. 279) *The Spirit of the Liturgy*, pp. 55-56
13 (p. 280) *God and the World*... pp. 223, 224-225
14 (p. 281) *Salt of the Earth*... pp. 26-27
15 (p. 282) *Mary, The Church at the Source*, pp. 34-35

16 (p. 283) *The Spirit of the Liturgy*, pp. 177-178, 184
17 (p. 284) *God Is Near Us*... pp. 39, 40-41
18 (p. 285) *God Is Near Us*... pp. 46-47
19 (p. 286) Homily, December 8, 2005, www.vatican.va
20 (p. 287) Homily, December 8, 2005, www.vatican.va
21 (p. 288) Homily, December 8, 2005, www.vatican.va
22 (p. 289) Homily, October 23, 2005, www.vatican.va
23 (p. 290) *God and the World*... pp. 425, 426-427
24 (p. 291) *God and the World*... pp. 77, 80-81
25 (p. 292) ZENIT, ZE05060923
26 (p. 293) ZENIT, ZE05060923
27 (p. 294) ZENIT, ZE05060923
28 (p. 295) *God and the World*... pp. 83-84
29 (p. 296) *Salt of the Earth*... pp. 27, 28, 29, 30
30 (p. 297) *Pilgrim Fellowship of Faith*... pp. 121-122

OCTOBER

1 (p. 300) *Salt of the Earth*... pp. 20, 22
2 (p. 301) Homily, October 2, 2005, www.vatican.va
3 (p. 302) *Co-Workers of the Truth*, p. 303
4 (p. 303) *Seek That Which Is Above*, pp. 130-132
5 (p. 304) *God and the World*... pp. 279, 280
6 (p. 305) *In the Beginning*... pp. 44-45
7 (p. 306) *God and the World*... pp. 318-319
8 (p. 307) *Principles of Catholic*.... pp. 344-345
9 (p. 308) *Truth and Tolerance*... pp. 78-79
10 (p. 309) *Truth and Tolerance*... pp. 148-149
11 (p. 310) *L'Osservatore Romano*, (1932), p. 3
12 (p. 311) Homily, April 9, 2006, www.vatican.va
13 (p. 312) Homily, December 8, 2005, www.vatican.va
14 (p. 313) Message, January 1, 2006, www.vatican.va
15 (p. 314) Message, January 1, 2006, www.vatican.va
16 (p. 315) Message, January 1, 2006, www.vatican.va

17 (p. 316) Message, January 1, 2006, www.vatican.va
18 (p. 317) *L'Osservatore Romano*, (1939), p. 7
19 (p. 318) *L'Osservatore Romano*, (1939), pp. 7-8
20 (p. 319) *Truth and Tolerance*... pp. 87-89
21 (p. 320) ZENIT, ZE05052023
22 (p. 321) *Pilgrim Fellowship of Faith*... pp. 157, 158-159
23 (p. 322) *Homiletic & Pastoral Review*, pp. 10-11
24 (p. 323) *On The Way To Jesus Christ*, pp. 70-71
25 (p. 324) *Many Religions*... pp. 69, 70-71
26 (p. 325) *Many Religions*... pp. 73-74, 76-77
27 (p. 326) *Truth and Tolerance*... pp. 55-56
28 (p. 327) Address, March 22, 2006, www.vatican.va
29 (p. 328) *Mary, The Church at the Source*, pp. 39-41
30 (p. 329) *L'Osservatore Romano*, (1939), p. 8
31 (p. 330) *God and the World*... pp. 189-190

NOVEMBER

1 (p. 332) *The Spirit of the Liturgy*, pp. 110-111
2 (p. 333) *God and the World…* pp. 129-130
3 (p. 334) *Co-Workers of the Truth*, p. 350
4 (p. 335) *Many Religions…* pp. 84-85
5 (p. 336) *Co-Workers of the Truth*, p. 35
6 (p. 337) *Principles of Catholic…* pp. 49-50
7 (p. 338) *Pilgrim Fellowship of Faith…* p. 286
8 (p. 339) *Pilgrim Fellowship of Faith…* p. 287
9 (p. 340) *Pilgrim Fellowship of Faith…* pp. 292-293
10 (p. 341) *Pilgrim Fellowship of Faith…* pp. 289-290, 291
11 (p. 342) *Behold The Pierced One…* pp. 117-118
12 (p. 343) *A Turning Point…* pp. 175-177
13 (p. 344) ZENIT, ZE05042402
14 (p. 345) *God and the World…* p. 63
15 (p. 346) *God and the World…* p. 70

16 (p. 347) *God Is Near Us…* p. 82
17 (p. 348) *God Is Near Us…* p. 83
18 (p. 349) *L'Osservatore Romano*, (1932), p. 1
19 (p. 350) Address, March 29, 2006, www.vatican.va
20 (p. 351) Homily, April 13, 2006, www.vatican.va
21 (p. 352) *God Is Love…* p. 22
22 (p. 353) *The Feast of Faith…* pp. 116-117
23 (p. 354) *Introduction to Christianity*, p. 251
24 (p. 355) *Seeking God's Face*, 2006, www.vatican.va
25 (p. 356) *Seeking God's Face*, pp. 64-65
26 (p. 357) *Co-Workers of the Truth*, p. 377
27 (p. 358) *Truth and Tolerance…* p. 205
28 (p. 359) *God Is Near Us…* pp. 137, 139-140
29 (p. 360) *God Is Near Us…* pp. 140-141, 143
30 (p. 361) *God Is Near Us…* pp. 144-145

DECEMBER

1 (p. 364) *Dogma and Preaching*, pp. 71-72
2 (p. 365) *Seeking God's Face*, pp. 74-75
3 (p. 366) *Co-Workers of the Truth*, p. 106
4 (p. 367) *A New Song…* pp. 27, 28
5 (p. 368) *Seeking God's Face*, pp. 77-78
6 (p. 369) ZENIT, ZE05121420
7 (p. 370) ZENIT, ZE05121420
8 (p. 371) *Daughter Zion…* pp. 70-71
9 (p. 372) *Co-Workers of the Truth*, pp. 390-391
10 (p. 373) *God and the World…* p. 207
11 (p. 374) *Dogma and Preaching*, pp. 19-20
12 (p. 375) *On The Way To Jesus Christ*, pp. 73-74
13 (p. 376) *Dogma and Preaching*, p. 21
14 (p. 377) *Dogma and Preaching*, pp. 22-23
15 (p. 378) *Co-Workers of the Truth*, p. 407
16 (p. 379) *Principles of Catholic…* pp. 79-80

17 (p. 380) *Daughter Zion…* pp. 40-41
18 (p. 381) *Dogma and Preaching*, pp. 23-24
19 (p. 382) *Dogma and Preaching*, pp. 80, 81
20 (p. 383) *Dogma and Preaching*, pp. 85-87
21 (p. 384) *Dogma and Preaching*, pp. 90, 91
22 (p. 385) *Pilgrim Fellowship of Faith…* pp. 165-166
23 (p. 386) *Pilgrim Fellowship of Faith…* pp. 164-165
24 (p. 387) *God Is Near Us…* pp. 11-12
25 (p. 388) *God Is Near Us…* pp. 23-24
26 (p. 389) *God Is Love…* pp. 16-17
27 (p. 390) *God Is Love…* p. 18
28 (p. 391) *God Is Love…* p. 21
29 (p. 392) *L'Osservatore Romano*, (1768), p. 6
30 (p. 393) *Behold The Pierced One…* pp. 104, 105-106
31 (p. 394) *Co-Workers of the Truth*, pp. 48-49

Benedictus cover quote: *A New Song…* p. 144

Index of Illustrations

JANUARY

Page 14: *Madonna of Mercy*, F. Granacci (style), 16th c. © 1990, Photo Scala, Florence.

Page 15: *The Creation of the earth, dividing the waters, creation of the heavens, creation of plants*, French psalter, last quarter 13th c., M.730, f.9, detail © 2003, Pierpont Morgan Library / Art Resource / Scala, Florence.

Page 16: *Christ and the Apostles*, Byzantine Icon, 17th c. © Picture Desk / Dagli Orti.

Page 17: *The Vision of the Three Magi*, R. Van der Weyden, 15th c. © BPK, Berlin / J.P. Anders.

Page 18: *Blessing Christ*, Giotto, 14th c. © 1990, Photo Scala, Florence.

Page 19: *The Adoration of the Magi*, Master of the Altarpiece of Scottish Abbey, 15th c. © akg-images / E. Lessing.

Page 20: *The Three Kings*, P. Hey, 20th c. © Bridgeman Giraudon / Christie's, London.

Page 21: *The Baptism of Christ*, Fra Angelico, 15th c. © Picture Desk / Dagli Orti.

Page 22: *The Last Judgement*, P. Bares, 16th c. © Picture Desk / Dagli Orti.

Page 23: *Noah Releasing the Dove from the Ark*, Italian Mosaic, 13th c. © 1990, Photo Scala, Florence.

Page 24: *The Adoration of the Magi*, A. della Robbia, 15th c. © akg-images.

Page 25: *Vision of St. Bernhard of Clairvaux*, F. Lippi, 15th c. © akg-images / Rabatti-Domingie.

Page 26: *Ruth and Booz*, N. Poussin, 17th c. © All rights reserved / RMN, Paris.

Page 27: *Noli me Tangere*, Fra Angelico, 15th c. © akg-images / Electa.

Page 28: *Let the Children Come to Me*, C. Vogel von Vogelstein, 19th c. © 1990, Photo Scala, Florence.

Page 29: *The Storm on the Sea of Galilee*, Rembrandt, 17th c. © Bridgeman Giraudon / Isabella Stewart Gardner Museum, Boston, MA, USA.

Page 30: *The Apostles' Mission* © All rights reserved.

Page 31: *The Last Supper*, A. del Castagno, 15th c. © Picture Desk / Dagli Orti.

Page 32: *The Good Samaritan*, P.R. Morris, 19th c. © Bridgeman Giraudon / Blackburn Museum and Art Gallery, Lancashire, UK.

Page 33: *The Sermon on the Mount*, Fra Angelico, 15th c. © 1990, Museo di San Marco, Photo Scala, Florence.

Page 34: *The Adoration of the Name of Jesus*, El Greco, 16th c. © Bridgeman Giraudon.

Page 35: *Calling of St. Matthew*, Caravaggio, 17th c. © akg-images / Rabatti-Domingie.

Page 36: *The Baptism of Christ*, Armenian Illumination, 14th c. © All rights reserved.

Page 37: *Christ and the Apostles*, Byzantine Icon, 17th c. © Picture Desk / Dagli Orti.

Page 38: *The Conversion of St. Paul*, Caravaggio, 17th c. © Bridgeman Giraudon.

Page 39: *The First Miraculous Draught of Fish*, J.J. Tissot, 19th c. © Bridgeman Giraudon / Brooklyn Museum of Art, New York, USA.

Page 40: *The Baptism of Clovis*, French Illumination © All rights reserved.

Page 41: *Job Mocked by his Wife*, G. de La Tour , 17th c. © P. Bernard / RMN, Paris.

Page 42: *The Prophet Elijah*, Russian School, 17th c. © Bridgeman Giraudon.

Page 43: *St. Joseph with Jesus*, B.E. Murillo, 17th c. © 1998, Photo Scala, Florence.

Page 44: *The Trinity*, El Greco, 16th c. © Bridgeman Giraudon.

FEBRUARY

Page 46: *St. Luke Painting the Virgin*, M. Van Heemskerck, 16th c. © Bridgeman Giraudon.

Page 47: *The Visitation*, J. Fouquet, 15th c. © Bridgeman Giraudon.

Page 48: *St. Joseph*, P. Annigoni, 20th c. © 1990, Photo Scala, Florence.

Page 49: *The Transfiguration of Christ*, Armenian Manuscript, 14th c. © Picture Desk / Dagli Orti.

Page 50: *Noli me Tangere*, Illumination © All rights reserved.

Page 51: *Raising of Lazarus*, Giotto, 14th c. © akg-images / Cameraphoto.

Page 52: *Ecce Homo*, A. Ciseri, 19th c. © akg-images / Rabatti-Domingie.

Page 53: *The Fall*, H. Van der Goes, 15th c. © Bridgeman Giraudon.

Page 54: *The Good Samaritan*, D. Fontebasso, 18th c. © Picture Desk / Dagli Orti.

Page 55: *Christ and the Adulteress*, L. Cranach, 16th c. © Museum of Fine Arts, Budapest, Hungary.

Page 56: *The Crucifixion*, Masaccio, 15th c. © 2000, Photo Scala, Florence.

Page 57: *The Multiplication of Loaves*, French Manuscript, 15th c. © BNF, Paris.

Page 58: *The Ascension of Christ*, Souvigny Bible, 12th c. © Picture Desk / Dagli Orti.

Page 59: *The Voice in the Desert*, J.J. Tissot, 19th c. © Bridgeman Giraudon / Brooklyn Museum of Art, New York, USA.

Page 60: *The Pentecost*, Miniature, 16th c. © IRHT.

Page 61: *The Flight into Egypt*, Giotto, 14th c. © Bridgeman Giraudon.

Page 62: *St. Peter*, L. Memmi, 14th c. © Bridgeman Giraudon.

Page 63: *The Procession of St. Gregory*, P. de Limbourg, 15th c. © Bridgeman Giraudon.

Page 64: *The Dormition of the Virgin*, Master of Santa Maria del Campo, 15th c. © Bridgeman Giraudon.

Page 65: *The Burning Bush*, Ravenna Mosaic, 6th c. © Picture Desk / Dagli Orti.

Page 66: *Christ's Temptation in the Desert*, Lanslevillard Fresco, 15th c. © Picture Desk / Dagli Orti.

Page 67: *St. Peter on his Throne*, Masaccio, 15th c. © 1990, Photo Scala, Florence.

Page 68: *The Christ and St. John*, Manerius Bible, 12th c. © All rights reserved.

Page 69: *The Woman taken in Adultery*, Rembrandt, 17th c. © Bridgeman Giraudon.

Page 70: *The Coronation of the Virgin*, D. Velazquez, 17th c. © 1990, Photo Scala, Florence.

Page 71: *The Glorification of the Cross*, G. Tiepolo, 18th c. © akg-images / Cameraphoto.

Page 72: *Ruth and Booz*, N. Poussin, 17th c. © All rigths reserved / RMN, Paris.

Page 73: *The Stigmatization of St. Francis of Assisi*, Sassetta, 15th c. © The National Gallery, London.

Page 74: *Pieta*, L. Lotto, 16th c. © akg-images / Electa.

MARCH

Page 76: *The Last Supper*, P. Lorenzetti, 14th c. © akg-images / E. Lessing.

Page 77: *The Agony in the Garden*, Fra Angelico, 15th c. © 1990, Museo di San Marco, Photo Scala, Florence.

Page 78: *Blessing Christ*, L. Bastiani, 15th c. © Picture Desk / Dagli Orti.

Page 79: *The Transfiguration*, G. di Benedetto, 14th c. © BNF, Paris.

Page 80: *The Crucifixion*, Fra Angelico, 15th c. © 1990, Museo di San Marco, Photo Scala, Florence.

Page 81: *The Liberation of St. Peter*, Raphael, 16th c. © 1990, Photo Scala, Florence.

Page 82: *The Visitation*, R. Van der Weyden, 15th c. © akg-images.

Page 83: *St. Peter Visited in Jail by St. Paul*, F. Lippi, 15th c. © Bridgeman Giraudon.

Page 84: *Christ and the Canaanite Woman*, J. Colombe, 15th c. © Bridgeman Giraudon.

Page 85: *Stars and Cross*, Ravenna Mosaic, 5th c. © Picture Desk / Dagli Orti.

Page 86: *Christ and Samaritan Woman*, H. Siemiradzki, 19th c. © akg-images.

Page 87: *Christ at Emmaus*, Rembrandt, 17th c. © 1999, Musée Jacquemart André / IDF / Scala.

Page 88: *The Creation of Eve*, G. di Benedetto, 14th c. © BNF, Paris.

Page 89: *St. Sebastian tended by St. Irene*, G. de la Tour, 17th c. © Picture Desk / Dagli Orti.

Page 90: *The Holy Family*, B. Luini, 16th c. © C. Jean / RMN, Paris.

Page 91: *The Entry into Jerusalem*, P. de Limbourg, 15th c. © Bridgeman Giraudon.

Page 92: *The Holy Trinity*, Illumination, 14th c. © All rights reserved.

Page 93: *St. Matthew*, G. Reni, 17th c. © Bridgeman Giraudon.

Page 94: *St. Sebastian tended by St. Irene*, G. de la Tour, 17th c. © Picture Desk / Dagli Orti.

Page 95: *The Crucifixion*, Masaccio, 15th c. © 2000, Photo Scala, Florence.

Page 96: *The Last Judgement*, R. Van der Weyden, 15th c. © J. Michot.

Page 97: *St. Barbara*, R. Campin, 15th c. © Bridgeman Giraudon.

Page 98: *Wheatfield with Sheaves*, V. Van Gogh, 19th c. © Bridgeman Giraudon.

Page 99: *Abraham's Three Visitors at Mambre*, Ravenna Mosaic, 6th c. © Picture Desk / Dagli Orti.

Page 100: *The Annunciation*, F. Lippi, 15th c. © Bridgeman Giraudon.

Page 101: *Presentation in Temple*, Master of Paciano, 14th c. © akg-images / Rabatti-Domingie.

Page 102: *Jesus in the Temple*, S. Martini, 14th c. © akg-images.

Page 103: *St. Martin of Tours dividing his Cloak*, S. Martini, 14th c. © Picture Desk / Dagli Orti.

Page 104: *The Deposition from the Cross*, Fra Angelico, 15th c. © Picture Desk / Dagli Orti.

Page 105: *The Sower*, V. Van Gogh , 19th c. © akg-images.

Page 106: *The Coronation of the Virgin*, L. Monaco, 15th c. © 2004, Photo Scala, Florence.

APRIL

Page 108: *Morning in the Reisengebirge*, C.D. Friedrich, 19th c. © akg-images.

Page 109: *Initial E with Christ sending out the Apostles*, Antiphonary, Italy, third quarter 15th c., M.584, f.4, detail. © 2004 Pierpont Morgan Library / Art Resource / Scala, Florence.

Page 110: *The Fall*, L. Cranach, 16th c. © akg-images.

Page 111: *The Washing of the Feet*, Giotto, 14th c. © Picture Desk / Dagli Orti.

Page 112: *The Last Supper*, Ingeburge Psalter, 13th c. © Bridgeman Giraudon.

Page 113: *The Crucifixion*, M. Grunewald, 16th c. © Bridgeman Giraudon.

Page 114: *Mary Magdalene*, G. de La Tour, 17th c. © akg-images / E. Lessing.

Page 115: *The Light of the World*, W.H. Hunt, 19th c. © Bridgeman Giraudon / Manchester Art Gallery, UK.

Page 116: *The Resurrection of Christ*, J. Serra, 14th c. © Picture Desk / Dagli Orti.

Page 117: *The Resurrection of Christ*, M. Grunewald, 16th c. © Picture Desk / Dagli Orti.

Page 118: *Christ and Samaritan Woman*, H. Siemiradzki, 19th c. © akg-images.

Page 119: *Holy Women at the Sepulcher*, Fra Angelico, 15th c. © 1990, Museo di San Marco, Photo Scala, Florence.

Page 120: *The Red Sea*, J.J. Besserer, 17th c. © akg-images.

Page 121: *Doubting Thomas*, Caravaggio, 16th c. © akg-images.

Page 122: *The Conversion of St. Paul*, B.E. Murillo, 17th c. © akg-images / E. Lessing.

Page 123: *Noli me Tangere*, Fra Bartolomeo, 16th c. © akg-images / E. Lessing.

Page 124: *The Transfiguration*, Perugino, 15th c. © 1999, Photo Scala, Florence.

Page 125: *The Avignon Pieta*, E. Quarton, 15th c. © Bridgeman Giraudon / P. Willi.

Page 126: *St. John in Patmos*, P. de Limbourg, 15th c. © Ojéda / RMN, Paris.

Page 127: *The Madonna giving her Girdle to St. Thomas*, B. Gozzoli, 15th c. © 1990, Photo Scala, Florence.

Page 128: *Jeremiah*, St.-Vaast Bible, 11th c. © All rights reserved.

Page 129: *The Ascension of the Holy Spirit*, J. Fouquet, 15th c. © Bridgeman Giraudon.

Page 130: *The Renunciation of Queen Elizabeth of Hungary*, J. Collinson, 19th c. © All rights reserved.

Page 131: *The Last Supper*, German School, 15th c. © Bridgeman Giraudon / The Barnes Foundation, Merion, Pennsylvania, USA.

Page 132: *The Holy Sacrament and Two Angels*, French School, 15th c. © Bridgeman Giraudon / Glasgow University Library, Scotland.

Page 133: *Noli me Tangere*, Fra Bartolomeo, 16th c. © akg-images / E. Lessing.

Page 134: *The Pentecost*, English Illumination, 11th c. © Rouen Library, France.

Page 135: *St. Joachim*, Hungarian School, 15th c. © Picture Desk / Dagli Orti.

Page 136: *The Good Shepherd*, P. de Champaigne, 17th c. © Bridgeman Giraudon.

Page 137: *The Adoration of the Mystic Lamb*, H.&J. Van Eyck, 15th c. © Bridgeman Giraudon.

MAY

Page 138: *The Visitation*, M. Albertinelli, 16th c. © 1996, Photo Scala, Florence.

Page 140: *Madonna of Magnificat*, S. Botticelli, 15th c. © akg-images / E. Lessing.

Page 141: *The Birth of John the Baptist*, Hispano-Flemish Workshop, 15th c. © Picture Desk / Dagli Orti.

Page 142: *The Birth of John the Baptist*, D. Ghirlandaio, 15th c. © 1990, Photo Scala, Florence.

Page 143: *The Annunciation*, Garofalo, 16th c. © Bridgeman Giraudon.

Page 144: *The Annunciation*, Fra Angelico, 15th c. © Picture Desk / Dagli Orti.

Page 145: *Ruth and Booz*, N. Poussin, 17th c. © All rigths reserved / RMN, Paris.

Page 146: *Offering to the Virgin Mary*, S. St.-Jean, 19th c. © Studio Basset.

Page 147: *The Pentecost*, L. de Morales, 16th c. © Bridgeman Giraudon.

Page 148: *Madonna and Child*, L. Monaco, 15th c. © Bridgeman Giraudon.

Page 149: *Madonna with the Rosary*, M. Stanzione, 17th c. © 1990, Photo Scala, Florence.

Page 150: *The Annunciation* © All rights reserved.

Page 151: *Ave Maria at the Crossing*, G. Segantini , 19th c. © akg-images.

Page 152: *The Annunciation*, S. Botticelli, 15th c. © akg-images / E. Lessing.

Page 153: *The Transfiguration*, Raphael, 16th c. © akg-images / Nimatallah.

Page 154: *Noli me Tangere*, Fra Angelico, 15th c. © akg-images / Electa.

Page 155: *The Ascension*, J. Fouquet, 15th c. © Bridgeman Giraudon.

Page 156: *The Ascension*, J.-F. de Troy, 18th c. © Bridgeman Giraudon.

Page 157: *The St. Zeno of Verona Altarpiece*, A. Mantegna, 15th c. © Bridgeman Giraudon.

Page 158: *The Presentation in the Temple*, A. Lorenzetti, 14th c. © akg-images / E. Lessing.

Page 159: *The Last Supper*, J. de Juanes, 16th c. © Bridgeman Giraudon.

Page 160: *The Coronation of the Virgin*, L. Monaco, 15th c. © 2004, Photo Scala, Florence.

Page 161: *Blessing in Church*, French School, 15th c.

Page 162: *The Good Samaritan*, P.R. Morris, 19th c.

Page 163: *The Adoration of the Mystic Lamb*, H.&J. Van Eyck, 15th c.

Page 164: *The Baptism of Christ*, Fra Angelico, 15th c.

Page 165: *The Annunciation*, O. Gentileschi, 17th c.

Page 166: *The Pentecost*, English School, 12th c.

Page 167: *The Annunciation*, El Greco, 16th c.

Page 168: *The Baptism of Christ*, P. de Limbourg, 15th c.

Page 169: *The Seven Joys of the Virgin*, Master of the Holy Family, 15th c.

Page 170: *The Visitation*, J. Strub, 16th c.

JUNE

Page 172: *The Red Sea*, French Miniature, 14th c.

Page 173: *The Nativity*, L. Lotto, 16th c.

Page 174: *The Trinity*, H. von Bingen, 12th c.

Page 175: *Christ in the House of Martha and Mary*, J. Vermeer, 17th c.

Page 176: *Ruth and Booz*, N. Poussin, 17th c.

Page 177: *The Entry into Jerusalem*, Russian School, 16th c.

Page 178: *The Multiplication of Loaves*, French Manuscript, 15th c.

Page 179: *The Supper at Emmaus*, T. Bigot, 17th c.

Page 180: *Noli me Tangere*, Duccio di Buoninsegna, 14th c.

Page 181: *The Adoration of the Mystic Lamb*, H.&J. Van Eyck, 15th c.

Page 182: *Christ and the Cross*, Italian Mosaic, 4th c.

Page 183: *The Last Supper*, Fra Angelico, 15th c.

Page 184: *The Ascension*, J. Fouquet, 15th c.

Page 185: *The Adoration of the Shepherds*, F. de Zurbaran, 17th c.

Page 186: *Moses receiving the Tablets of the Law*

Page 187: *The Supper at Emmaus*, R. Ghirlandaio, 16th c.

Page 188: *St. Mark*, French School, 15th c.

Page 189: *The Adoration of the Mystic Lamb*, H.&J. Van Eyck, 15th c.

Page 190: *Abraham's Three Visitors at Mambre*, Ravenna Mosaic, 6th c.

Page 191: *The Last Supper*, M. di Nardo, 15th c.

Page 192: *The Last Supper*, J. de Juanes, 16th c.

Page 193: *Christ with Peasant Family*, F. von Uhde, 19th c.

Page 194: *The Crucifixion*, J. Canavesio, 15th c.

Page 195: *The Voice in the Desert*, J.J. Tissot, 19th c.

Page 196: *The Miraculous Draught of Fishes*, G. di Benedetto, 14th c.

Page 197: *Ave Maria at the Crossing*, G. Segantini, 19th c.

Page 198: *The Calling of Peter and Andrew*, D. Ghirlandaio, 15th c.

Page 199: *Payment of the Tribute Money*, Masaccio, 15th c.

Page 200: *St. Paul preaching*, Illumination, 16th c.

Page 201: *The Calling of Peter and Andrew*, D. Ghirlandaio, 15th c.

JULY

Page 202: *Wheatfield with Sheaves*, V. Van Gogh, 19th c.

Page 204: *The Assumption*, Titian, 16th c.

Page 205: *The Labours of Man*, The Liebana Beatus, 10th c.

Page 206: *Moses receiving the Tablets of the Law*

Page 207: *The Angel refusing Gifts from Tobias*, G. Biliverti, 17th c.

Page 208: *The Crucifixion*, J. Canavesio, 15th c.

Page 209: *The Last Supper*, Giotto , 14th c.

Page 210: *The Baptism of Christ*, Perugino, 15th c.

Page 211: *The Annunciation*, L. Costa, 15th c. © akg-images.

Page 212: *The Visitation*, Master of Lluça, 13th c. © Picture Desk / Dagli Orti.

Page 213: *Christ and the Canaanite Woman*, J. Colombe, 15th c. © Bridgeman Giraudon.

Page 214: *The Presentation in the Temple*, Titian, 16th c. © 1990, Photo Scala, Florence.

Page 215: *The Pentecost*, English School, 12th c. © Bridgeman Giraudon / Glasgow University Library.

Page 216: *St. Luke painting the Madonna*, R. Van der Weyden, 15th c. © 1990, Photo Scala, Florence.

Page 217: *The Annunciation*, El Greco, 16th c. © akg-images / E. Lessing.

Page 218: *The Entry into Jerusalem*, Russian School, 16th c. © Bridgeman Giraudon.

Page 219: *Salvator Mundi*, F. Pourbus I, 16th c. © Bridgeman Giraudon.

Page 220: *The Crucifixion*, M. Grunewald, 16th c. © Bridgeman Giraudon.

Page 221: *Angel of Tobit*, Husayn, 17th c. © Arnaudet / RMN, Paris.

Page 222: *St. Benedict in Prayer*, Master of Messkirch, 16th c. © All rights reserved.

Page 223: *The Adoration of the Shepherds*, A. Mengs, 18th c. © All rights reserved.

Page 224: *The Last Supper*, A. del Castagno, 15th c. © Picture Desk / Dagli Orti.

Page 225: *Virgin and Child*, W. Dyce, 19th c. © Bridgeman Giraudon.

Page 226: *The Presentation in the Temple*, Titian, 16th c. © 1990, Photo Scala, Florence.

Page 227: *The Stigmatization of St. Francis of Assisi*, Giotto, 14th c. © 1990, Photo Scala, Florence.

Page 228: *The Prophet Elijah*, Russian School, 17th c. © Bridgeman Giraudon.

Page 229: *The Adoration of the Magi*, T. di Bartolo, 14th c. © 1990, Photo Scala, Florence.

Page 230: *The Annunciation*, F. Francia, 16th c. © akg-images.

Page 231: *The Last Judgement*, Fra Angelico, 15th c. © akg-images / E. Lessing.

Page 232: *The Creation of Eve*, G. di Benedetto, 14th c. © BNF, Paris.

Page 233: *Christ and the Apostles*, Byzantine Icon, 17th c. © Picture Desk / Dagli Orti.

Page 234: *The Last Judgement*, R. Van der Weyden, 15th c. © J. Michot.

AUGUST

Page 236: *Initial E with Christ sending out the Apostles*, Antiphonary, Italy, third quarter 15th c., M.584, f.4, detail.

© 2004 Pierpont Morgan Library / Art Resource / Scala, Florence.

Page 237: *The Annunciation*, Fra Angelico, 15th c. © Picture Desk / Dagli Orti.

Page 238: *The Pilgrims at Emmaus*, F. de Zurbaran, 17th c. © Picture Desk / Dagli Orti.

Page 239: *The Ascension of Christ*, French Psalter, 13th c. © All rights reserved.

Page 240: *Angel of Tobit*, Husayn, 17th c. © Arnaudet / RMN, Paris.

Page 241: *The Transfiguration*, Fra Angelico, 15th c. © 1990, Photo Scala, Florence.

Page 242: *Madonna of Mercy*, F. Granacci (style), 16th c. © 1990, Photo Scala, Florence.

Page 243: *Christ Mocked*, Fra Angelico, 15th c. © 1990, Photo Scala, Florence.

Page 244: *The Sacrifice of Isaac*, Caravaggio, 17th c. © 1991, Photo Scala, Florence.

Page 245: *The Agony in the Garden*, S. Botticelli, 16th c. © Bridgeman Giraudon.

Page 246: *The Tree of Jesse*, French School, 13th c. © Bridgeman Giraudon.

Page 247: *Noah's Ark*, Master of Sir John Fastolf, 15th c. © Picture Desk / Bodleian Library.

Page 248: *The Penitent St. Jerome*, Giampietrino, 16th c. © Bridgeman Giraudon.

Page 249: *Virgin and Child*, Boccacino, 16th c. © All rights reserved.

Page 250: *The Assumption*, J. Ferrer, 15th c. © Picture Desk / Dagli Orti.

Page 251: *The Last Judgement*, R. Van der Weyden, 15th c. © J. Michot.

Page 252: *The Assumption*, B.E. Murillo, 17th c. © All rights reserved.

Page 253: *St. Francis' Renouncement*, Giotto, 14th c. © Bridgeman Giraudon.

Page 254: *The Adoration of the Shepherds*, F. de Zurbaran, 17th c. © Grenoble Museum, France.

Page 255: *The Annunciation*, M. Albertinelli, 15th c. © 2004, Photo Scala, Florence.

Page 256: *St. Joseph with Jesus*, B.E. Murillo , 17th c. © 1998, Photo Scala, Florence.

Page 257: *The Newborn Child*, G. de La Tour, 17th c. © akg-images / E. Lessing.

Page 258: *St. Joseph and the Christ Child*, El Greco, 16th c. © Bridgeman Giraudon.

Page 259: *Christ blessing*, Giotto, 14th c. © 1990, Photo Scala, Florence.

Page 260: *The St. Denis Altarpiece*, H. Bellechose, 15th c. © Bridgeman Giraudon.

Page 261: *The Adoration of the Magi*, Master of the Altarpiece of Scottish Abbey, 15th c. © akg-images / E. Lessing.

Page 262: *St. Augustine and St. Monica*, A. Scheffer, 19th c. © Bridgeman Giraudon.

Page 263: *The Stigmatization of St. Francis of Assisi*, Giotto, 14th c. © 1990, Photo Scala, Florence.

Page 264: *The Liberation of St. Peter*, Raphael, 16th c. © 1990, Photo Scala, Florence.

Page 265: *The Ascent of the Blessed*, J. Bosch, 15th c. © Bridgeman Giraudon.

Page 266: *The Good Shepherd*, H.O. Tanner, 20th c. © The Newark Museum / Art Resource / Scala.

SEPTEMBER

Page 268: *The Last Supper*, Ingeburge Psalter, 13th c. © Bridgeman Giraudon.

Page 269: *The Risen Christ*, S. Rosa, 17th c. © Bridgeman Giraudon.

Page 270: *The Transfiguration*, Fra Angelico, 15th c. © 1990, Photo Scala, Florence.

Page 271: *St. Thomas*, M. Schongauer, 15th c. © All rights reserved.

Page 272: *The Washing of the Feet*, Giotto, 14th c. © Picture Desk / Dagli Orti.

Page 273: *The Last Supper*, M. di Nardo, 15th c. © Bridgeman Giraudon.

Page 274: *The Annunciation*, M. Albertinelli, 15th c. © 2004, Photo Scala, Florence.

Page 275: *The Birth of the Virgin Mary*, P. da Cortona, 17th c. © akg-images / Rabatti-Domingie.

Page 276: *Jonah and the Whale*, G. Trubert, 15th c. © BNF, Paris.

Page 277: *The Pentecost*, El Greco, 16th c. © akg-images.

Page 278: *Christ Asleep in his Boat*, J.J. Meynier, 19th c. © Bridgeman Giraudon.

Page 279: *Christ blessing*, F. Gallego, 15th c. © Picture Desk / Dagli Orti.

Page 280: *The Stoning of St. Stephen*, French Sacramentary, 12th c. © BNF, Paris.

Page 281: *The Adoration of the Mystic Lamb*, H&J. Van Eyck, 15th c. © Bridgeman Giraudon.

Page 282: *The Deposition*, G. dai Libri, 15th c. © Bridgeman Giraudon.

Page 283: *The Education of the Virgin*, Workshop of L. de La Hyre, 17th c. © Bridgeman Giraudon.

Page 284: *The Annunciation*, Armenian Miniature, 14th c. © All rights reserved.

Page 285: *The Sacrifice of Isaac*, Caravaggio, 17th c. © 1991, Photo Scala, Florence.

Page 286: *The Temptation*, Miniature, 15th c. © All rights reserved.

Page 287: *The Calling of Peter and Andrew*, D. Ghirlandaio, 15th c. © 1990, Photo Scala, Florence.

Page 288: *Dead Christ*, H. Memling, 15th c. © Picture Desk / Dagli Orti.

Page 289: *The Adoration of the Mystic Lamb*, H&J. Van Eyck, 15th c. © Bridgeman Giraudon.

Page 290: *The Madonna giving her Girdle to St. Thomas*, B. Gozzoli, 15th c. © 1990, Photo Scala, Florence.

Page 291: *The Creation*, J. Fouquet, 15th c. © Bridgeman Giraudon.

Page 292: *The Meeting of Joachim and Anne*, Giotto, 14th c. © Picture Desk / Dagli Orti.

Page 293: *The Mystic Marriage of St. Catherine*, Anonymous, 15th c. © Hungarian National Gallery.

Page 294: *The Holy Family*, N. Halle, 18th c. © Bridgeman Giraudon

Page 295: *The Agony in the Garden*, S. Botticelli, 15th c. © Bridgeman Giraudon.

Page 296: *The Nativity*, Giotto, 14th c. © Bridgeman Giraudon.

Page 297: *Madonna of Roses*, S. St.-Jean, 19th c. © Arnaudet / RMN, Paris.

OCTOBER

Page 298: *Initial E with Christ sending out the Apostles*, Antiphonary, Italy, third quarter 15th c., M.584, f.4, detail. © 2004 Pierpont Morgan Library / Art Resource / Scala, Florence.

Page 300: *Christ with Peasant Family* , F. von Uhde, 19th c. © akg-images / E. Lessing.

Page 301: *The Labours of Man*, The Liebana Beatus, 10th c. © Picture Desk / Dagli Orti.

Page 302: *The Sower*, J.F. Millet, 19th c. © Bridgeman Giraudon / Museum of Fine Arts, Boston.

Page 303: *St. Francis preaching*, Giotto, 14th c. © Bridgeman Giraudon.

Page 304: *The Apostles' Mission* © All rights reserved.

Page 305: *The Adoration of the Shepherds*, L. Lotto, 16th c. © akg-images / E. Lessing.

Page 306: *Madonna of the Rosary*, G.B. Paggi, 17th c. © Bridgeman Giraudon.

Page 307: *The Multiplication of the Loaves*, French Missal, 16th c. © All rights reserved.

Page 308: *The Crucifixion*, French Miniature, 13th c. © BNF, Paris.

Page 309: *The Creation of the earth, dividing the waters, creation of the heavens, creation of plants*, French Psalter, last quarter 13th c., M.730, f.9, detail © 2003, Pierpont Morgan Library / Art Resource / Scala, Florence.

Page 310: *Christ's entry into Jerusalem*, Lanslevillard Fresco, 15th c. © Picture Desk / Dagli Orti.

Page 311: *St. Martin of Tours dividing his Cloak*, S. Martini, 14th c. © Picture Desk / Dagli Orti.

Page 312: *The Presentation in Temple*, Master of Paciano, 14th c. © akg-images / Rabatti-DominMé.

Page 313: *The Fall*, H. Van der Goes, 15th c. © Bridgeman Giraudon.

Page 314: *Noah's Ark*, Master of Sir John Fastolf, 15th c. © Picture Desk / Bodleian Library.

Page 315: *The Ascension of Christ*, French Psalter, 13th c. © All rights reserved.

Page 316: *The Assumption*, T. di Bartolo, 15th c. © akg-images.

Page 317: *The Baptism of Christ*, El Greco, 16th c. © Bridgeman Giraudon.

Page 318: *The Annunciation* © All rights reserved.

Page 319: *The Burning Bush*, Ravenna Mosaic, 6th c. © Picture Desk / Dagli Orti.

Page 320: *Jacob's Ladder*, Avignon School, 15th c. © Picture Desk / Dagli Orti.

Page 321: *St. Matthew*, G. Reni, 17th c. © Bridgeman Giraudon.

Page 322: *The Presentation in the Temple*, V. Carpaccio, 16th c. © akg-images / Cameraphoto.

Page 323: *The St. Denis Altarpiece*, H. Bellechose, 15th c. © Bridgeman Giraudon.

Page 324: *The Presentation in the Temple*, A. Lorenzetti, 14th c. © akg-images / Rabatti-DominMé.

Page 325: *The Seven Joys of the Virgin*, Master of the Holy Family, 15th c. © Bridgeman Giraudon.

Page 326: *The Adoration of the Magi*, Fra Angelico, 15th c. © Bridgeman Giraudon.

Page 327: *The Nativity*, Giotto, 14th c. © Bridgeman Giraudon.

Page 328: *St. Luke*, A. Mantegna , 15th c. © Bridgeman Giraudon.

Page 329: *The Last Supper*, J. Huguet, 15th c. © 1990, Photo Scala, Florence.

Page 330: *The Crucifixion*, G. Canavesio, 15th c. © Picture Desk / Dagli Orti.

NOVEMBER

Page 332: *The Resurrection of Christ*, M. Grunewald, 16th c. © Picture Desk / Dagli Orti.

Page 333: *Light and Colour*, W. Turner, 19th c. © All rights reserved.

Page 334: *The Last Judgement*, P. Bares, 16th c. © Picture Desk / Dagli Orti.

Page 335: *The Pentecost*, Miniature, 16th c. © IRHT.

Page 336: *St. Bartholomew between St. Agnes and St. Cecilia*, Master of the Bartholomew Altar, 16th c. © akg-images.

Page 337: *The Creation of Eve*, G. di Benedetto, 14th c. © BNF, Paris.

Page 338: *The Adoration of the Mystic Lamb*, H&J. Van Eyck, 15th c. © Bridgeman Giraudon.

Page 339: *The Pentecost*, English Illumination, 11th c. © Rouen Library, France.

Page 340: *The Crucifixion*, E. Schiele, 20th c. © Bridgeman Giraudon / Christie's, London.

Page 341: *Jonah and the Whale*, G. Trubert, 15th c. © BNF, Paris.

Page 342: *St. John in Patmos*, P. de Limbourg, 15th c. © Ojéda / RMN, Paris.

Page 343: *The Deposition from the Cross*, Fra Angelico, 15th c. © Picture Desk / Dagli Orti.

Page 344: *The Adoration of the Mystic Lamb*, H&J. Van Eyck, 15th c. © Bridgeman Giraudon.

Page 345: *Moses receiving the Tablets of the Law* © All rights reserved.

Page 346: *The Festival of the Rosary*, A. Durer, 16th c. © Bridgeman Giraudon.

Page 347: *The last Supper*, J. Huguet, 15th c. © 1990, Photo Scala, Florence.

Page 348: *Deposition from the Cross*, Fra Angelico, 15th c. © Picture Desk / Dagli Orti.

Page 349: *Noah Releasing the Dove from the Ark*, Italian Mosaic, 14th c. © 1990, Photo Scala, Florence.

Page 350: *The Transfiguration*, A. Previtali, 15th c. © 1997, Scala, Florence.

Page 351: *St. Philip Neri*, G. Tiepolo, 18th c. © 1990, Photo Scala, Florence.

Page 352: *The Martyrdom of St. Thomas*, Master Francke, 15th c. © Bridgeman Giraudon.

Page 353: *St. Cecilia*, N. Poussin (attr. to), 17th c. © Bridgeman Giraudon.

Page 354: *St. John in Patmos*, P. de Limbourg, 15th c. © Ojéda / RMN, Paris.

Page 355: *St. Martin and the Beggar*, El Greco, 16th c. © akg-images / J. Martin.

Page 356: *The Star of Bethleem*, F. Leighton, 19th c. © akg-images.

Page 357: *The Assumption*, F. Lippi, 15th c. © 1992, Photo Scala, Florence.

Page 358: *The Last Judgement*, Fra Angelico, 15th c. © akg-images / E. Lessing.

Page 359: *Jacob's Ladder*, Avignon School, 15th c. © Picture Desk / Dagli Orti.

Page 360: *The Last Supper*, Fra Angelico, 15th c. © Bridgeman Giraudon.

Page 361: *The Nativity*, French Sacramentary, 12th c. © BNF, Paris.

DECEMBER

Page 362: *The Newborn Child*, G. de La Tour, 17th c. © akg-images / E. Lessing.

Page 364: *Christ in the Garden of Olives*, P. de Limbourg, 15th c. © Bridgeman Giraudon.

Page 365: *The Visitation*, M. Albertinelli, 16th c. © 1996, Scala, Florence.

Page 366: *The Crucifixion*, E. Schiele, 20th c. © Bridgeman Giraudon / Christie's, London.

Page 367: *Christ among the Doctors*, Pinturicchio, 16th c. © 1990, Photo Scala, Florence.

Page 368: *The Visitation*, J. Pontormo, 16th c. © Picture Desk / Dagli Orti.

Page 369: *The Annunciation*, Fra Angelico, 15th c. © Picture Desk / Dagli Orti.

Page 370: *Immaculate Conception*, G.B. Tiepolo, 18th c. © Picture Desk / Dagli Orti.

Page 371: *The Annunciation*, O. Gentileschi, 17th c. © 1992, Photo Scala, Florence.

Page 372: *The Adoration of the Shepherds*, A. Mengs, 18th c. © All rights reserved.

Page 373: *The Crucifixion*, M. Grunewald, 16th c. © Bridgeman Giraudon.

Page 374: *The Tree of Jesse*, French School, 13th c. © Bridgeman Giraudon.

Page 375: *Virgin of Guadalupe*, J. de Villegas, 18th c. © akg-images.

Page 376: *Christ and the Apostles*, Byzantine Icon, 17th c. © Picture Desk / Dagli Orti.

Page 377: *Simeon in the Temple*, Rembrandt, 17th c. © All rights reserved.

Page 378: *The Nativity*, R. Campin, 15th c. © Bridgeman Giraudon.

Page 379: *The Adoration of the Shepherds*, Caravaggio, 17th c. © Picture Desk / Dagli Orti.

Page 380: *The Nativity*, Maître Francke, 15th c. © Bridgeman Giraudon.

Page 381: *The Adoration of the Shepherds*, F. de Zurbaran, 17th c. © Grenoble Museum, France.

Page 382: *The Nativity*, Byzantine Mosaic, 12th c. © Picture Desk / Dagli Orti.

Page 383: *The Nativity*, F. Barocci , 17th c. © akg-images.

Page 384: *Holy Night*, F. von Uhde, 19th c. © akg-images / E. Lessing.

Page 385: *The Annunciation*, Fra Angelico, 15th c. © Picture Desk / Dagli Orti.

Page 386: *The Annunciation*, M. Schongauer, 15th c. © Bridgeman Giraudon.

Page 387: *Virgin and Child*, Master of Moulins, 15th c. © Bridgeman Giraudon.

Page 388: *The Nativity*, Giotto, 14th c. © Bridgeman Giraudon.

Page 389: *The Nativity*, Maître Francke, 15th c. © Bridgeman Giraudon.

Page 390: *The Celestial Court*, J. Colombe, 15th c. © Bridgeman Giraudon.

Page 391: *The Meeting of Joachim and Anne*, Giotto, 14th c. © Picture Desk / Dagli Orti.

Page 392: *The Nativity*, R. Campin, 15th c. © Bridgeman Giraudon.

Page 393: *The Flight into Egypt*, B.E. Murillo, 17th c. © 1998, Photo Scala, Florence.

Page 394: *The Stoning of St. Stephen*, French Sacramentary, 12th c. © BNF, Paris.

Courtesy of the Ministero Beni e Att. Culturali Italiano: pages 28, 33, 56, 77, 80, 95, 106, 119, 138, 149, 160, 214, 226, 229, 241, 243, 244, 270, 285, 350, 365, 371.

Publisher: Pierre-Marie Dumont
Editor-in-Chief: Peter John Cameron, O.P.
Senior Editor: Romanus Cessario, O.P.
Contributors: J. Augustine Di Noia, O.P. , and Brian Mulcahy, O.P.
Assistant to the Editor: Catherine Kolpak
Administrative Assistant: Jeanne Shanahan
Coordinator, Design and Cover Design: Solange Bosdevesy
Iconography: Isabelle Mascaras, Anaïs Acker, Domitille de Catelbajac
Assistants to the Editorial Staff: Diaga Seck, Emmanuelle Lebrun, Aude Bertrand
Proofreaders: Sr. Mary Paul Thomas Maertz, O.P., Janet Chevrier
Production: Anne Marmey